Friends
So
Different

Friends So Different

Essays on
Canada and the United States
in the 1980s

Edited by
Lansing Lamont
and
J. Duncan Edmonds

Published for the Americas Society
by
University of Ottawa Press
Ottawa • London • Paris

© University of Ottawa Press, 1989
Printed and bound in Canada
ISBN 0-7766-0263-2

Canadian Cataloguing in Publication Data

Main entry under title:

Friends so different: essays on Canada and the
United States in the 1980s

ISBN 0-7766-0263-2

1. Canada—Relations—United States. 2. United
States—Relations—Canada. I. Lamont, Lansing,
1930- . II. Edmonds, J. Duncan (James Duncan),
1936-

FC249.F74 1989   303.4'8271'073   C89-090195-3
F1029.5.U6F74 1989

69870

UNIVERSITÉ   UNIVERSITY
D'OTTAWA   OF OTTAWA

This book has been made possible in large part through the generous
assistance of the William H. Donner Foundation

Design: Judith Gregory

To
John Wendell Holmes, 1910–1988
Diplomat, historian, wise counselor and friend

The Americas Society is the pre-eminent forum in the United States for the discussion of Western Hemisphere issues. Its core mission is to improve Americans' understanding of the political, economic and cultural values of other hemispheric nations. The Society, with roots dating back to the mid-1960s, is a non-profit organization based in New York. It enjoys a nation-wide membership of about a thousand leaders in American business, public affairs and the arts. Its chairman is David Rockefeller and its president is Ambassador George Landau.

The Canadian Affairs program of the Americas Society was formed in 1981 and is now the leading public forum in the United States for the discussion of bilateral issues. It seeks to inform an influential constituency of Americans on all important aspects of the Canadian experience, as well as on problems of major concern to Canadian–American relations.

The William H. Donner Foundation, established in 1962 and based in New York City, is a national philanthropic organization dedicated in part to the advancement of knowledge and understanding of Canada in the United States. The Foundation has underwritten the Americas Society/ Canadian Affairs' Visiting Associate program, which has attracted a number of the contributors in this book. The Foundation has also provided funds toward the publication cost of this book.

Contents

Foreword

Canada and the United States share one of the closest and most important relationships that exist anywhere between two countries. In light of Canada's role as the immediate neighbor and largest trading partner of the United States, it is essential that Americans have a more comprehensive understanding of Canada and the Canadian peoples: their heritage, their institutions, their culture, their attitudes and approach to life. For, despite our strong sense of communion, there are great differences between us. The Americas Society believes that greater awareness and appreciation of these differences will help to strengthen the bonds of the Canadian–American alliance. We hope that this book contributes to that cause.

David Rockefeller

Acknowledgments

The editors are indebted, of course, to those contributing essayists whose generous offering of their time and talents ensured the completion of this book.

We are particularly grateful to Vera Lucas of Ottawa and now Victoria. Her patient and always professional preparation of the edited manuscripts was an invaluable contribution to the project. As well, we deeply appreciate the support of the Americas Society, in particular that of its president, George Landau, and the staff of Canadian Affairs.

Final publication of this work owes much to the enthusiasm and wise counsel of Toivo Roht, Director of the University of Ottawa Press, and to the caring editorial guidance and patience of Jennifer Wilson, our editor.

Contributors

Perrin Beatty was Canada's Minister of National Defence when he gave this address to the Americas Society on December 10, 1987. Educated at the University of Western Ontario, he was first elected to the House of Commons in 1972. He served in a number of Cabinet positions before being appointed to the defense post, where he became the architect of the Mulroney government's plan to expand Canada's military establishment. Mr. Beatty now serves as Minister of Health and Welfare.

Peter Brimelow is a senior editor with *Forbes* magazine. He was educated at the University of Sussex, England, and Stanford University. An experienced financial journalist, he held high editorial positions with Canada's *Maclean's* magazine and the *Financial Post* before moving to the United States to work for *Barron's* and then *Forbes*. Mr. Brimelow regularly contributes columns to the *Wall Street Journal*, *The Times* of London and the *Financial Post*. Author of several books, notably *The Patriot Game*, he began work on this article as the 1987–88 Americas Society Visiting Associate.

McGeorge Bundy is Professor of History at New York University. Born in Boston and educated at Yale College and Harvard's Society of Fellows, he has been a student of international affairs since 1945, when he wrote *On Active Service* with the Secretary of War, Henry Stimson. In the following years, he taught American foreign policy at Harvard where he became Dean of the Faculty of Arts and Sciences. He went on to serve as Special Assistant for National Security Affairs at the White House during the nuclear crises in Berlin and Cuba and, later, as President of the Ford Foundation. Mr. Bundy's latest book, *Danger and Survival*, a history of the nuclear era, has been widely acclaimed. This address was given to the Americas Society in November 1981.

William Diebold is a noted authority on international economic policy. He was educated at Swarthmore College, Yale Graduate School and the London School of Economics. His long association with the Council on Foreign Relations began in 1939 when he was appointed as a Rockefeller research fellow. After a post-war stint with the State Department's Division of Commercial Policy, he returned to the Council, serving in a succession of posts before becoming its Director of Economic Studies. As a member of the Americas Society/Canadian Affairs Advisory Board, he prepared this essay especially for this book.

Charles F. Doran is Professor of International Relations and Director of the Center of Canadian Studies at Johns Hopkins University's School of Advanced International Studies in Washington, D.C. He was educated at Harvard College and Johns Hopkins University. A political economist and longtime Canadianist, he has served as President of the Association of Canadian Studies in the United States. His many articles and books include *Forgotten Partnership: U.S.–Canadian Relations Today*. This essay is based on his Americas Society talk given on October 31, 1983.

Lawrence S. Eagleburger was Assistant Secretary of State for European and Canadian Affairs at the time this talk was given on October 1, 1981. A graduate of the University of Wisconsin, he entered the State Department in 1957 and pursued a distinguished diplomatic career before retiring in 1984 as Under Secretary for Political Affairs. For the next five years he served as President of Kissinger Associates, an international consulting firm. In 1989, President Bush appointed Mr. Eagleburger as Deputy Secretary of State.

J. Duncan Edmonds, a co-editor of this book, delivered the lecture, on which his essay is based, in January 1986 while serving as Visiting Associate of the Americas Society.

Annette Baker Fox is Associate Research Scholar at the Institute of War and Peace Studies at Columbia University, where she and her late husband, William T.R. Fox, served as founding directors of the Canadian Studies Program. She was educated at Wellesley College and at the University of Chicago, from which she received her Ph.D. In 1987, she was awarded the Donner Medal by the Association for Canadian Studies in the United States. Dr. Fox is author, co-author or co-editor of more than half a dozen books on international subjects. This paper was delivered to the Americas Society on October 13, 1981.

Michael A. Goldberg is Herbert R. Fullerton Professor of Urban Land Policy in the Faculty of Commerce and Business Administration at the University of British Columbia. His scholarly work has dealt over the years with a range of policy issues related to urban land and housing markets. Recently he has turned his attention to the development of international financial centers.

Allan E. Gotlieb served as Canada's Ambassador to the United States from 1981 to 1988. Before that, he had enjoyed a distinguished career in government service, rising through the ranks of the Department of External Affairs to become Under-Secretary of State. He retired from the diplomatic service in 1989 to enter law practice. He spent a term as William Lyon Mackenzie King Visiting Professor of Canadian Studies at Harvard, and currently serves as Chairman of the Canada (Arts) Council. The paper in this book was given as a talk as he concluded his tenure as Ambassador.

John W. Holmes made a lasting contribution to Canadian foreign policy as a career diplomat, teacher and historian. He joined the Department of External Affairs in 1943, retiring as Assistant Under-Secretary in 1960 to become President of the Canadian Institute of International Affairs. Subsequently, he was Visiting Professor of International Relations at the University of Toronto and York University. His more than fifty articles and books included the definitive account of Canadian foreign policy from 1943 to 1957, *The Shaping of Peace*. His first paper in this book was delivered to the Americas Society on October 1, 1981. He had been working on the epilogue until a few weeks before his death in 1988.

Mark MacGuigan, Secretary of State for External Affairs under Prime Minister Trudeau, subsequently served as Minister of Justice and Attorney General before being appointed to the Federal Court of Canada in 1984. He was previously a Professor of Law at the University of Windsor and Osgoode Hall. He was first elected to Parliament in 1968. This address was delivered to the Americas Society on September 30, 1981, while he was Foreign Minister.

John Meisel is Sir Edward Peacock Professor of Political Science at Queen's University and former Chairman of the Canadian Radio-Television and Telecommunications Commission. He was serving in the latter post when he delivered his talk to the Americas Society on March 11, 1983. Professor Meisel was educated at the University of Toronto and the London School of Economics. One of his country's best-known commentators, he is the author of several books and articles on Canadian politics.

John Mercer is a Professor of Geography at Syracuse University. He has studied and written widely on urban social issues, including those related to the elderly, to housing and to urban governance. With Michael Goldberg, he is the co-author of *The Myth of the North American City: Continentalism Challenged*. Their paper was especially prepared for this book, although based on an earlier lecture given to the Americas Society.

Mavor Moore is a cultural critic, actor and educator. He was Dean of Performing Arts and Drama at York University and Chairman of the Canada (Arts) Council from 1979 to 1983. He has lectured widely and contributes a weekly column on cultural affairs to *The Globe and Mail*. Mr. Moore's career in theater, film, radio and television has earned him numerous awards, among them the Order of Canada. This essay is based on a talk he gave to the Americas Society on February 4, 1982.

The Rt. Hon. Brian Mulroney is Prime Minister of Canada. A native of Quebec, he was educated at St. Francis Xavier University and Laval University. His executive and labor negotiating skills helped elevate him to the presidency of the Iron Ore Company of Canada. Subsequently, he entered public life, becoming leader of the Progressive Conservative Party in 1983. Mr. Mulroney was elected Prime Minister in 1984 and re-elected in 1988. This speech was delivered to the Americas Society on March 28, 1988.

Jacques Parizeau, a Professor of Economics at the University of Montreal's Ecole des Hautes Etudes Commerciales, is leader of the Parti Québécois in the province of Quebec. He served as Minister of Finance in the government of Premier René Lévesque, who founded the separatist Parti Québécois and led it to power in the late 1970s. Mr. Parizeau received his Ph.D. from the London School of Economics. He is the author of numerous articles that have been widely published in Canada. His essay was delivered as an Americas Society's lecture on May 9, 1985.

Gérard Pelletier, one of the so-called "Wise Men" of the early Trudeau Administration, was educated at the University of Montreal. He had a noteworthy career in Quebec journalism before being elected to the federal Parliament in 1965. He held several prominent Cabinet positions with the Trudeau government before being appointed Canada's Ambassador to France in 1975. As Permanent Representative with Canada's Mission to the United Nations from 1981 to 1984, he delivered the Americas Society lecture, on which this essay is based, in January 1982.

John Roberts was Canada's Minister of the Environment when he delivered this talk on March 8, 1982. He was educated at the University of Toronto and Oxford University, England, before entering public life. He served in the Department of External Affairs and was first elected a Member of Parliament in 1968. He held several other important portfolios in the Trudeau government. Mr. Roberts is currently Professor of Politics at Concordia University in Montreal.

Gordon Robertson is Fellow-in-Residence and former President of the Institute for Research on Public Policy, Ottawa. He was educated at the universities of Saskatchewan, Toronto and Oxford before beginning a distinguished career in Canada's civil service. Under various federal governments, he served successively as Deputy Minister of Northern Affairs and Natural Resources, as Commissioner of the Northwest Territories and, for twelve years, as Secretary to the Cabinet for Federal–Provincial Relations in the Privy Council Office. Mr. Robertson currently serves as Chancellor of Carleton University. He was a member of the Americas Society/Canadian Affairs Advisory Board when he prepared his article especially for this book.

Nicholas Stethem, Managing Director of the Strategic Analysis Group in Toronto, has written widely on defense matters. A graduate of the Royal Military College of Canada, he served with the armed forces in Canada and Europe before beginning his career in 1975 as a commentator and adviser on military and national security affairs. His articles have appeared in major Canadian newspapers and professional journals. He was the 1986–87 Americas Society Visiting Associate when he gave the talk on which this paper is based.

James H. Taylor is Under-Secretary of State for External Affairs, the second-highest ranking diplomatic post in the Canadian foreign service. Educated at McMaster University, he went on to study at Oxford as a Rhodes Scholar. Mr. Taylor joined the Department of External Affairs in 1953. He has held a succession of important posts since then, including that of Ambassador to NATO from 1983 to 1985. This address was given to the Americas Society on April 15, 1987.

Anthony Westell is Director of the School of Journalism at Carleton University, Ottawa. One of Canada's outstanding journalists, he began his career in London and, after emigrating to Canada, served as a top editor and bureau chief with leading publications, including *The Globe and Mail* and *Toronto Star*. He is the author of several books. Mr. Westell was on leave as political columnist for the *Star*, serving as the 1983–84 Americas Society Visiting Associate, when he gave this talk on January 27, 1983.

Robin W. Winks, Professor of History and Master of Berkeley College at Yale, is an author and scholar of wide-ranging interests. As founding director of Yale's Canadian Studies program and now Chairman of its Committee on Canadian Studies, he has written knowledgeably about that country. His many articles and books also encompass British and Commonwealth history, the art of mystery writing and the role of academics in the Central Intelligence Agency. He earned his Ph.D. at Johns Hopkins University. This lecture was given to the Americas Society on December 13, 1981.

General Introduction

The beginning of the 1980s should have been promising for Canadian–American relations. Ronald Reagan devoted a full quarter of his announcement for the presidency to the importance of relations with Canada and Mexico. He spoke enthusiastically about the concept of a North American "accord." In his first trip outside the United States, the new President journeyed to Ottawa to meet with Prime Minister Trudeau.

Despite these auspicious signs, relations between the United States and Canada, the world's two largest trading partners and North America's two closest strategic allies, had in fact markedly deteriorated over the previous two decades. By the start of the 1980s, as both countries appeared to accelerate the aggressive pursuit of their respective national interests, some observers believed the relationship had reached an all-time low.

That may surprise those many Americans and Canadians who consider themselves almost mirror images of each other. Yet, this was in many ways a clash of two distinct nationalisms—and the collision course had been set more than a century before.

Nationalism, "the type and image of our souls" in the words of Walter Lippmann, had stamped itself in contrasting ways on the psyches of these two North American peoples. From the start their political roots had diverged, the American Founding Fathers championing life, liberty and the pursuit of happiness and their Canadian counterparts espousing, under the British North America Act, peace, order and good government. Gradually, those divergent precepts had refined themselves into profoundly differing attitudes: Canadians came to accept and rely on the idea of government as protector and intervener on behalf of their interests; Americans developed a well-honed skepticism of government as a potential threat to their individual liberties.

Culturally, the esprit de corps of the two nations had also evolved through starkly different experiences. America, born in revolution, its unity redeemed through civil war, survived to forge an assertive national identity. Canada, born of compromise, the molding of two proud and separate British and French cultures, found its struggle for national identity painfully protracted, even today not yet fully resolved. A third nationalism, economic, had spun off from the conflicting views of Canadians and Americans about the role of government in their lives, the sanctity of capitalist free enterprise and its right to operate at will in foreign markets. The tensions here stemmed largely from the imbalance between the two economies and Canadians' consequent overweening sense of disadvantage at having to compete with a neighboring market ten times the size of their own.

For most of the century following Canada's assumption of nationhood in 1867, these two sets of historically different nationalisms only on rare occasions abraded to the point of open conflict. The "manifest destiny" and annexationist syndromes played themselves out among Americans in the late 1800s. Congress in 1911 revived them briefly but sufficiently to lend credence to Canadians' slogan of "No Truck or Trade with the Yankees," thus dooming hopes for an historic Canada–U.S. Reciprocity Agreement at the time. In the post–Second World War era, however, friction between the two countries intensified as the relationship grew more complex. The United States assumed a more ambitious international role, and the historic personal camaraderie between the Presidents and Prime Ministers became frayed amid the whirl of conflicting larger forces.

The easy days of Roosevelt and Mackenzie King, of Eisenhower and St. Laurent, were overtaken by nuclear arms imperatives that bred antagonism between Diefenbaker and Kennedy, by a Vietnam War that sowed discord between Lyndon Johnson and Lester Pearson, and by the rude realities of international commerce that led to the American import surcharge in 1971 and a falling-out between President Nixon and Trudeau. It was that surcharge, aimed principally at Japan but damaging to Canada as well through its sideswipe effect, that provoked Ottawa's latent nationalism and drove it to assert a significantly more independent foreign policy based in part on the so-called "third option" strategy. Canada—already at odds with the United States over its continued ties to Cuba, its muted disapproval of American policy in Vietnam and its reluctance to join the Organization of American States (OAS) in this hemisphere—now sought for itself a role even more removed from the United States: that of the West's chief proponent of Third World interests. Canada set out to establish, among other things, closer trade and investment links with Asian and South American countries.

At the same time, Ottawa, having regarded with deepening concern the massive penetration of American investment and branch-plant business in Canada throughout the post-war period, decided to initiate a more aggressive economic nationalism through such measures as the Foreign Investment Review Act and, later, the National Energy Program (NEP). The Foreign Investment Review Act, which established the Foreign Investment Review Agency (FIRA) and was designed to screen out those foreign firms whose businesses were deemed of insufficient benefit to Canada, immediately struck hostile sparks within the American investment community. The NEP, one of whose major roles was to "Canadianize" the American-dominated oil and gas industry in Canada, created instant controversy on both sides of the border. Alarmed, too, at the influx of American magazines and television programming in Canada, the government in Ottawa set out to enforce minimum levels of Canadian-oriented programming on the nation's television screens. It also revoked the tax benefits of Canadian firms advertising on American broadcasting stations along the border and sent *Time* magazine's Canadian operation packing.

This rather un-Canadian testiness not only characterized a determinedly sovereign nation's response to external forces. It indicated as well a new confidence resulting from Canadians' success in dealing with a series of internal challenges and crises of their own. The long nightmare of the Quebec separatism crisis, threatening the very fabric of Canadian federation, had ended with the Quebec referendum of 1980, reaffirming that province's desire to remain within the national fold. The patriation of Canada's Constitution in 1982, severing the last formal link to Great Britain, had been achieved in spite of formidable legal obstacles and provincial opposition. Still to come was the long overdue energy accord between Ottawa and the disgruntled Canadian West, which helped dissipate the separatist murmurings in that region. Finally, the introduction of Canada's own new Charter of Rights and Freedoms, coming nearly two centuries after America's Bill of Rights, had provided further symbolic evidence of Canada's mounting self-assuredness.

Enter, right, the galloping Reagan Era. The new Republican President sought not only to repeal the notion of an expansive federal government overseeing all aspects of America's public weal, a notion nurtured to reality during the decades of the Democrats' New Deal and Great Society. Reagan's election also heralded an administration imbued with its own strongly nationalistic traits, an ideology committed to making America "stand tall" again around the world. The Reaganauts would move to erase America's guilt-ridden memories of Vietnam and Watergate. They would return the nation to a bolder, self-interested posture, restoring its diplomatic prestige abroad, its military and economic power at home. In particular, the Reaganauts, far more than previous administrations, cherished their strong ties to American business, to American entrepreneurship, to the concept of government championing as well as protecting the forces of a free market everywhere.

It was almost inevitable that the feisty nationalists of Reagan's Washington would sooner or later have to deal with the contentious nationalists of Trudeau's Ottawa. The clash came sooner, hard on the heels of Ottawa's toughening of FIRA and its imposition of the NEP in late 1980. Ottawa's perception was that, after two decades of increasing dominance of Canada's airwaves and business sectors by American interests, Canadians were fully justified in asserting their cultural and economic sovereignty through countermeasures. Washington's perception was that the countermeasures were unfairly restrictive and unjustly discriminatory toward American and other foreign investors. Relations, according to one senior American official, were "sliding dangerously toward crisis."

It was both an inauspicious and an opportune juncture to launch a new public affairs program in America that would introduce Canada and the Canadian perspective to an influential American audience.

For too long, otherwise intelligent and informed Americans had casually accepted the caricature of Canada, sketched in the *National Lampoon,* as a sort of arctic Nebraska, rarely visited by anyone but the Queen and illiterate sport fishermen. Most Americans seemed benignly disposed toward Canada, despite the skirmishing at the government level, but were vaguely unsure whether it should be treated as a continental wilderness treasure or a burgeoning industrial power (in fact, the world's seventh-largest). What seemed clear, as the 1980s arrived, was that many Americans of goodwill who wished to do business in Canada had only a faint comprehension of the country and of the people they would be dealing with. If Canadians had felt abused over such issues as fishing rights because they had misunderstood the role of the American Senate, American executives sounded hurt to the point of outrage that Canadians—the very extension of themselves, right?—would have invoked such unfriendly measures as the Foreign Investment Review Act and the NEP.

This prevalent misconception in the United States—that Americans and Canadians are virtually indistinguishable from each other—has been potentially damaging to the relationship. Just because they look alike, for the most part talk alike, and share many similar social and economic values, many well-meaning Americans left themselves vulnerable to disappointment and hard feelings as Canadians, late on, began to assert a more muscular sense of nationhood.

If America, as the lead nation, was henceforth to avoid the sort of estrangement that resulted from habitual ignorance of or indifference toward Canada, it would have to redouble its efforts to inform itself about the country and, most importantly, about those *differences* that distinguish the two peoples as proudly separate friends and neighbors. It was to that end that the Canadian Affairs program of the Americas Society was founded in 1981.

The Americas Society was the brainchild of David Rockefeller, perhaps the most influential private-sector figure in his country. Housed in a handsome, historic landmark building in upper

Manhattan, the Society operates as the premier international forum concerned with Western Hemisphere issues. It is a non-partisan, non-profit organization that seeks to foster greater understanding between the United States and its hemispheric neighbors. For many years the Society's work had been oriented largely toward Latin America and the Caribbean. The political, social and economic problems of those regions were, and continue to be, urgent and compelling.

By late 1980, however, Rockefeller and his fellow trustees felt the need for a full-fledged public affairs program that would bring Canada and the Canadian perspective into sharper focus for a sizable community of business, cultural and public affairs leaders in the New York area. Economic, environmental and other problems between Ottawa and Washington had sparked growing awareness in the United States that continued misunderstandings about Canadian purposes and attitudes were undermining not only intergovernment relations but also effective long-range private sector ties between the two countries. "For both sides, flexibility and communication must be the watchwords if we are to avoid irreparable damage to the relationship," warned America's Under Secretary of State for Economic Affairs, Myer Rashish, in a speech given during that period at the Americas Society.

In December 1980, at a dinner for Rockefeller in Toronto, the idea for a New York-based Canadian Affairs program was given the blessing of a number of prominent Canadian businessmen, led by the Bank of Nova Scotia's Cedric Ritchie. He and the heads of seven other Canadian and American companies, as well as the Donner Foundation of Canada, pledged an initial underwriting to launch the program. Its founding director, Lansing Lamont, was hired from the world of American journalism where he had served as a Washington and foreign correspondent for *Time* magazine, notably as its chief correspondent in Canada during the early 1970s.

It was Lamont's task to air before an American audience in New York not only those issues vital to the Canada–U.S. relationship, but the whole spectrum of the Canadian experience—political, economic and cultural. His program would augment in a different way the educational work already being ably carried out in Canadian studies programs at a number of American universities. The newest Canadian Affairs forum, though it regularly presented scholarly lectures by distinguished

Canadian and American professors, was from its start a variegated program aimed primarily at informing senior business and professional leaders about Canada in a non-academic setting. Its viewpoint, as far as possible, was neither partisan nor pedantic.

The Canadian Affairs program's purpose would be fulfilled through a rigorous schedule of conferences, seminars, round-table briefings, discussion groups and exhibitions. The speakers would be men and women of achievement from the Canadian world of arts, business, government, journalism and academe. Interspersed with the Canadians would be American experts familiar with Canada and bilateral issues. One of these, the Under Secretary of Commerce for International Trade, Lionel Olmer, was shortly to note in an address to the new forum:

> The Center for Inter-American Relations [later renamed the Americas Society] could not have chosen a better time to establish its Canadian Affairs program. We are faced with a unique period in our bilateral relationship . . . I welcome the efforts of this distinguished Center in bringing about better understanding between our two great countries.

Americas Society/Canadian Affairs, as it came to be known after the Center for Inter-American Relations was phased into the Americas Society, launched itself formally in October 1981. Its first events—a no-holds-barred speech by Canadian External Affairs Minister Mark MacGuigan at the program's inaugural dinner, followed the next day by a luncheon address of equal bluntness from the United States' Assistant Secretary of State for European Affairs, Lawrence Eagleburger— all too plainly exposed the reigning antagonisms of the day. Some of the Americans present found the Canadian's candor offensive; others wondered whether the new program was an unnecessary amplifier of disputes that might best be kept muffled. The Canadians, on the other hand, welcomed the chance to convey their feelings, unrestricted by diplomatic protocol, to a weighty audience of New Yorkers, and Canada's press eagerly reported the remarks of both speakers. As it was, the era of quiet Canadian–American diplomacy had long since passed. Americas Society/Canadian Affairs was born amidst a rhetorical fire-fight between the two countries. For better or worse, the program garnered attention from the start and seldom skirted an issue from that time on.

Over succeeding years, as Canadian Affairs gained a reputation as the premier forum of its kind, more than 200 leading Canadians and Americans from all walks of life journeyed to New York to participate in its programs. Government ministers, Cabinet members and lawmakers addressed the forum's growing audience. The procession included: political leaders like Robert Bourassa, David Peterson and Peter Lougheed; historians like the late and venerated John Holmes of Canada, and McGeorge Bundy, former adviser to presidents; authors and journalists like Margaret Atwood, Pierre Berton, Robert MacNeil and Richard Gwyn; scholars like Yale's Robin Winks; cultural figures like Yousuf Karsh and Arthur Erickson; diplomats like former Ambassadors Kenneth Taylor and Gérard Pelletier; and business statesmen, from Northern Telecom's Edmund Fitzgerald to the Bank of Montreal's William Mulholland. In March 1988, Canada's Prime Minister Brian Mulroney addressed an overflow Americas Society audience at New York's Plaza Hotel.

As the procession of speakers lengthened, their talks and articles began to form an impressive testament to the variety and strengths of the Canadian–American relationship. Cumulatively, they shaped an unsparing, richly textured portrait of Canada and the bilateral relationship in this decade, its evolution from the slough of the early eighties to the era of Shamrock summitry and the more open-door policies of a new Conservative government.

The idea of a book, an anthology of the most publishable of these many talks at the Americas Society/Canadian Affairs forum, took shape as certain patterns emerged from the welter of insights and opinions expressed. The theme of national sovereignty—the need to understand the *differences* that distinguish the character of Canadians from that of Americans—was the great constant. As Robert Johnstone, then Canada's Deputy Minister of International Trade, put it in an early talk:

We are not Americans. We have not, like the sheep in the Whiffenpoof Song, simply gone astray across some notional boundary line. We are citizens of a distinct sovereign state. Sovereign not only in the legal sense. Sovereign because of all the things in our history that over the years have gone to make us different from others.

The Canadian speakers could be, and often were, sharply critical of their own government's policies. But what shone through much of the time was an inherent appreciation of government's assertive role in their nation's development. Monique Bégin, Trudeau's Minister of National Health and Welfare, made the point sweepingly at one round-table luncheon. Throughout its history, she observed, Canada has been the recipient of benevolent public enterprises launched by its governments: publicly owned and operated hydroelectric power systems, a national railway system, provincially owned and operated telephone systems, the Canadian Broadcasting Corporation, Air Canada and Petro-Can, a publicly owned oil company. Given this record, Bégin concluded, it is not surprising that Canadians have put in place a host of universal social security measures, including a national health insurance program that is more comprehensive than anything in America. Journalist Richard Gwyn, a frequent visitor to the forum before he became the *Toronto Star*'s chief European correspondent, wrote that Canadians do not lobby and fight for their rights against government "because in the collective perception the government is *theirs*. They assume it is working for them." A novel perception, some Americans might feel.

Especially valuable was the gamut of national perspectives that speakers brought to such issues as nuclear disarmament, East–West relations and women's rights. To hear Canada's Ambassador to the United Nations on the disarmament question, or its former Ambassador to Moscow Geoffrey Pearson on the psychology of Soviet–American relations, was to comprehend the considerable disparity in Canadian and American views about the great challenges of our time. Closer to home, Canada's traditional diffidence about involving itself in larger hemispheric concerns, reserving its right to complain when the United States takes the lead in such matters, was personified by New Democratic Party leader Edward Broadbent and challenged by Professor Robin Winks, Yale historian and founder of that university's Canadian Studies program. Americans, listening to Canadian speakers project their views about such troubling spheres of influence as Moscow and the Middle East, might have sensed the irony of Canada's constructive engagement overseas contrasted with its quasi-isolationism within the Americas. At the same time, a mutuality of interests prevailed on occasion, as when Canadian

Affairs hosted *Women as Leaders in North America: Bridges and Barriers*, a 1985 conference in New York that convened more than a hundred prominent feminists and women of achievement from both countries. "American women can take heart from our success in their own struggle for the Equal Rights Amendment," declared Flora MacDonald, Canada's Minister of Employment and Immigration. Geraldine Ferraro, the 1984 Democratic Vice Presidential candidate, recalled the woman in Toronto who handed her a piece of paper to sign. "It's for my nine-year-old daughter," the woman said, "who's going to be the first female Prime Minister of Canada."

There was more than enough introspection. Canadians, discussing their cultural battles and regional frustrations, veered from barrel-chested chauvinism to wry skepticism. The cultural conflicts that have engulfed Quebec and anglophone Canada evoked passions in many a speaker, while audiences were quick to grasp the wintry resentment of Westerners alienated from both a distant federal government and a Toronto–Montreal axis that has so long dominated Canada's culture and politics. Allan Fotheringham, the irreverent columnist for *Maclean's* magazine, predicted (wrongly) at a Canadian Affairs press panel session in 1982 that Trudeau's exit from the Prime Minister's office would "suck out the alienation and hatred" in Canada's West and eradicate the last seeds of separatism in that region. French-Canadian author Dominique Clift, on the same panel, sounded the death knell for Quebec nationalism. New forces, including the advent of an aggressive business-oriented society in Quebec, had led to "a breakdown in the nationalists' focus on the nation-state as the chosen instrument for the expression of French cultural values." All the same, the *New York Times*'s Henry Giniger concluded, the regionalism issue would continue to complicate efforts to achieve real lasting unity in Canada. Only when the lopsided political domination by populous Ontario and Quebec ceased, or some reform of Canada's archaic Senate occurred, would the regional grievances of the Western and Maritime provinces dissipate. And that time was far off, if ever.

Always, however, the recurring theme in these Americas Society/Canadian Affairs talks was the bilateral one. While Canadians and Americans share common interests and face many similar challenges, they view the bilateral relationship from markedly differing perspectives. For Canadians, America's dominance and huge scale of operation are continuing preoccupations. For Americans, saddled with other international priorities, the effort has been to fit Canada and Canadians' interests into a broader world context. It is almost as if at times the United States wished that the bilateral tie, per se, did not exist.

The fact that these talks were given to a largely American audience should be borne in mind by readers. Many of the Canadians were outspoken in their criticism of American policy and perspectives. Canadians have always been comfortable giving advice to Americans. Americans, recognizing Canadians' sensitivity in dealing with the larger dominant partner in the relationship, have customarily tended to let Canadians take the initiative in areas of bilateral contentiousness, from acid rain to protective trade practices. The cultivation in some influential Canadian circles of anti-American feeling is seldom returned in kind in the United States. There, the more basic problem is not anti-Canadianism but rather an unshakable incomprehension as to why Americans should even want to know enough about Canadians to dislike them. It is this, not the particulars of acid rain or tariffs on British Columbia timber exports, that exasperates Canadians. It is this well of amiable ignorance that we hope this book can in some small way help drain.

Friendships, to survive and flourish, have to be based on something more profound than neighborly goodwill. Canadians and Americans need as friends to read each other with far more awareness and empathy. We need to better understand each other's history, economics and serious culture. We need to appreciate our fundamental distinctions in order to cope with our more immediate differences. We need as close friends to track the subtleties in our respective political and social systems, to feel out each other's attitudes and mindsets, in order to avoid those unnecessary collisions that jar the relationship.

Friends So Different, the product of Americans and Canadians who have played contributing roles in the bilateral saga, explores not only the issues but also the spirit that animates this historic alliance. It illuminates, we hope, the deeper national values and character that belie the cliché that we are one homogenous North American family separated only by an artificial border. We are in fact two proudly peaceable kingdoms, contiguous but clearly delineated by our differing approaches to the world and to one another.

L.L.
J.D.E.
January 1, 1989

Part I

Canadian–American Relations

In December 1981, a *Time* magazine poll reported that Americans, by an approval rating of 90 per cent, considered Canada their most trusted ally. That must have seemed a particularly ironic twist for Canadian and American business and government leaders who, in that very period, were experiencing severe strains in the bilateral relationship. No shots had been exchanged across the more than 5 000 miles of undefended border, but the shouting across it had reached high-decibel levels.

The public in both countries clung to the old verities of common Canadian–American bonds and shared values: two pluralistic, immigrant societies with a shared notion of human rights and a common commitment to democratic practices; a general similarity in world outlook; a generally shared cultural milieu; and a pair of vibrant economies based on the creative role of the private sector.

Yet, these connective values had become background harmony to the dissonant clangor of two nations, starkly *un*comparable in influence and power, which for the last decade or so had become increasingly aggressive in pursuing their respective national interests. The frequent collision of these interests, especially in the economic sector, led to a souring in relations.

Canadians might argue, as New Democratic Party leader Edward Broadbent did before the Americas Society, that Canada was taking sharply restrictive economic measures not simply out of emotional jingoism or some form of banal anti-Americanism, but in order to free its economy from dependence on the United States. But many Americans refused to buy this argument, accusing Canada of unfairly changing the established rules of bilateral investment and business procedure in their country.

At the same time, veteran diplomats on both sides deplored the lack of any systematic approach to Canada–U.S. relations, the absence of any strategic planning apparatus and the ritual reliance by both governments on *ad hoc* approaches to important issues, in spite of the enormous volume of transborder dealings and the complex web of interrelationships between the two countries. Further unsettling to adherents of the quiet diplomacy that had characterized Canada–U.S. relations for most of the twentieth century was the turn toward a more strident public conduct of the relationship via the media and other channels. The tactic of lobbying more assertively for national interests, using the other country's legislative branch as a target, was first invoked by Canada's embassy in Washington. A new era, with new rules for managing the relationship, had begun.

Against this background, a quartet of leading American and Canadian opinion- and policy-makers addressed the state of the bilateral relationship in the fall of 1981. They were: John Holmes, the distinguished Canadian diplomat and historian; Annette Baker Fox, author and founder of the Canadian Studies program at Columbia University; Mark MacGuigan, Canada's Minister of External Affairs; and Lawrence Eagleburger, the United States' Assistant Secretary of State for European and Canadian Affairs. The issue of private versus public diplomacy was addressed a year later by Anthony Westell, a prominent Canadian journalist and the 1983–84 Americas Society Visiting Associate.

John W. Holmes

Crises in Canadian–
American Relations:
A Canadian Perspective

A problem about Canada is that it is odd man out.

Foreign offices and schools of international affairs never know with whom to associate us. In spite of our many similarities with the United States or with Jamaica or Brazil, it is hard to see us as a typical American state. We have as much in common with West European democracies. But within the North Atlantic Treaty Organization (NATO), for example, which is seen so often as a European–American dumbbell, we are hard to classify. In our forms of government we are associated most easily with our Commonwealth partners, Australia and New Zealand.

Canada has been called a regional power without a region. We suffer from this uniqueness by being misunderstood. We also suffer, more seriously in my view, from a lack of informed criticism by foreigners. Because we do not fit their patterns, the foreign policy élite in the United States and their sophisticated journals have virtually ignored the Canadian fact. The American financial media, which can hardly ignore a country more important to them than the European Economic Community (EEC) or Japan, display a frightening lack of understanding of Canadian history, politics, and economics. Because American comment on Canada is so customarily bland, I find the malevolent animosity of the *Wall Street Journal* refreshing. Its editors at least take us seriously as an adult nation even if they do not understand what makes us tick. That lack of understanding at the moment presents a serious threat to a relationship which has been a model of civilized behaviour to the world.

We need the consistent and critical attention of those Americans who recognize that foreign countries, however close, are complex and that their economics and politics cannot be comprehended in a vacuum. There is a small band of scholars and concerned citizens in the United States who might be called Canadianists, probably smaller than the number of Albanianists. Some of the best of them have recently published a thoughtful paper for the Atlantic Council entitled "United States Policy Towards Canada." That is a subject I have never seen treated in *Foreign Affairs* or *Foreign Policy*, although those publications do produce from time to time a token article on The Good Neighbor—written, of course, by a Canadian. Canadians write obsessively about their policies towards the United States; but because American scholars rarely if ever write about American policy towards Canada, discussion of the relationship is intellectually lopsided. One result is that Canadians can get away too easily with nonsense on the subject.

Most worrying to Canadians is the volatility of American policy and attitudes. Last year, after our diplomats in Teheran sheltered Americans, there were "Take-a-Canadian-to-Lunch" weeks from New York to San Diego. This year, according to American business journals, we are selfish ingrates unfit for the Western industrial club. We have been misjudged in both cases.

The problem is the lack of depth in American understanding. All right, Canada is boring. Any game is boring until you know the rules. So with Canadian–American relations. Students of conflict, as well as editors, prefer at least a little violence. But this Canada–U.S. relationship might prove to be normalcy itself. Surely, we aim for a world in which government and international relations are as boring as possible. In Canada only our possible fracture seems to attract attention. Canadians tend to see their genius in that they evolved from colonies into a state through peaceful means without either revolution or civil war, a process comfortable for our citizenry but very poor theatre otherwise.

The best speech an American official ever made about Canada was by President Nixon in Ottawa in 1972 when he advocated a more mature attitude towards the relationship. His remarks were aimed at those Canadians who were assessing American policy in ideological terms that did not really fit North America. They whined and grieved instead of regarding our differences as inevitable, perpetual, and negotiable. Less materially pecunious than Americans, they had to be morally purer. Unlike the Mexicans, they saw themselves as Canadians "so near to God, so far from the United States." Since then, I think Canadian attitudes have matured considerably, sobered by a little adversity, but also as a result of growing confidence in their nation's economic strength.

I am less sure that American attitudes towards Canada have matured. We are still regarded as a child-nation to be praised on principle and given stern warnings, but not to be taken seriously as an item on a foreign affairs agenda. President Carter never found time in his travels for a secondary capital like Ottawa. He explained this lapse by saying there were no problems he knew of at a time when Canadians thought they had a very long list. President Reagan came quickly after his election. Yet, we seem to be back in the old pattern—pat-on-the-shoulder rhetoric, nothing but goodwill at the top, while the issues go unresolved and tensions are aggravated. Telling Americans, as Reagan did, that they ought not to regard Canadians (or Mexicans) as foreigners, does not seem a very mature way, however sweetly intended, to approach the Canadian dimension of American foreign policy.

Canada, after all, is the amalgamation of colonies, from the Atlantic to the Pacific, which for various reasons did not want to become part of the great republic. The American misjudgement of Canada goes back to the illusions of the Revolution. It was assumed that it was imperial Britain that held the Canadians in thrall, that Canadians would welcome liberation and join the new United States as soon as they could. So "manifest destiny" did not require military action. The British, however, had mixed feelings about the value of Canada to them in the age of free trade; and Americans finally realized that it was the stubborn Canadians themselves who did not want to celebrate the Fourth of July.

Canada was viewed with suspicion as a toehold of monarchism on a republican continent, monarchism being then regarded with much the same antipathy as communism is today. The Dominion of Canada, established in 1867, was seen in Washington as an insult— "this semi-independent and irresponsible agency," President Grant called it. I suppose Grant was right, and I think Canadians should always bear in mind that we cut "manifest destiny" for the United States in half, that we remain a persistent affront to the spirit of 1776, and that the United States owes us nothing. Americans, on the other hand, might bear in mind that the founders of English Canada were largely refugees from the revolutionary terrorists in Boston and Philadelphia.

It is to the everlasting credit of the United States that we were allowed to establish our dominion without violent interference, although not until the beginning of this century did the American government reluctantly accept the existence of Canada as a permanent fact. While Teddy Roosevelt howled against us in the spirit of Sumner and Seward, those elsewhere, who believed that the Republic must employ high principles in dealing with other countries, worked quietly behind the scenes with Britons and Canadians of goodwill to produce the Boundary Waters Treaty of 1909 and the International Joint Commission (IJC). The IJC is an inspired mechanism for equitable relations between unequal states, for which the more powerful country deserves the most credit.

It is this basic instinct for fair play, not charity, on which Canada must count; and it seems especially necessary to recall this history whenever our relations become shrill, as they are at present.

In the fairytale atmosphere in which we have shrouded North American relations, it has been considered bad form to touch on ancient hostilities and conflicts which nice people don't have. It seems, however, a sounder basis for good relations to recognize that it was not ever thus, that this relationship in fact has been a triumph of reason over emotion, of pragmatism over ideology. At the moment, we are in great danger of ruining our good reputation by an unseemly shouting match that is about real conflicts of interest, but is clouded with ideological distortion that feeds on itself. We ritually say we are different, a good and welcome thing. But in practice an unwelcome intolerance intrudes, as now, when we realize how *real* the differences are.

These differences, which are causing tension at the moment, are misinterpreted as ideological, whereas they are really the pragmatic consequences of two very different economic, political, and social situations. We chew the same gum, but our political lives are distinct. The interests of a super- and a lesser power—with their different histories; different social, ethnic, and linguistic conditions; different federal systems with dissimilar allocation of powers—must necessarily serve their governments in differing ways. The essential difference is in sheer size and clout. If Canadians tend to be collectivists and Americans to be individualists, the reason is that Americans have a lot more individuals. It has nothing to do with Karl Marx. Canada has one overweening problem that the United States does not have: that of living beside a superpower. For us, the problem has advantages as well as disadvantages.

The charge laid against Canada in Congress and on Wall Street these days is *nationalism*. The accusation varies in intensity— from rational assessments of the National Energy Policy (NEP) and Foreign Investment Review Agency (FIRA) as antithetical to American business interests to ludicrous comparisons of Canadian policies with those of the Third World and of Prime Minister Trudeau's proposals with those of socialist states.

Americans and their government have every right to challenge Canadian policies that affect their interests. Canadians themselves are by no means agreed on the wisdom of the NEP or FIRA. What is worrying is the failure of Americans to see why Canadians feel as they do about the ownership of their resources, or the need to protect their press and media from American free enterprise. I have yet to see an American attack on our NEP, official or editorial, which cites the simple, eloquent statistics on foreign ownership in our respective countries and asks what Americans would do in comparable situations. The loaded language of the American press on the subject helps us understand the resentment of the Third World against Western journalism.

If you want to be subtly misled on almost every fact, read an article published in *Fortune* last April called "Trudeau's War on U.S. Business." It states consistently, for example, that Canada invited the American companies to develop its national resources, conveying the impression that this was a kind of United Nations aid and development project. Canada certainly welcomed foreign investment, as did most other countries, including the United States when it was developing its economy. The multinationals have surely not lost money over their

Canadian operations. It is constantly said that our policy is one of discrimination against Americans, but there is no evidence that any foreign country has been treated worse than another. The first companies taken over by the Canadian national oil company, Petro-Can, with generous compensation, were Belgian and French. Fantasies about expropriation, the confusing of Canadianization with nationalization, have helped create the current miasma in Canada–U.S. relations.

"Trudeau's policy." One of the disparaging misinterpretations of our so-called "economic nationalism" is that it is the personal whim of the Prime Minister, a deliberate effort to unify our distracted country by setting up a foreign devil. We did not take that charge seriously until it appeared in a *New York Times* editorial, creating in one stroke a considerable degree of apoplexy in Canada. What especially upsets those of us who have spent our lives calming the more hallucinated Canadian nationalists and arguing for reason across the border is the ignorance that that kind of article displays of the dynamics of Canadian policy.

This is no "new wave of nationalism." To begin with, Pierre Trudeau is ideologically anti-nationalist. His coming to power coincided with a maturing of the Canadian economy and a consequent insistence on a greater share of native control. It was given a shove by the Nixon–Connally surcharge of 1971 which seemed to imply that we could have a happy trading relationship with the United States provided the balance was not in our favour. This "nationalism" was thus an idea whose time had come. No government could have resisted it. It was in the tradition of the historic National Policy proclaimed by Sir John A. Macdonald, the great Conservative leader, after the United States' rejection of reciprocity in 1866.

In the world at large, the energy crisis and the increased competitiveness of international trade have driven all countries, including the United States, to enlist the power of the state to protect and promote the national interest in the world economy. We are all trying, through the General Agreement on Tariffs and Trade (GATT) and the Organization for Economic Cooperation and Development (OECD), to put brakes on these interventions. And we are all trying to use the rules to our own advantage. If Canada seems to Americans more wicked than others—the French, the Japanese, or the Mexicans—it is because Americans are discovering that Canada really matters more to them than Japan or the EEC on which they lavish their attention. It is also because in the past Canada has been the most docile, with a degree of foreign ownership of its economy beyond that of any other developed country.

Why do Americans accept stricter rules by the British and Norwegians over foreign control? Is it because, half-consciously, they regard Canada as a kind of fiefdom, a country which, not being foreign, ought to know its place? Why this discrimination against Canada?

The effort to increase Canadian ownership of its energy resources to even 50 per cent may not prove wise. But it is almost inevitable at a time when we, like others, face grave problems of unemployment and national debt. To be called raving nationalists by Americans at a time when, in our eyes, the United States seems gripped by a heady nationalism of its own, seems hardly fair. American complaints about Canadian restrictions on trade and investment are matched by Canadian complaints of comparable practices in a number of American states. Americans never seem to think nationalism is a term that can be applied to them.

One noted Canadian economist, a recent convert from American citizenship, suggested that xenophobia would be a more appropriate word to describe the fears that have beset America about the Saudis, the Japanese, and the aggressive Canadians who are trying to buy up Dallas and other pockets of Americana. When Congressmen were told that the attempt by Seagrams to take over Conoco was part of a Canadian plot to buy out the United States, Edgar Bronfman, Seagrams' chairman, asked whether "the Canadian minnow is about to swallow the American whale." He noted facetiously that, in order to have the same relative significance for the American economy as increasing American direct investment in Canada has for the Canadian economy, Canadian direct investment in the United States would have to increase to about $375 billion instead of declining to the $7 billion which it has recently. Furthermore, the idea that Seagrams, Olympia & York, and other corporate predators are tools of the government in Ottawa strikes Canadians as slightly hilarious. Having spent years trying to persuade paranoid Canadians that the multinational corporations are not agents of an American conspiracy, I was dismayed to find the argument used even more paranoiacally in reverse.

Between states of unequal size and wealth simple reciprocity is a dubious policy. There is an arguable case that Canadian actions contravene GATT and OECD rules and that the United States could rally some European countries in support. Don't tempt us too far, for we can argue that those rules were made to favour the interests of the powerful. That is why we insisted on an exemption in the so-called national treatment resolution in the OECD. We defied the United States on those grounds, too, over the Law of the Sea, allying ourselves with Third World complaints about the old law of the sea. If our attitudes often seem ambivalent, remember that we are in part a developing country and that, as regards multinational companies, say, we have much in common with the Third World.

At the basic political level, America's and Canada's forms and philosophies of government are substantially different. We have a parliamentary system of responsible government; you believe in the separation of powers. There is much to be said for both systems, but yours, which may represent the ultimate in internal democracy, presents all other countries with difficulties that grow larger as the world grows more interdependent.

In our system, as in most other countries, the government can negotiate agreements and be confident of ratifying them. Any agreement negotiated by the American Administration, however, is subject to endless review by Congress which often seems to regard itself as beyond international law and not bound by the accepted procedures of ordinary states. That is why Canadians were so upset by the refusal of Congress even to consider the East Coast Fisheries and Maritime Boundary agreements of 1979. American and Canadian negotiators had worked arduously for years to reach the kind of equitable bargain that characterizes civilized countries. It was accepted by the United States government, at least that part of it which represents the only government with which we can bargain. No foreign government can negotiate with the American Senate and lobbying the Senators seems a distasteful intrusion into the domestic affairs of a friendly state, incompatible with our idea of good government and good neighbourliness.

We are told insistently by Americans that the American Constitution is something we should have become accustomed to by now. Yet, in our view, the assertion of Congressional control over foreign policy has increased disturbingly since Watergate and Vietnam. We think there is a fundamental unfairness in what our respective constitutions require of each other. It is true there are situations in which the Canadian federal government lacks the power to force provincial governments to do what the United States wants, but basically our internal problems of jurisdiction are ours to settle. Washington has a comparable difficulty with recalcitrant states. Still, the degree of difficulty presented by each nation's constitutional handicaps is in no way comparable. In any case, the misbehaviour of our provinces is matched by the discrimination practised by state and municipal governments in the United States.

Our concern is aggravated by our inability to obtain reliable agreements from Washington on things that matter very much to us: for example, the issue of the Alaska pipeline to which we have made expensive commitments; acid rain, and other forms of pollution which seriously threaten our environment. We are often unable even to get the divided powers in Washington to listen to our views on these issues. In our mutual interest we need countless agreements and understandings at all levels, but new attitudes in Congress threaten our workmanlike relations. We worry because Congress seems increasingly subject to whimsical regional pressures and therefore unable to take a balanced view of the bilateral relationship as a whole.

In this century we have felt that in crises we could appeal to the State Department or to the White House, to someone willing to consider our arguments even if he did not agree. We wonder now to whom we can turn. Who speaks or negotiates for the United States? I am not suggesting our claims be accepted as valid, that we are always in the unchallengeable right. We do, however, want to bargain and conclude transactions that are binding.

Yet, that appears too difficult for America's friends and allies because of what Samuel Huntington has called "the absence in America of a 'state' in the European sense"—or, for that matter, in the Canadian, Australian, or Japanese sense. A reviewer of Huntington's new book, *American Politics*, noted that Americans have always viewed government as inherently illegitimate, have given it power grudgingly, and then objected to its exercise. "Until recently," the reviewer wrote, "this obduracy had a certain charm; it was a luxury America could afford. Now, we face a world less amenable to our influence, which might suggest the time has come to get our act together" (Andrew Hacker, *New York Times Book Review*, November 15, 1982, p. 3).

Canadians recognize that Americans have a beautiful Constitution, but we wish they would realize how difficult it is to be an ally of a country that cannot make binding commitments. If our systems of government differ, so, too, do our philosophies. The American Constitution is dedicated to "life, liberty, and the pursuit of happiness" for the individual. Canada's has the stated aim of "peace, order and good government." The struggling colonies that linked themselves together to form the preposterous Dominion of Canada had to be practical. Ours has always been a functionalist approach. We did not for practical reasons seek *independence* from Britain because we needed Britain for our markets, our defence, and as a deterrent to "manifest destiny" from the outside. There was no use cutting off our noses in the name of some fashionable ideology like anti-colonialism. We worked out with the British a peaceful evolution of self-government with mutual respect. That experiment set the pattern for the transformation of the world's greatest empire into a Commonwealth and it saved the world oceans of blood in the process. If the French had followed our example, America would have been saved from Vietnam. Ours was a triumph of functionalism over ideology.

We are the least ideologically nationalist state in the Western world. Inevitably, Americans judge our nationalism in their own terms and conclude that we are a failed model of themselves. Therefore, they exaggerate the significance of our divisions.

We do not pretend or want to be a unified nation-state. We have two nations and two languages to start with, and vast regional diversities that stretch our central control. That is our condition, not our weakness. It is part of our concept of freedom—freedom from the demands of conforming to an oppressive nationalism. We have a long tradition of civil argument but not of civil war. If we press to gain greater control over our economy and resources, it is because we must do so to survive in this competitive new world. We have our own kind of order and good government, our own history, and a land we love and desire to preserve. We will not sacrifice these simply for the more efficient organization of our continent.

We have, because of our circumstances, very different views of the role of government in our economic and social life. Our governments have been more interventionist because they had to be. We had to have our own railways, airlines, broadcasting, and television because American transport and communications would not serve our needs. Most of these enterprises have been initiated in the past by Conservative governments, federal and provincial, which normally sing the praises of free enterprise and voice a low opinion of socialism.

That is a very Canadian, functionalist view, and it is totally unideological. We do not for a moment suggest that our kind of government is applicable to the United States with its vast industry. Americans make a great mistake if they think that this so-called Canadian nationalism is the fad of one or two individuals in Ottawa. No Canadian government would at the moment act differently, because what Americans call our nationalism is a widely and deeply based feeling. It is in no sense a recrudescence of the more ideological and often anti-American nationalism of the sixties, fueled by American radicals. Our economy has reached a higher level of maturity; and we are going to do whatever is practical to raise the level of national control and ownership.

As the less powerful country on this continent, Canada has always had to stake out fences for protection, not from American imperialism but from the force of continental pressures. There is no way we will accept the "free enterprise" organization of the continent, for we are not equal partners. International free enterprise is American nationalism. Canadians must stake out a place for their cultural activities, for the media that serve our needs, and we must make sure that our resources are prudently used. We cannot accept supra-sovereign authority. At the same time, we have traditionally welcomed bodies like the IJC or the Permanent Joint Board on Defense which, while preserving the sovereignty of each government, seek equitable solutions to bilateral problems. On the other hand, let us not exaggerate the barriers. They leave room for an unusually free border between two healthy states rather than between one superpower and one depressed, put upon, lesser neighbour.

Whether in a spirit of generosity or retaliation, Americans tend to talk of reciprocity in their dealings with Canada. Yet, this is too simplistic a formula for so complex a relationship. Canadians have no right to ask for favours; and they should drop that silly tone of grievance when they resist American policies, the David-versus-Goliath syndrome. Strict reciprocity would cause Canada often to suffer inordinately; its punitive application by the United States could also be counterproductive. Because of our contrasting situations, tit-for-tat policies on, for example, the imposition of border broadcasting taxes or the restriction of investment may hurt us little or even serve our ends. The principle we need is one of discriminating management.

There are substantial differences as well over foreign policy arising from our different roles in the world. Canadians are willing allies in world politics, allies not just of the United States but of NATO as a whole. It has never been a question of Canada's adopting a radically contrary position to that of the United States on basic world issues; that is not because we are under constraint, but because we see the basics in similar terms.

We in our own way were as much the originators of NATO as the Americans. A medium power with our own historical traditions, playing a peripheral rather than decisive world role, we have differed mainly from the United States in perspectives and tactics. Soviet-American détente always seemed particularly important for us because we lie between the superpowers. For us, international institutions—the United Nations, NATO, the Commonwealth—are essential because only through them can we exert any impact. That is why we have been dismayed by the American volte-face over the Law of the Sea. Not only do we see in that move a loss of protection of our own interests. The Law of the Sea endeavour has seemed to us one of the greatest efforts at multilateral diplomacy in the history of mankind, one which cannot be allowed to fail.

We are accused of not pulling our weight in NATO, and there is a case to be made against us. Americans should understand, however, that the increasing tendency in Europe and the United States to regard NATO as a bilateral Europe–U.S. alliance, leaving Canada out of consideration, increases the sense in Canada that NATO is someone else's alliance. Would it not be better to return to what has been the

Canadian view of NATO from the beginning—a community of states seeking a common defence, not a strategic dumbbell?

The Europeans may like to preserve the myth of a European position, but North America is a geographical, not a political, entity; there is no such thing as a North American position. Canadians agree with the United States on many issues, but on many others our perspectives are closer to those of the Germans, while the British are closer to the Americans. Would it not be healthier to regard inevitable differences among the allies as natural variations of opinion among fourteen countries rather than a breach between the United States and Europe, a breach which effectively serves the interests of our antagonists, but which is not in accordance with the facts?

There are many Canadians who think we should spend more on defence. Others argue that the assigned percentages of expenditure are set according to the assessments of the great powers as to what *they* wish to spend, and that the great powers do that for their own economic and strategic reasons. In an age of extravagant technology we cannot afford to gamble in the area of defence. For Canada, furthermore, it is a strategic necessity to maintain our sway over the largest country in the alliance—to maintain, for example, an expensive civilian infrastructure along an important NATO frontier, the Arctic. I say this not to justify our actual defence policy but to remind our American friends that the view from the North is conditioned by unique factors.

Differences between Ottawa and Washington—on issues ranging from Central America to Southern Africa to the role of the United Nations—are differences of 45 degrees, more or less. If we have not shouted over our disagreements, it is due to the fundamental loyalty America's allies feel towards the United States and also, I should add, to nervousness about a mood in Washington that seems less tolerant than in times past. We are worried, furthermore, by the recrudescence of that anarchical force of anti-Americanism in the world, which threatens not only the United States but the larger world order we cherish. If we do differ, it is not out of anti-Americanism but rather a desire to save our champion from what seems to us to be harmful mistakes.

We recognize the singular role that accompanies the special responsibility of the United States in the NATO alliance. At the same time, none of us can accept in principle those practices whereby the United States takes unilateral decisions, over Afghanistan, for example, and then makes the test of unity and loyalty our willingness to follow an American policy we regard as unwise.

Finally, there is the question of Canada and the Americas. Canada has never joined the Organization of American States (OAS). The reason originally was attributed to American concern at having a Trojan horse from the wicked British Empire infecting the pure republican climate of the Americas. There were other circumstances, however: our over-extended commitments to other international organizations, as well as, frankly, a reluctance to get mixed up in U.S.–Latin American disputes. We thought we might end up in the OAS either supporting the United States and looking like an American satellite or voting to support the Latins and getting Congress mad at us. I am describing, not applauding, this policy. For the moment, I suspect the desire to avoid antagonizing the stout hearts in Washington makes us even more cautious. In the OAS, furthermore, members vote up or down on decisions, which is why we prefer bodies like NATO and the Commonwealth where the members seek consensus.

Remember also that the Western Hemisphere, as Americans see it, is a product of American and Latin American history rather than a conclusion based on geography. Canada's links have been largely in the Northern Hemisphere. There is strong support in Canada for increasing ties with Mexico or Venezuela, Brazil or Peru. We have always enjoyed close relations with our sister nations in the Commonwealth Caribbean. Indeed, our ties with Mexico are growing stronger. President Lopez Portillo and Prime Minister Trudeau have met three times this past year. You in the United States are being surrounded.

The idea of a North American accord, advanced by President Reagan and others during the last American election, was greeted with suspicion in Mexico and Canada. Both smaller countries feared, probably without justification, that the United States wanted to share their oil resources. Having been present at the first trilateral summit at White Sulphur Springs in 1956, I can see advantage in periodic meetings of the three heads of government. The United States, however, must recognize the difference between a consultation and a briefing, as at White Sulphur Springs. First on the agenda of such a meeting should be a careful listening to Canadian views on the Arctic and to Mexican views on Central America. Canada, along with Venezuela and Mexico, agreed to participate in President Reagan's so-called Caribbean Basin Initiative, although all three of us have serious doubts about Washington's approach to the problems of that area.

History and geography, I am afraid, have made Canada a country unlike others, no more virtuous, just unique. It was tiresome of our forefathers to have made life inconvenient for orderly American minds. But I fear Americans will have to spend some time seeing our frailties and strengths for what they are if the United States is to cope successfully with its senior economic partner. This is a plea, then, for pragmatism and tolerance, qualities that have led Canadians and Americans to set an example to the world. If we can avoid the abstractions and sit down at the table, if we can subdue the rhetoric and look at the facts, we will better serve the interests of both peoples.

Resistance to the United States is endemic in the Canadian tradition. Anti-Americanism, on the other hand, has not been seen for many years. My fear is that present American attitudes and policies might well rekindle the flames of ideological anti-Americanism in Canada. The latent America-bashers have gained ammunition from the evidence that editors and Congressmen can be so easily misled on bilateral matters by vested interests in the United States. If we can lower the temperature, we can turn our attention to those pioneering proposals for new mechanisms of diplomatic consultation, conflict avoidance, and early-warning provisions that could dramatically alter the current fractious climate. It would surely be more to the point than all this talk of retaliation or going it alone.

I recall once, at a Commonwealth Conference, a Nigerian identifying the spirit of the Commonwealth as a "willingness to listen to each other with forbearance." It is that which has held the Commonwealth together over the decades in spite of frequent lapses. The Commonwealth is an association of sovereign states with no supra-sovereign authority and no voting. In that respect it resembles the North American community which has the same requirement for tolerance. For without tolerance and goodwill this blessed but unequal relationship of ours cannot continue. Even that is not enough without a clearer understanding of our differences.

It is worth remembering that we, Canada and the United States, co-habit this continent in the modern way, out of wedlock; neither of us wishes to risk the perils of marriage or, for that matter, divorce.

Annette Baker Fox

Crises in Canadian–American Relations: An American Perspective

The so-called crises in Canadian–American relations recur almost cyclically, regardless of specific precipitating causes. The ups and downs in atmospherics that surround the treatment of issues arising between the two governments are familiar to those who follow the bilateral relationship. The current unpleasantness, headlined by the mass media, boils up, simmers a bit, then subsides, to be replaced temporarily by a more amicable feeling.

These fluctuations have become particularly noticeable since the Second World War, which marked a major watershed in Canadian–American relations. Prior to the war, Americans seldom thought of Canada, especially as an independent state, since its sovereignty dates only from 1926. Even during the war, some American leaders continued to regard Canada as a kind of surrogate for Great Britain. Our wartime collaboration, however, was so close as almost to obliterate national boundaries in some defense activities. Furthermore, collaborators from both countries formed personal associations so intimate that the habit of cooperation lasted for a long period after the war. This was especially marked among the two nations' armed services. The Americans failed to note that their Canadian counterparts always carefully guarded their ultimate freedom to disengage or at least to limit the scope of the collaboration.

This sort of inattention, added to our common tendency to regard Canadians as "just like us" (forgetting the French Canadians), made it peculiarly difficult for Americans later on to understand the efforts of the Canadian government to act in more autonomous ways. Americans, to whom the notion of a continental energy policy or some other form of "continentalism" seemed economically rational, were surprised at the strongly negative reaction of Canadians. The latter perceived these concepts as efforts to "erase the border." Their responses and counteractions were often interpreted in Washington as unfriendly anti-Americanism, whereas the intention of the Canadians had been primarily one of enhancing their ability to control their own national destiny.

A brief catalog of some earlier post-war "crises" in bilateral relations may provide a better sense of their transitory nature. McCarthyism, during the early fifties, generated numerous conflicts with the Canadians, including one so bitter that it outshadowed all the rest: the suicide of Herbert Norman, a highly respected Canadian diplomat and Canadian Ambassador in Cairo, who had been branded a Communist sympathizer by McCarthy. Secretary of State Dulles's "globalmania" proved even more unpalatable to America's unwilling Canadian partners than had Dean Acheson's cavalier treatment of Canada's objections to Washington's headstrong leadership in the Korean War. The recalcitrance of Prime Minister Diefenbaker to American strategic concerns during the Cuban missile crisis is another example of those instances where Canadian government leaders sought to restrain their impulsive ally from what they regarded as overly provocative acts. More recently, Washington's prosecution of the Vietnam War provided ever more opportunities for friction between the United States and a disapproving Canadian government, which eventually abandoned the tradition of "quiet diplomacy" in its dealings with the United States.

Turning from global foreign policy questions to economic matters, one is reminded that relations between the two countries touch on many different kinds of issues. General harmony on one set of issues may coincide with intense disharmony on another set.

For a long time, American and Canadian officials have worked together on the world scene to bring about acceptance of the principle of unfettered world trade. (This has not precluded protectionist acts by both governments on occasion; rather, it signifies a preference by both countries for opening up markets as freely as possible.) Suddenly, President Nixon and his Secretary of the Treasury, John Connally, in their August 1971 announcement of a "new economic policy" —including a 10 per cent surcharge on imports into the United States— administered a shock to the Western world. It was felt most intensely in Canada, which had become accustomed to being excepted from whatever economic restrictions the United States imposed on others. This watershed action catalyzed a movement, already apparent within much of Canada's leadership, to disengage from what had become an uncomfortably close trade and investment relationship with the United States. The growing concern among thoughtful Canadians over their ability to control their own economy found a response in the Trudeau government.

Other federal acts had already limited foreigners, principally Americans, in such traditionally restricted areas of the Canadian economy as radio, television, transportation and banking. Canada, particularly during the Tokyo Round of GATT (General Agreement on Tariffs and Trade) negotiations, continued to work with the United States to reduce trade barriers between them. The objective, at least in terms of import duties, has been for the two countries to approach something almost as unrestricted as a free trade area, although the principle itself is very unpopular in Canada. Thus, the Canadian government's efforts to diversify its trading partners, following the Nixon shock, were regarded as legitimate by American officials, perhaps because they were confident that close trade ties would continue. The story, however, turned out differently with respect to investment and energy matters. Canada's initiatives here, which triggered unfavorable reaction in the United States, were considerably more restrictive.

The Foreign Investment Review Act was calmly accepted at first by the United States government. It merely required foreigners proposing to make a direct investment in Canada to show how such an enterprise would redound to the benefit of the host country. Application of the Act was also accepted as fair and unexceptionable, especially since almost all proposals for such investment were accepted. Recently, however, the administrative conditions have seemed to be stiffening, with hints of review and retroactive restraints that alarm potential American investors and government officials. Retroactive moves are especially anathema to them. (It was already a source of friction when the First National City Bank of New York took over Canada's Mercantile Bank in the 1960s.)

Most controversial, in Canada as well as the United States, was the sudden inauguration a year ago of the National Energy Program (NEP). American critics in the oil and gas industry believe the NEP's provisions are inconsistent with those promises made by Canada when it accepted in 1976 the Organization for Economic Cooperation and Development (OECD) code on the treatment of multinational corporations, specifically those related to non-discriminatory treatment of such enterprises. Efforts to "Canadianize" the petroleum industry appear to be leading to rules giving Canadian companies an unfair advantage in competition with American subsidiaries based in Canada. Resentment is understandable even if the ultimate objective is acceptable.

Americans have come to understand that Canadian petroleum supplies on which they had depended for two decades are limited; they have accepted the need of the Canadian government to assure the country it will fill domestic needs first. Natural gas is another matter. Canada's abundant supply could well be used by American consumers, but the gas is available at a set cost which many regard as uneconomically high. A lot of American industry spokesmen and public officials believe that if American companies have the money to purchase raw materials abroad, foreign sellers should be ready to strike a bargain regardless of the long-term economic and social requirements of their country.

Americans are only beginning to realize that Canada, rich as it is in valuable natural resources, is not a limitless source for immediate purchase. A lot of exploration and development of Canadian resources was carried on by American companies to satisfy American markets, engendering the attitude that somehow these American entities were not quite "foreign." There was bound to be friction as Canadians became increasingly sensitive to the fact that important decisions about the exploitation of their resources were made south of the border.

Canada's federal and provincial governments have thus taken steps to control the development of these resources, to the dismay of many American energy companies doing business in the north.

As for Canadian direct investment in the United States, which is rapidly growing, the shoe is on the other foot. Partly due to the appeal of the larger market, as well as to government restrictions within Canada, Canadian entrepreneurs are turning south. One major target is American real estate. This involves a paradox. Several Canadian provinces place restrictions on the sale of real property to all foreigners, but such restrictions are rare in the United States. All at once, Americans are beginning to experience, on a modest scale, what has been a long-standing concern in Canada. Some Americans also resent the easy access to scarce capital funds that have been made available to enterprising Canadian corporations. Canadians taking the initiative in these areas, not simply reacting to American moves, has been a novel experience.

On environmental issues, however, it has traditionally been Canada that has initiated complaints about the pollution of Canadian land, water and air emanating from the greater industrial activity on the American side. A critical issue is acid rain, generated on both sides of the border, but most of it issuing from the United States. Acid rain is killing much of the life in the myriad lakes of Ontario and Quebec. Made aware of the issue, Americans have been sympathetic, recognizing it as a common problem requiring a joint solution. But the American government has been exacerbatingly slow to act, under mounting political pressure to have coal substituted for oil and to ease regulations in the development of energy. Some Americans are also inclined to remind Canadians that their own industrialization along the border contributes to the problem more than they are frequently willing to acknowledge.

Those concerned about the long-range impact of air pollution across the border may hope for an eventual bilateral Clean Air Agreement comparable to the Great Lakes Water Quality Agreement of 1972, before irreparable damage is done to the lakes and forests of both countries.

So far, I have focused on state-to-state relations between Canada and the United States. However, a wise American observer, President Emeritus John Dickey of Dartmouth, has commented on the "transcending, transnational, public–private mix" of the relationship. By way of noting that the Ottawa–Washington connection is only the tip of the iceberg, Dickey wrote that "the fabric of U.S.–Canadian relations is so closely knit below the governmental level that the substance of relations between the two countries is more likely to be found there than in the usual catalog of interstate relations." Most of these contacts produce few headlines or get mentioned on the business page of the *New York Times* and the *Wall Street Journal*. For bonds between the two peoples exist in all aspects of their social lives, as well as their economic transactions: religious, cultural, educational, professional, scientific, sport, visual and performing arts. A narrowly American perspective on these relationships would contradict their very nature. In the conduct of these ties, controversy seldom divides the participants along national lines.

At the same time, along with the growth of so many complex transnational contacts, another trend has taken hold during the latter part of this century: governments intervene and public policy dominates in areas of social activity where affairs were once conducted only on private terms. Though this situation is marked now in both countries, Canadians have accepted for much longer the legitimacy of a government role in the social arena. Indeed, today's crises in Canadian–American relations can be traced in part to diverging attitudes on the appropriate role for government. While the Reagan Administration is withdrawing from all sorts of government regulation, leaning ideologically toward private responsibility in fields that Americans once accepted as public, the Trudeau government is moving in the opposite direction.

One explanation for Canada's moves to speed up efforts to control aspects of the economy that earlier had been left alone is that the constitutional crisis in Canada has pushed the Trudeau government into attempts to reassert command. Binding a disparate nation together, the constant concern of every Canadian Prime Minister, is a particularly urgent priority for Mr. Trudeau and his advisers. Paradoxically, their efforts to ensure strong national decision-making out of Ottawa in the name of all Canadians provoke even more intensely the provinces' determination to preserve or even extend their own autonomy. Since the provinces already enjoy greater jurisdictional powers than the American states, vis-à-vis the federal government, it is hard for Americans to grasp the sensitivity of Canada's constitutional issues.

These issues originate from an historical experience very

different from the American one. Yet Americans, mostly ignorant of Canada's tradition, find it hard to understand why Canadians don't accept the same ideals of national unity and centralized decision-making on national problems. Most Americans, for example, would not widely favor an independent Quebec.

Despite the restraint exercised by Americans over Canada's constitutional crisis, we will inevitably be affected by the outcome, even if indirectly. Thus, efforts to assess the consequences have been undertaken by such study groups as the Atlantic Council and the Council on Foreign Relations, whose members are concerned about the "balkanization" of Canada. Businessmen have been especially apprehensive about the enhanced intervention of government in Canada's economy, both federal and provincial. They also worry about provincial governments interfering in interprovincial trade in ways that would be unconstitutional in the United States. At the same time, American businessmen frequently ignore the fact that some provinces oppose the federal government's restraints on foreign direct investment, investment which the provinces wish to encourage, not frighten away.

Americans' puzzlement over the role of Canada's provinces matches Canadians' worry over the separation of powers in the American system, especially Congress's capacity to interfere with or override executive efforts to reach understandings with the Canadian federal government. Some Congressmen, it is true, have been better friends to Canada than certain American Administrations, notably President Nixon's. Still, the subtly different political processes in the two countries help generate misunderstandings and ignorance within the United States. For example, Americans are used to slow-moving decision-making at the national level, where a myriad of conflicting private and public interests have to be reconciled. So they are unused to the fact that in Canada a major policy change can be speedily enacted, for example the NEP, which was made possible by a House of Commons vote at the command of the Prime Minister. Americans expect to see binding regulations ensue in Canada, as they would if a Congressional act were to be implemented in the United States, where the legality of the regulations would likely be upheld in the courts. Instead, they observe a process of persuasion following legislative enactment, with far less reliance on judicial enforcement. Some of our ignorance of how Canadian policy is adopted and executed is attributable to the more secretive character of Canadian decision-making. Also, Americans seldom realize the greater tendency of Canadians to accept the legitimacy of the government's actions without challenge, the assumption being that public officials are better qualified to make judgments on complex matters.

Despite differences in the policy-making process, Canada and the United States share one overriding characteristic: they are pluralist societies in which the many crisscrossing interest groups and economic sectors are so powerful that it is difficult for governments to exert absolute control over them. Thus, Canadian companies have escaped government controls in their own country by expanding their operations in the United States. And earlier, American industries established subsidiaries in Canada to avoid those tariff barriers, especially duties on manufactured goods, erected to protect Canadian industry.

Canadians are fond of emphasizing a point that seems to color their view of the relationship, to wit, that they have a population only one-tenth the size of America's (as well as an economy of the same ratio), most of it stretched out across an enormous territory and concentrated in areas contiguous to the United States. Indeed, their sense of vulnerability is seldom appreciated by Americans. Yet, for a number of the more contentious bilateral issues the ratio seems not one to ten but closer to one to one. For some American border communities, the pollution coming from the Canadian side may be even greater than that crossing the border at the same point into Canada. At the same time, despite the population imbalance in favor of the United States and the preponderance of American magazines, books and television broadcasts that reach Canadians, Canadians seem to enjoy an ability to approach or lobby influential American groups and to speak publicly more often and with more forthrightness in the United States than Americans tend to do in Canada.

Perhaps because they feel there is more balance in the relationship than Canadians do, American officials talk more about "reciprocity" in their dealings with Canada. "Reciprocity" may be a dirty word to those Canadians who have become accustomed to having allowance made for their smaller size and capacity to influence events. But Canadians are likely to hear the word with increasing frequency. For we are currently witnessing not only a cyclical rise in friction between the two countries, but also probably a long-term, secular trend affecting the relationship.

Canada has now become a leading industrialized country, sovereign in every sense of the word. It has demonstrated the capacity to command its own economy contrary to the wishes or preferences of outsiders. Two decades ago, Americans had to be reminded of Canada in the context of "The Neighbor Taken For Granted," the subject of a conference and book sponsored by the American Assembly at Columbia University. Just recently, the Atlantic Council in Washington has issued a report, "The Neighbor We Cannot Take For Granted." The titles say much about the change in perspective. Yet, both Canadians and Americans have been slow to realize the significance of this trend on Canada's part toward greater self-reliance. Even less is it appreciated by other industrialized countries in the West, which may tend to focus more on power as an extension of military might. However, the wealth and experience of Canada have been amply recognized of late in the summit meetings of leading Western nations. Thus, American officials, not surprisingly, are expecting the Canadian government to live up to its responsibilities and not continue identifying Canada with those still-developing countries that merit special allowance for their weakness.

This last is a particularly American perspective, one which identifies the writer as a political scientist observing the relationship from south of the border. I might have assumed a different role and tack—for example, that of the American tourist delighted with the services and holiday attractions of Canada. I might have adopted the viewpoint of a New England state governor meeting with the premiers of Quebec and the Maritime provinces to address such problems as ease of transportation and distribution of energy supply. I might have taken the perspective of an American automobile company seeking a share of available government subsidy in Canada for locating a new plant; or that of an American fisheries industry seeking a fair share of the ocean's resources from what used to be the high seas, but is now a carefully delineated fishing ground marked by 200-mile off-shore economic zones that were claimed early by Canada and later by the United States.

The occasional suggestion on either side that some linkage of essentially unrelated issues might improve the bargaining power of one side with the other is usually resisted. One basic reason why representatives from two pragmatic nations know that linkage will not work is that they understand the need to insulate controversies rather than extend their scope to include potentially volatile issues that have no practical connection to the problem at hand. Until now, at least, Canadian leaders have realized the folly of weakening their bargaining hand in an area where they are strong by allowing the issue to be combined with one in an area where they are weaker. But as they watch the muscle-flexing of the American Congress in areas of concern to Canada, they may wonder whether they can continue on that course. Will Congress follow the executive branch in recognizing that linking unrelated issues in a package deal may cost more than any conceivable gains? As long as the constituencies they represent oppose having their interests traded to their disadvantage for gains accruing to some other unrelated group, Congressmen will probably recognize the impracticality of the linkage course.

Canadian or American, we share one common perspective: there is no place in the relationship for threats of retaliation against actions taken by one of the partners. Both are too vulnerable; the injury would be mutual. With few exceptions this principle has been long understood and accepted by both parties. In this period of heightened friction between our two governments, it is appropriate that a group like the Americas Society should seek to enlighten its membership—and the broader American constituency—by offering long-term perspectives on the bilateral relationship. Thus, the Society and its Canadian Affairs program become part of that intricate network of private Canadians and Americans which in so many ways transmits a more enduring sense of the Canada–U.S. relationship than the alternating moods of their national governments.

With greater understanding by Americans of the contrasting perceptions on either side, the recurrent crises in Canadian–American relations may gradually diminish in intensity, if not in frequency. At least we can be spared the unpleasant surprises that occur when expectations are violated by neighbors who, contrary to conventional wisdom, are not in all respects just like ourselves.

Mark MacGuigan

The Search for Nationhood:
Defining Canada's
National Interest

Today, we often hear that the policies of Canada are vexing the Canadian–American relationship. Yet, unless and until Americans both inside and outside government appreciate more fully the rationale for Canadian economic policies, the goal of managing the relationship effectively will prove elusive. We have to understand each other, or we risk talking right past each other.

Let me cite several political facts of Canadian life. First, all Canadians think of themselves as self-appointed experts on the United States. Second, all Canadians believe they know just what needs to be done to straighten out Canada–U.S. relations. Third, while Canada–U.S. relations tend to get buried on page 48 of the *New York Times*, they are big box-office in Canada. Thus, on one side we have perceived general omniscience and on the other relative disinterest. These facts of the political environment affect the way politicians in Canada have to deal with the question of our relationship.

Precisely because the Canada–U.S. relationship is a potentially volatile topic, successive Canadian governments have emphasized the importance of conducting relations with the United States on a businesslike and case-by-case basis. The emphasis has been on dealing with bilateral difficulties in a direct, low-key manner, not through negotiations in the press. Over the years, the United States has welcomed this rational, problem-solving approach, and the state of the relationship reflected this. Beyond the obvious utility of these methods, the genuine respect and warmth existing between the two peoples made that way of doing business natural.

There *have* been difficulties. In 1971, the United States implemented a number of economic policy decisions in the trade area—the so-called "Nixon shock"—that were nothing short of traumatic for Canadian policy-makers at the time. Those decisions subsequently reinforced Canadians' determination to strengthen national control over their economy.

But it is with a general history of cooperation in mind that I address a set of American concerns, some of which have recently prompted American officials to express public surprise at what they call Canada's nationalist and short-sighted policies.

Clearly, important elements of the American private sector, as well as Congress and the Administration, see a disturbing change in Canadian economic policies. In addition to "nationalist" and "short-sighted," the terms most often used to characterize our supposedly sudden shift in direction are "interventionist," "restrictive," and "discriminatory." In the view of some prominent Americans, it is no longer possible to look northward and "recognize" the Canada they thought they knew.

Accompanying this general concern is a more specific complaint, voiced mostly by corporate spokesmen, that the "rules of the game" have been abruptly changed in Canada, and that this amounts to unfair treatment. The companies involved have not hesitated to act on their convictions and to seek support in their country, often from their friends in Congress.

This level of alarm is unjustified; yet, to a degree it is understandable, since the commercial and economic stakes are high. More than 21 per cent of American foreign direct investment worldwide is in Canada, amounting to more than $38 billion. So there is a strong degree of exposure involved. At the same time, two-way trade between the two countries in 1980 totalled some $90 billion, making this the largest trading relationship in the world. The point is that *neither* side wishes to jeopardize economic links of such importance.

A key to minimizing that jeopardy is knowledge. If Americans knew more about Canadian realities, they would recognize that these realities are not threatening to American interests. Rather, they reveal a country in the process of strengthening itself not at the expense of others, but in a way that will in fact result in a more capable neighbour and ally for America.

What is happening in Canada today is no less than the enhancement of our nationhood. The domestic debates taking place over the nature of our government have their roots in the original bargaining which led to Confederation more than a hundred years ago. Less well known perhaps is the ongoing debate over economic development policy that has paralleled the political discussion. These two strands are converging now as the constitutional issue nears a decisive stage and as the main direction of economic development policy is clarified. The combined effect of this coming of age in Canada may startle you as our nearest neighbour. But if our lines of communication remain clear, the prospect should not be too unsettling.

Prime Minister Trudeau summed it up as he introduced President Reagan in the House of Commons on March 11 this year:

> In the years to come the United States will be looking at a dynamic neighbour to the North. By putting its own house in order Canada will grow confident in itself. We will establish more clearly where our interests lie and we will pursue them with renewed vigour. One thing will remain unchanged, however: our deep friendship for the United States.

What we hope our American friends realize is that, in economic terms, this clarifying of national interest is based on political traditions and economic structures measurably different from their own. More than 200 years ago our paths diverged, although our goals remained much the same. The parting of the ways led to different political institutions and, when compared with different geographic circumstances as well, to different attitudes about the role of government.

An example is the degree to which Canadian governments have historically felt the need to intervene in national life in order to knit together and develop a huge, under-populated country. Among the results of this intervention are: government-supported national television and radio networks; national airlines; the Canadian National Railway family of companies; and a host of other government undertakings designed to mobilize capital, technological, and human resources on a scale of effort and risk which the challenges of our nation's development require. The need for, and the public's familiarity with, government intervention in the Canadian economy remain fixed in our country.

At the same time, government intervention represents a pragmatic Canadian response to a particular set of circumstances; it by no means reflects any philosophical discomfort with the role of private enterprise. The private sector has been and will remain the driving force behind Canada's economic development. We share the perception that one of the best guarantors of a free society is a free economy. But Canada's economic development needs to be as coherent and forward-looking as possible in terms of the overall benefits to Canadian society. For those reasons Canadian governments, provincial as well as federal, are at ease with their responsibilities for judicious intervention in the development process.

This is directly due in part to a second fundamental difference between the two countries: the structure of their economies. Canada's economy is one-tenth the size of America's and more heavily dependent on primary resource industries. The manufacturing base in Canada is narrower and, to a significant degree, foreign-controlled. Although Canadian and American economic interests run parallel in many respects, they also diverge in important and specific ways. Over the past twenty years, the public debate about the degree to which such divergence was desirable has centred on the question of foreign ownership. While Canadians acknowledge the benefits that foreign investment has brought them, it became clear by the early 1970s, after a decade of study, that there were significant costs involved as well. These costs include the negative effects on the performance of the economy from the locating of so many of its command centres outside Canada; inadequate research and development opportunities for our engineers and scientists; and, due to the branch-plant phenomenon, serious constraints on Canada's potential for developing greater trade prospects. In particular, the events of 1971, with the imposition of the 15 per cent surtax by Nixon and Connally, left us feeling suddenly vulnerable.

Accordingly, in 1974 we established a foreign investment review process, with the task of screening foreign investment for "significant benefit" to Canada. As of August 1981, the Canadian government had an approval rate of 90.5 per cent for applications by American investors, hardly grounds for suggesting that they have been subjected to harsh treatment.

Even now, after seven years of the Foreign Investment Review Agency (FIRA), foreign ownership figures in Canada are at a level which would simply not be tolerated in the United States. For example, according to the latest available figures, foreign investment in the United States accounted for *5 per cent* of the mining industry and *3 per cent* of the manufacturing sector; the comparable Canadian levels are 37 per cent and 47 per cent, a stark contrast. In 1978, non-residents controlled about 30 per cent of all non-financial industries in Canada; the comparable American figure was about 2 per cent. And, while only two of the fifty largest firms in the United States are foreign-controlled, nineteen of the fifty largest firms in Canada are foreign-controlled.

The reason for Canadian action on foreign investment must be clearly understood. No country could allow these levels of foreign involvement to continue indefinitely. No country ever has. Having determined that the amount of foreign ownership and control in Canada was a concern, we chose to deal with the problem totally in accordance with our international undertakings. There has been no question of nationalization, confiscation, or forced sale. Foreign investors have simply been told the conditions under which they would be welcome.

Canada needs and wants foreign investment that will benefit all parties concerned. Foreign companies and individuals will continue to do business profitably in Canada. I do not believe that those who are complaining about our policies are, in fact, arguing that they have lost money on their investments. Certainly not. By comparison with other countries, there are few more secure places to invest money than Canada.

In the energy sector, the cause of much recent anxiety has been Canada's National Energy Program (NEP). Given the special significance that the energy sector has for Canada's economic development, the NEP is founded on three basic principles: *security* of supply and ultimate independence from the world oil market; *opportunity* for all Canadians to participate in the energy industry, particularly oil and gas, and to share in the benefits of its expansion; and *fairness*, with a pricing and revenue-sharing regime that recognizes the needs and rights of all Canadians, with respect to the development of all of Canada's regions.

One aspect of the NEP which has been much misunderstood is "Canadianization." The objective here is to increase that share of the oil and gas industry owned and controlled by Canadians—to 50 per cent of the industry, a decade from now. In the strategy to achieve this most legitimate objective, the emphasis is on *making room* for Canadian oil and gas companies in Canada, not on *forcing out* foreign companies. There is no question that we intend to give Canadian companies the opportunity to grow more quickly. What we have not intended or done is to make the operations of large international oil firms unprofitable. For example, the net cost to American firms exploring in Canada will remain lower than in the United States.

But we are dealing with an extraordinary situation. Throughout the 1950s and 1970s, non-residents owned nearly 80 per cent and controlled more than 90 per cent of Canadian oil and gas assets. They also controlled nearly 100 per cent of the assets employed in refining and marketing operations. Canada did not have a single Canadian multinational oil company, not even a small one. We did not have a vertically integrated domestic company, until Petro-Canada acquired Pacific Petroleum in 1978.

Before the NEP, an unintended by-product of the Canadian government's policies was increased foreign ownership. New windfall profits, due to increases in oil and gas prices, favoured those firms already in the business with the largest production; most were foreign-owned. These same foreign-owned firms were also the main beneficiaries of the earned depletion allowance. Thus, the pre-NEP policy framework virtually guaranteed that the big foreign-owned resource companies would get bigger.

No other developed country faced this predicament. Indeed, it is a predicament tolerated by no other country, period. By 1980, the Canadian oil and gas industry—74 per cent of it foreign-owned and 81.5 per cent of it foreign-controlled—generated almost one-third of all the non-financial sector profits in Canada. Without substantial changes, enormous power and influence in Canada was destined to fall into a few foreign hands. We therefore decided that we had to act, and act promptly.

Unlike some other countries, however, Canada has preferred the carrot to the stick. The operations of foreign firms in my country are still very profitable; to the extent that they increase Canadian ownership, they can now be even more so. Certainly, the rules of the game have changed from ten, twenty, or thirty years ago, just as perceptions, needs, and situations have changed. But the changed rules are clear. They can be ignored to the detriment of future balance sheets, or they can be used advantageously by foreign-owned corporate citizens of Canada who are sensitive to our national environment and to the opportunities there for profitable investment.

In addition, the NEP gives foreign companies an incentive to acquire Canadian shareholders and partners. To the extent they do, the companies can benefit from higher exploration grants just like firms which are already more than 50 per cent Canadian-owned. It is worth noting that many foreign-controlled companies are quietly rearranging their affairs in Canada to take advantage of the NEP, thus allowing for continued growth and prosperity in our country.

As for the assertion that recent takeovers of foreign-controlled Canadian oil and gas subsidiaries by Canadians have been at "firesale" prices under the NEP, I refer you to the biggest single takeover since the NEP, the purchase of Hudson's Bay Oil and Gas from Conoco. It was at a price that Conoco itself has termed fair and reasonable; the price included a premium of 52 per cent above the pre-NEP stockmarket price. The highest premium of all, 67 per cent, was won by St. Joe's Minerals for the "forced" sale of Candel Oil Ltd., in order to deflect a takeover attempt on St. Joe's itself. Not bad business for an alleged shotgun wedding. By comparison, the average premium in over sixty takeovers in Canada since 1978 was 35 per cent. And, as a matter of note, the takeover fever in Canada began long before the NEP, involving Canadian as well as foreign firms in other sectors besides energy.

One should not leave the impression, however, that these American concerns and Canada's responses to them define the larger state of relations between us. On our side, we see the United States' own record on trade and investment as hardly unblemished. Measures have been taken, for example, to assist American industrial sectors having trouble with foreign competition. "Buy America" preferences abound. Indeed, there are sectors of the American economy from which foreign investors are simply excluded. And Canada is still awaiting action from the United States on shared environmental and fisheries issues.

Raising these problems affords little pleasure. It does, however, help put the bilateral relationship in better perspective. For Canada, the state of relations with the United States is a crucial matter, full of political sensitivity. And energy and investment questions lie at the heart of the relationship. The Canadian government has developed policies in these areas that command broad national support. It has sought to take American concerns into account, but the main lines of our policies are set. They are set because they correspond to the firm wish of the people of Canada. They are in the political mainstream, and also in the mainstream of a larger, wider current of Canadian economic and political history. These policies are not the product of short-term political expediency. Their genesis can be traced back through at least two decades of spirited and intensive national debate. It would be a mistake to suppose that a Canadian government would be able or willing to resist the historical momentum of our country's growing determination to exert control over its own economic destiny.

It is the reality of the Canada–U.S. relationship that our two different countries can grow separately in their own ways, yet retain bonds of friendship and respect through a common heritage of basic values—values of the sort we have protected together in two world wars, in Korea, in Iran, in the North Atlantic Treaty Organization, and in the North American Air Defence Agreement. These values find their ultimate expression in the countless personal links which are the fabric of our relationship. In the long run, those values and links define the quality of our kinship.

Canada and the United States have followed distinct paths from the beginning. Our challenge has always been to contain and channel our disagreements so that they do not impede the steady flow of friendship. We must continue to accept those responsibilities. But we must do more. We must visualize our relationship, including our problems, in a world perspective. In a turbulent world, those few like-minded countries such as ours cannot afford to be distracted from jointly achieving our common goals of freedom, justice, democracy, and friendship among all peoples.

Lawrence S. Eagleburger

American–Canadian Relations

The United States and Canada appear to be at one of those watersheds that we reach from time to time in our relationship. I only hope that what I have to say will serve to improve the quality of our dialogue. For how we manage life together on this continent is too important for both of us to become hostage to the vagaries of special interests or the enthusiasms of headlines.

The conventional symbol of the uniqueness of Canadian–American relations is our 5 500 miles of open, undefended border. Yet, that border was far from peaceful in the early years. The conversion of the U.S.–Canada border to a peaceful and unguarded frontier began with an international negotiation that led to a constructive act of statesmanship, the Rush–Bagot Agreement of 1817. The Rush–Bagot Agreement provided for disarmament on the Great Lakes, setting an example that led to disarmament on land as well. It proved the means to overcome hostility and set the American and Canadian peoples upon the path of peaceful resolution of their disputes, working out problems to mutual advantage.

Since 1817, Canada and the United States have built their relationship on the foundation of constructive diplomacy laid out by the Rush–Bagot Agreement. Not that we no longer have problems.

Indeed, the newspapers have lately been full of accounts of our differences with Canada. Yet, can anyone believe that two such vibrant societies as ours could live in such close proximity, with so many contacts and so much business, without inevitably facing tough and sometimes intractable problems? What is special about our relationship is not the number or quality of our differences, but rather the habit we have developed of handling them with real maturity. In creating this tradition, the United States and Canada have learned to resolve peacefully even the most contentious issues, such as boundary disputes. Indeed, much of the U.S.–Canada border was established through a process of negotiation or arbitration. This was possible only because both sides were willing to work hard to find mechanisms and seek solutions that were mutually acceptable. A total of 142 years and 22 treaties were required to define and demarcate the land border between our two countries. Today, the United States and Canada follow this same pattern in seeking to delineate offshore boundaries. For example, the United States has ratified the East Coast Boundary Treaty which provides for submitting the disputed boundary in the Gulf of Maine to international arbitration. We hope for early Canadian ratification. We also wish to reach agreement with Canada on a means of settling the disputed offshore boundaries on the West Coast, and off Alaska and Yukon.

The great significance of the settlement of these frontier disputes is that the United States and Canada, as Adlai Stevenson once observed, "have long since given up the idea of using force, and have accepted in our relations with one another the rule of law, of mediation, of peaceful adjustment." But accepting these high principles in theory is not enough. We must work continually to implement them. Improving U.S.–Canada relations, or even maintaining them at a satisfactory level, requires a conscious and sustained effort on both sides and at many levels. It requires, first, an effort to understand each other better. It also requires that each country formulate its domestic policies with due regard to potentially significant adverse impacts on the other. Most of all, it requires that we be able to talk and listen to each other as we lay out our concerns. The alternative is to risk establishing a pattern of action and reaction, whether in our newspapers or in our parliaments, that would in time be massively painful to all of us. We have a responsibility to our people, on both sides, to avoid over-reactions which could have negative consequences not only for our countries, but for the free international trade and investment environment on which both our countries ultimately depend.

In the United States, the will to achieve more fruitful relations with Canada begins at the highest levels of government. President Reagan has often spoken of his special desire for closer relations among the countries of North America. As a symbol of his desire for closer ties with Canada, he made his first trip abroad as President to Ottawa. We on the American side must be prepared to make the sustained efforts in all areas of U.S.–Canada relations that are required to further the effort President Reagan has personally begun.

Yet, Americans do not always make as strong an effort as they should to understand our Canadian neighbors and the ways their perceptions differ from our own. We do not always appreciate the difficulties caused for Canada by the great disparity in the size of our two countries. We think of ourselves as a friendly giant, as indeed we are. But, as Prime Minister Trudeau has pointed out, when a mouse is in bed with an elephant, however well intentioned the elephant, the mouse must be conscious of the elephant's every twitch. While this image neglects cases in which the mouse may be biting the elephant, it conveys something of the feeling that Canadians have about the relationship and suggests why it is important always to bear in mind the effects of our actions on our neighbors.

Another important Canadian perception, not always well understood or appreciated by Americans, is the general feeling of unease many Canadians have about the high degree of foreign ownership of Canadian industry. Some 55 per cent of Canadian manufacturing is foreign-controlled; in certain economic sectors the figure is higher—68 per cent in petroleum and natural gas, 76 per cent in transportation equipment, for example. We may feel that Canadians' unease about this phenomenon is unwarranted. We know that the free flow of foreign investment is a key factor in development, in creating jobs and increasing national income. We also know that in the modern world multinational corporations make every effort to ensure that their operations fully recognize the goals and objectives of the host countries where they operate, and that they contribute to those goals. We must also remember, however, that every country has the sovereign right to set the terms under which foreign investment takes place within its borders. Thus, we do not challenge the "Canadianization" goals of Canada's energy and investment policies. Our concerns about these programs relate to the *means* proposed to achieve the objectives.

Canadians sometimes feel that we in the United States tend to ignore their problems when we focus on our domestic or international concerns. This is more often a perception, or misperception, than a reality. I can assure you that this Administration is listening and is trying to deal constructively with concerns raised by Canada, concerns that often center on the problems of transboundary air pollution or our fisheries relationship.

On the fisheries issue, the Administration recognized when it came to office that serious concerns had developed in Canada over the failure of the American Senate to ratify the East Coast Boundary and Fisheries agreements. President Reagan withdrew the Fisheries Treaty, recognizing it was unratifiable, and succeeded in achieving ratification of the Boundary Treaty. His action makes possible a fair settlement of the boundary dispute with Canada in the Gulf of Maine area, on the basis of international arbitration, and provides a foundation on which to build a future fisheries relationship between our two countries. The Administration and the Canadian government have also reached the negotiated settlement of a major dispute over albacore tuna fishing on the West Coast. The dispute had led in 1979 to Canadian seizures of American fishing boats and to an American embargo of tuna imports from Canada. The Albacore Tuna Treaty, which has been ratified by both countries and which took effect on July 29, permits American and Canadian albacore fishermen to search for albacore tuna in each other's fishery zones and to have reciprocal access to a selected list of each other's ports.

On transboundary air pollution, the United States and Canada are working toward the same goals. A series of joint work groups has been busily engaged for over a year, defining the dimensions of the problem and exploring possible approaches to deal with it. Negotiations for a U.S.–Canada agreement on transborder air pollution have been formally opened at the same time as the American government is seeking a renewal of its basic legislation in this area, the Clean Air Act. Canadian interests will be kept very much in mind during this latter process.

We approach this problem with an acute awareness of the high level of concern in Canada about acid rain and the acidification of Canada's lakes, rivers and streams. We know that many areas in the United States have comparable concerns; indeed, the original impetus on this issue came from the American Congress. What we find disturbing is the public perception of the air pollution issue in Canada—that virtually all the blame for acid rain must be placed at our doorstep. Quite frankly, this perception is based on what we believe are a number of misconceptions. Let me try to set the record straight:

—The United States is an international leader and pace-setter in controlling air pollution. While our record is not perfect, our accomplishments are noteworthy.

—A rough comparison of the amounts of sulfur dioxide generated in the United States and Canada would show us to be far ahead of Canada in controlling this pollutant, considered the most significant source of acid rain. With ten times the population of Canada and more than ten times the industrial base, the United States could be expected, without any pollution controls, to produce more than ten times as much sulfur dioxide as Canada. In fact, we produce only about five and one-half times as much. Even at that level, we realize we create problems for ourselves and for our neighbors, problems that must be resolved.

—The United States has strict mandatory standards for new sources of air pollution. Scrubbers to remove sulfur dioxide are required on new coal-burning power plants in the United States, but not in Canada, although neither country requires they be installed on old plants. The United States has equipped 84 coal-fired power plants with scrubbers and 34 more are being equipped. Canada has built or has under construction a number of large new coal-burning power plants along the U.S.–Canada border that are not equipped with scrubbers.

I do not cite these facts out of any desire to criticize Canada's air pollution control program. We all recognize that such programs are expensive and must be designed by each country according to its own national objectives and fiscal constraints. But it is important for all concerned to understand that dealing with transboundary air pollution requires a joint effort by both countries. It is the responsibility of political leaders on both sides of the border to make this clear to their respective publics. The United States should do its share but should not be expected to carry a disproportionate share of the load. Achieving an equivalent level of control in the two countries, at an acceptable level, should be our objective.

An outstanding example of successful cooperation in the environmental area is the U.S.–Canada Great Lakes Water Quality Agreement. It has led to joint actions reversing a pattern of deterioration that could have led to the biological death of some of the Great Lakes. The results of this clean-up are visible in the lakes. We should remember, as we work on air pollution, that several years of hard work were required to reach an agreement on how to preserve the water quality of the Great Lakes.

Most of our working relationship with Canada covers areas of agreement and common perceptions, not disagreement and dispute. We cooperate closely and successfully through the International Joint Commission (IJC) on a host of problems involving transboundary water pollution, water levels and flows. In national security matters we remain the closest of allies, both within the North Atlantic Treaty Organization (NATO) and in our joint defense of North America. In international affairs, the United States and Canada share similar perceptions based on our common democratic heritage and commitment to freedom. We cooperate closely in many areas—in support of the peace process in the Middle East; in the Namibia Contact Group; on international security and disarmament matters; in opposing Soviet threats to Poland; in calling for Soviet withdrawal from Afghanistan; in programs for the resettlement of refugees from Southeast Asia; and, closer to home, in new initiatives to assist the peoples of the Caribbean Basin.

In bilateral relations, the sheer volume of our interactions in all fields—trade, investment, culture, tourism, family ties, transportation links—is almost immeasurable. Most of these transactions take place in harmony and without giving rise to problems that require governmental assistance. When government attention is required, the results are most often positive. There are exceptions, of course. Sometimes we voice our respective concerns and the response from the other side is not all one would wish.

Recently, Under Secretary of State for Economic Affairs Myer Rashish offered a thoughtful exposition of some very real concerns we have about the means chosen to implement Canada's energy and investment policies and the effects they would have on American interests. Mr. Rashish's speech to the Americas Society in May 1981 led to headlines in Canada such as: "U.S. Attacks Enrage Government" and "The Bullying of Canada." To describe as "bullying" these honest efforts on our part to discuss our legitimate concerns ought to worry us all. If we are to maintain a mature relationship, as I believe we must, the American and Canadian governments must continue to feel free to speak frankly to each other. We cannot be expected to remain silent about our important concerns, nor can we confine our exchanges entirely to private discussions behind closed doors. We have an obligation as democracies to keep our legislative bodies and our publics informed on the main lines of our policy as well as on the positions we take on the policies of others. Moreover, accurate and frank public discussion contributes to diminishing the risks of misunderstanding. And misunderstandings can make differences appear larger than they are.

The Canadian public is now aware of our opposition to some aspects of Canada's energy and investment policies. It may not understand our reasons, however. Perhaps this is because the basic "Canadianization" objective has been so well publicized, but less has been said about some of the means proposed to achieve that objective. We know Canadians are fair-minded people strongly committed to their international obligations and to playing a responsible role in the world trading system. So we have trouble reconciling some of the means contemplated to carry out "Canadianization" with those ideals of fair play.

        We do not oppose "Canadianization" of the oil industry, but we believe it could and should be achieved in ways that are consistent with accepted international principles and that are equitable to those who have made a major contribution in developing Canada's energy resources. We ask whether Canada's proposed National Energy Program (NEP) offers adequate or fair compensation, according to international standards. The government proposes to acquire retroactively a 25 per cent interest in oil that has been discovered on lands leased from the government. It offers compensation amounting to only a fraction of the estimated market value of the assets the government would acquire. A "grandfather clause" would avoid these problems of retroactive application and compensation. We ask also whether it is not reasonable to expect that Canada, having subscribed to the Investment Code of the Organization for Economic Cooperation and Development (OECD)— which endorses the principle of non-discriminatory or "national" treatment of foreign investment—would avoid such a major derogation of the principle of non-discriminatory treatment as that embodied in the NEP.

        As for the Foreign Investment Review Agency (FIRA), we fully accept Canada's right, according to accepted international standards, to set rules designed to ensure that proposed new foreign investment is in Canada's interest. Our concerns about FIRA's performance reviews and the new Committee on Industrial and Regional Benefits relate to potential trade-distorting effects. For example, a reduced tariff on an item, agreed to by Canada in a multilateral trade negotiation, has no value to us if an agency of the Canadian government tells companies that, in order to operate in Canada, they must agree to buy such items only from Canadian sources. This would impair our rights under the General Agreement on Tariffs and Trade (GATT). Another concern is FIRA's "extraterritorial" application to certain mergers or acquisitions that take place abroad. When the firm being acquired has a Canadian subsidiary, FIRA asserts the right to decide whether the acquiring firm may retain the Canadian subsidiary, even though there has been no change in the percentage of foreign ownership and, hence, no new investment in Canada.

All of our current problems have to be considered in the context of a uniquely positive and productive long-term relationship. Living as we do with such a high degree of interdependence, our only reasonable choice is to make our relationship work to our mutual advantage. We are convinced that with goodwill on both sides we can find solutions or accommodations to our problems. I feel certain that the Canadian government shares our commitment to achieving a closer relationship. As far as we are concerned, there are no problems that could not be resolved amicably through a process of mutual accommodation with full consideration for each other's interests.

Speaking at Queen's University, Kingston, Ontario, in 1938, President Franklin Roosevelt said:

> We, as good neighbors, are true friends, because we maintain our own rights with frankness . . . because we settle our disputes by consultation, and because we discuss our common problems in the spirit of common good.

The Roosevelt formula remains today as valid for Canadians and Americans as it did then. Indeed, neither nation has much choice. As Benjamin Franklin once observed: "Either we hang together or we will hang separately."

Anthony Westell

A Farewell to
Quiet Diplomacy

Those familiar with the work of the late John Porter, probably Canada's greatest sociologist, may remember that in his major book on Canadian society, *The Vertical Mosaic*, he had something to say about journalists. Without any formal training, he observed with an almost audible sniff, journalists seem prepared to write about anything. And indeed, here I find myself writing about a subject in which I have no formal training or even experience: diplomacy.

I once argued with Dr. Porter that the role of journalists was to rush in where academics feared to tread. Because we had no reputation for scholarship or wisdom to lose, we could perhaps air ideas that others with a vested interest in conventional opinion would not dare to broadcast. Most of the time, we doubtless would be wrong but, as our work was only transitory, that would not matter. Sometimes we might advance ideas that others could then take up and explore.

Let me qualify the title of this essay. Rather than delivering a farewell to Quiet Diplomacy, I propose to chart its relative decline in the face of the tendency to conduct our disputes in public, a modern trend that may be aptly defined as Public Diplomacy. There is a longer and sounder historical record, on the other hand, that defines Quiet Diplomacy. In his book *The Presidents and the Prime Ministers*, chronicling relations between heads of Canadian and United States governments over the past century, Lawrence Martin suggests that the state of the relationship depends to a great extent on the personal relations between the Prime Minister and the President of the day. If they get on well, goodwill permeates the two governments and problems can be solved by negotiation—or if not solved, buried by mutual consent. The great thing is to keep disputes out of public view, and so maintain the smiling image of the "Special Relationship." As Martin recalled it, this was more or less the message of two distinguished diplomats, Livingston Merchant and Arnold Heeney, in their notable report (*Principles for Partnership*, 1965) on how best to conduct the relationship: Keep it quiet.

Curiously, as Martin observed, the Merchant–Heeney report came out in the same year in which President Lyndon Johnson, in a towering rage, summoned Prime Minister Lester Pearson to Camp David, Maryland, to bawl him out for some mild thoughts Pearson had expressed about American policy in Vietnam. Martin quoted an eyewitness as saying that Johnson actually grabbed Pearson by the lapels, but that is disputed. There is no doubt, however, that it was a fearful row. In the interests of Quiet Diplomacy, Pearson had tried to keep the row private, but word leaked out. Back in Ottawa, he was asked at a Cabinet meeting what had really happened. By way of reply, Pearson said he was reminded of the story of the British policeman giving evidence at a murder trial. "My Lord," the policeman told the judge, "acting on information received, I proceeded to a certain address and there found the body of a woman. She had been strangled, stabbed and shot, decapitated and dismembered. But, My Lord, she had not been interfered with." At Camp David, Pearson explained in conclusion, he had at least not been "interfered with."

So much for Quiet Diplomacy. It has meant trying to keep one's rows private, keeping up a good front, seeking to work out problems through diplomatic channels, with high-level political greasing when necessary. This may or may not be desirable. In Martin's view, it succeeded over the years in creating an illusion of special friendship between Canada and the United States when in fact relations were often quite rocky. But my thesis is that the option of Quiet Diplomacy is no longer always available. Of course, a great deal of the day-to-day business between the two countries will continue to be conducted quietly by officials and ministers using diplomatic channels. Increasingly, though, we are going to see major issues thrashed out in public, and we had better get used to it. We may, in fact, have to invent some new institutions to manage those public issues that threaten to become major disputes endangering the relationship.

Diplomacy is going public for a couple of related reasons. One is that most of the relationship is already in the non-governmental sector; that is to say, the relationship is not primarily a matter of government talking to government, but of businessmen and others pursuing their private interests across the border. The second reason is the revolution in communications. It is commonplace now to say that television in particular has utterly changed the way in which domestic politics are conducted. We are slower to grasp that television and other forms of communication are also changing the way in which foreign relations are conducted.

Several respected authorities hold the view that most of the action in the bilateral relationship nowadays is indeed non-governmental. The Royal Commission on Conditions of Foreign Service printed a report in 1981 that noted the growing importance of the economic component in international relations and the increasing interdependence of national economies. It drew the lesson that private-sector, non-state figures—businessmen in particular—were increasingly involved in relations between states. The report observed that

> ... an increasing proportion of Canada's international relations is conducted by the business community. The impact on both the content and the method of conducting foreign affairs is considerable. The international arena is a "world of deals" in which political and economic influences play vital and complementary roles. Economic and trade issues must be fundamental to our international relations because economic clout is the basis of a strong bargaining position. On the other hand, political relationships are important to the kind of business deals a country can make; only governments, by maintaining presences abroad, can develop the political influence that creates a climate in which business deals can be made.

The Royal Commission seemed to be endorsing the view that, increasingly, governments and their agents, the diplomats, would be in the business of primarily servicing corporations doing business abroad.

Shortly before he was appointed Ambassador to Washington, Allan Gotlieb published an article on relations with the United States in which he bluntly stated: "The economic dynamics are those of the private sector and they are the bases of the relationship. Much of the substance of economic cooperation and interchange between the private sectors takes place on its own terms." Thus, many of the business players are multinational or at least binational corporations. They have loyalties, obligations and identities in both countries. They may be primarily American or primarily Canadian, but to an increasing degree they transcend national considerations and have therefore introduced a new element into the relationship. It used to be said with some truth that "multinational" was merely a euphemism for "American," but there is no denying the rapid increase of late in the number of Canadian corporations with substantial subsidiaries in the United States. Business has become increasingly continental in outlook and, as we have seen, increasingly orchestrates more and more dynamics of the Canadian–American relationship for its own score.

Businessmen are often fearful of the news media. Still, their public relations advisers and lobbyists are not above using the media to draw attention to their grievances and to put pressure on politicians to act on their behalf. If they have a cross-border problem and cannot privately persuade governments to correct it for them, companies or industries contrive to arrange things so that the problem soon becomes public. American industries have been able to enlist the press, particularly the business press, to considerable effect in their campaign against Canada's National Energy Program (NEP), its Foreign Investment Review policy, and Ottawa's border broadcasting decisions. It has been diplomacy by headline and editorial—diplomacy carried on by other means, to borrow a well-known phrase.

International trade unions as well are actors in the bilateral relationship, beyond effective control of the two governments. Then there are the environmental lobbies and other advocacy groups that thrive on publicity by drawing attention to problems that leap the border, like acid rain, and by seeking to influence public policy in both countries. In sum, the number of non-governmental actors in the relationship is increasing; the national governments in Ottawa and Washington are less and less able to impose their policies and priorities on events. Increasingly, they have become facilitators and problem-solvers for the private interests operating across the border.

The role of communications in the Canada–U.S. relationship is a vast one with many facets. The flow of business data across the border raises new and immensely difficult challenges to the concept of national sovereignty. The impact of cross-border broadcasting is substantial, although it appears that entertainment programs are probably more influential than news and information broadcasts in creating attitudes and expectations that find their way onto the political agendas of both countries. The results, of course, are far from predictable: Ottawa, for example, provides the largest audience and much of the financial support for public broadcasting (PBS) stations in northern New York, but what people in Ottawa mainly seem to watch is British programming. The focus, however, in this discussion of communications and diplomacy is on journalism, and television journalism in particular.

We can all agree that the style of journalism has changed substantially in the past twenty years. The news media have gone from being more or less neutral recorders of events on the public agenda, and therefore supporters of public institutions, to being participants in the political process. As Harrison Salisbury put it in his book about the New York Times, Without Fear or Favor, the media have at least ascended to their rightful role of Fourth Estate, co-equal with the other three branches of the American government. I am not prepared to go all the way with Mr. Salisbury, still less to agree that this is an unrelieved blessing for democracy. But he is right in perceiving that the news media have become a centre of power rather than simply a report of other centres. And, as a contending power, the media have become ever more adversarial in their relations with government.

The advent of television journalism has had enormous impact. Unavoidably perhaps, television dramatizes the news, presenting it as a form of entertainment. High value is placed upon conflict, prefer-ably between easily identified heroes and villains. Where conflict is lacking, television journalists seek to create it by aggressive interviewing in which politicians and others are led to take uncompromising positions. Newspapers unfortunately follow at times the dramatic style set by tele-vision, instead of offering more careful, balanced assessments. Journalism has not only itself become a more visibly forceful centre of power; it has also weakened some of the other, traditional centres while strengthen-ing others. For example, the media have usurped some of the important roles that were previously played by political parties in setting the public agenda, legitimizing party spokesmen and building a national consensus. One result of this, some believe, is that the media make it very difficult to create any consensus at all.

It is the nature of the media to seek out people with colourful opinions because their comments make exciting news. And of course there are people on both sides of the border whose interests lie in disrupting relations rather than smoothing them. There are national-ists in Canada, a few of whom proclaim dislike for the United States tantamount to anti-Americanism, and they are often given a hearing. In America, I doubt that anyone wastes breath fearing or hating Canada. But there are those with protectionist interests, and I remember a while ago a remarkable article in the *Washington Post* in which a well-known academic fairly gloated over his prediction that Canada was about to be divided into five parts. I am not saying that such views should not be heard, but I do think the media tend to give them more prominence than they deserve.

Another by-product of the media's more assertive role in bilateral diplomacy is that, by providing platforms to all kinds of spokes-men for more or less legitimate interests, the media seem to have dis-persed the decision-making process in Washington and, to a small extent, in Ottawa. In conducting relations with the United States now, it is no longer sensible for Canada to try to deal only with the executive branch of government. It is necessary for Ottawa to treat also with Congress, with the interest lobbies seeking to influence policy, and of course with the media. Much of this dealing must go on more or less in the public eye, although the media will not always notice it: news on the bilateral front goes in and out of fashion. Relations between Canada and the United States may attract little interest for long periods, but when some story comes along and catches attention, everything about the relationship becomes newsworthy and everybody with anything to say is given a platform. Put another way, the news media may ignore for months or years at a time the routine but festering problems of the relationship; then suddenly they will discover a crisis.

Still another fundamental way in which journalists and the media influence diplomacy has been observed most trenchantly by Robert Hershman, a CBS documentary producer, who studied the relationship of television to diplomacy while a Senior Associate at the Carnegie Endowment for International Peace. His message is summed up in the title of an article he wrote for the Television Quarterly— Diplomacy in a Television Age: Lights, Camera, Action!—in which he draws on such examples as the hostage crisis in Iran. Fortunately, relations between Canada and the United States do not command that sort of attention from television, but the article contains some pertinent lessons nonetheless. Mr. Hershman reminds us that, when television becomes interested in an event—a summit meeting between the President and the Prime Minister, for example—it tends by its very presence to change the way in which the actors behave. They address not each other, but their publics. Television then edits the film to project what it conceives to be an interesting or exciting view of the event. The politicians and diplomats find themselves responding not to the original event, or to each other, but to the view of the event that television has lodged in the public mind.

This, the reader may say, is a very good argument for Quiet Diplomacy, for conducting our relations away from the media eye. Indeed, the United States' Minister in Ottawa, Richard Smith, has argued in effect that the serious problems of the past couple of years were made worse by Public Diplomacy. In a speech, he said:

> The kind of problems we face will not be resolved by tossing speeches and press interviews across the border. They can only be effectively managed by hard, pragmatic—and quiet—diplomacy where each side not only recognizes the legitimate interests of the other but actively seeks to accommodate them.

Yet, for the reasons I have stated, Quiet Diplomacy will not often be possible. Too many of the actors are outside the control of government; too many have an interest in creating a public issue they hope will pressure government to act a certain way.

The media become then, if they are not careful, mere trumpets for interests in conflict across the border. Because journalists are not allowed to cover the civilized discussions of diplomats working out our problems through the application of pure reason—because, in short, they are not privy to the workings of Quiet Diplomacy—they report instead the atmospherics: the pointed statements of politicians seeking to impress their constituents, of businessmen seeking to protect their profits, of nationalists with hidden agendas. The image that emerges is not that of two neighbours with a history of friendship and cooperation seeking to work out very real problems, but of two countries in a frequent state of confrontation and crisis.

Still, unlike most of the diplomats, I don't agree that the lesson of recent years is that we should return to quiet, private diplomacy. Most of the time, anyway, the relationship will be quiet because the media will not be interested.

Part II

Canadian–American Issues

In the 1980s, most of the issues that divided Americans and Canadians were centered in three broad areas: environmental, economic and cultural.

Acid rain pollution, much of it generated by American industries, was the emotional touchstone by which Canadian–American environmental relations were judged and has been for Canada its most acute foreign policy issue in the eighties.

Such problems as cleaning up the Great Lakes and preventing toxic sewage from contaminating them and the Niagara River challenged environmental relations between the two countries throughout the decade. But acid rain—the systematic flow across the border of industrial air pollutants, falling to earth in acidic particles—threatened the equanimity of bilateral relations more than anything. Despoliation of pristine lakes and forests defined the issue on one side; expensive emission-control costs, with the threat of job lay-offs at affected plants, defined the issue on the other.

Canadians, concerned for the preservation of their lakes as a main recreational source and the growth of their forests as an economic-export base, accused the United States of avoiding serious commitment to resolve the problem jointly. The United States was alleged to be the source of at least 50 per cent of the acid deposition in Canada, while Canada was said to account for between 15 and 20 per cent of acid rainfall in the United States. The main source of industrial emissions in the United States centered in the upper Midwest region of heavy utility plants and rust-belt factories—an economically deprived sector, but also a politically important one. The Reagan Administration, not to mention Congress, was reluctant to further exacerbate conditions there.

The Canadian government, however, with support from the environmental movements in both countries, argued persuasively for action on the issue. The Canadians succeeded in bringing acid rain to the attention of the American people and getting the issue placed on the American public agenda. Few Canadians pressed the case with more vigor, and results, than the Minister of the Environment, John Roberts. In his essay here, Roberts marshals the argument for both countries taking joint action immediately to contain the acid rain threat.

Economic relations were dominated for most of the decade by the free trade issue: should Canadians repudiate their history and take a "leap of faith" into a freer trading arrangement with the United States? Or should they opt again for the status quo?

In purely economic terms the issue, as viewed by free trade advocates, was much the same as it had been in 1887 when Governor General Lord Lansdowne had declared that a commercial union with the United States "would be greatly to the advantage of the people of the Dominion." There would be more jobs; the price of goods would be lower.

In the 1980s, the advantages of a free trade agreement to both countries seemed just as obvious: the creation of hundreds of thousands of new jobs on each side of the border; a marked increase in the gross national product of each nation; the incentive to readjust and strengthen both economies to compete more effectively with other trading nations and blocs. Canada and the United States were each other's best markets by far. The United States exported more to Canada than to anywhere else—almost double what it exported to Japan, measurably greater than what it exported to Britain, France and West Germany combined. Fully 70 per cent of Canada's exports went to the United States.

"The relationship between our two countries is a prototype of the emerging global economy," Sylvia Ostry, Canada's Deputy Minister for International Trade and former Chief Economist for the Organization for Economic Cooperation and Development, pointed out in a speech to the Americas Society in early 1984. "Whole industrial sectors have become integrated. By the time a new Chrysler van is sold in Detroit, it is neither American nor Canadian but a North American hybrid."

Former American Under Secretary of State George Ball had commented some years earlier that Canada was fighting "a rearguard action against the inevitable," that sooner or later commercial imperatives would lead to the free movement of all goods across the border, resulting in "substantial economic integration, which will require for its full realization a progressively expanding area of political cohesion."

It was precisely this sort of prescient candor that unfortunately abraded the sensitivities of many Canadians, reawakening their latent nationalism, refueling all their old fears of American political and cultural aggrandizement. The argument *against* Canada entering into a free trade compact with the United States took its basic form in the words of one of its most respected public figures, Mitchell Sharp, former Minister of External Affairs. "To enter into a free trade arrangement with the United States," he said, "is to alter fundamentally the direction of Canadian policy, not so much in economic terms as in political terms. I do not think Canadians are prepared to do so."

In this section, three writers explore the free trade issue. The Canadians, Anthony Westell and Duncan Edmonds, both former Americas Society Visiting Associates, argue for the proposition that Canadians *are* prepared to enter an era of freer trade. William Diebold, a widely respected expert on trade matters, analyzes America's stake in a free trade accord with Canada.

Crucial to Canadians' argument against a free trade treaty has been the portent of *cultural*, as well as political, absorption by the United States. Canadians' fear of American cultural pervasiveness and the diminution of their own cultural identity has been a constant refrain of the eighties. The United States already exports across the border books, magazines, films, records and television programs in such volume that they seem almost to swamp the modest output of Canada's own cultural industry. While Canadians' fear on this score, as it relates to the free trade accord, has been largely baseless, it does carry high emotional potency because it reflects Canadians' concern over their susceptibility to what amounts to an imported culture.

Three out of every four books that Canadians read are imported. Ninety-seven per cent of movie screen time in Canada is devoted to imported films. Almost 90 per cent of record and tape sales goes to twelve foreign firms. Ninety per cent of available television screen time is taken by foreign programming. The overwhelming influence in all these imports is from the United States, reflecting American cultural norms and values. American television has very significantly affected culture in Canadian society, according to many older Canadians who worry they may be the first generation in their country to be raising, in effect, American children.

Suspicion among Canadians of a freer trading system and American motives in general derives not only from irritation over the fact that most Americans display a manifest indifference to, or a colossal ignorance of, Canadian culture. It reflects in a deeper sense the obsession with preserving at all costs whatever modest cultural identity Canadians may enjoy—from their diversely original literature to their bountifully talented performing arts.

Canadians remember that it was barely four decades ago that their country's arts scene was as bleak and environmentally fragile as their northern tundra. With rare exception, few fiction authors had amassed a body of distinguished work; the same applied to composers. Theater festivals were almost non-existent, television was embryonic, and film-making, aside from the government-owned National Film Board, was a torpid industry. Canada's dance and opera were undernourished arts at best. The scene today has been transformed. The performing arts burst with energy, more than 300 companies attracting audiences of some 12 million persons annually and contributing about $300 million to the gross national product. Film-making flourishes, broadcasting has become a multi-million-dollar international industry, and Canadian talents in both fields have crossed the border to register a major impact in the American entertainment world. Publishing in Canada— books, magazines, newspapers—thrives and stirs a range of national emotions.

Two lively figures from Canada's cultural scene, John Meisel and Mavor Moore, attempt in this section to define the meaning of cultural identity and why it remains a perennial concern of their countrymen. Meisel focuses on one aspect—broadcasting—of the efforts by Canada to restrain the tidal influx of cultural imports from abroad, while Moore essays a grand tour of the Canadian theater, past and present.

John Roberts

Acid Rain:
The Poison in Canadian–
American Relations

Twenty years ago, few members of the Americas Society would have thought environmental matters to be its proper concern. Twenty years ago, there were no government departments like mine today, devoted exclusively to environmental matters. Two decades ago, we thought of pollution as a local issue, best dealt with in a local way. Today, environmental stress is an international and inter-continental phenomenon.

The internationalization of environmental problems is but one of many changes that have taken place. The relative weight of these issues in the scale of human problems has increased dramatically as we have become sensitized to the enormous consequences that environmental alterations pose to our economies, our health, even to our survival.

At last we realize how important it is to get right the relationship between man and nature. If we get that relationship wrong, we risk triggering such fundamental changes on our planet that the human race may suddenly become as displaced as the dinosaurs which preceded it. We may one day be little more than curious objects of interest for the archaeologists among those more intelligent ants that Admiral Rickover has so reassuringly suggested will replace the human species.

A profound change has been occurring in the way people think about their environment. Air, water and soil were once regarded as unlimited free goods, to be used as anyone saw fit. Today, we recognize them as fundamental resources: rare, often irreplaceable once used up or befouled, assets that must be utilized but in ways that permit them to remain productive over the long term. We have finally absorbed the truth of the adage that "We did not inherit the world from our parents; we are borrowing it from our children."

Our belated awareness that air, water and soil are themselves resources has changed the economic and social context of environmental decision-taking among the world's developed societies.

The environment must be considered a factor of production, like labour, land and capital. As long as environmental factors are available at no cost, it is enticing to use them instead of those which cost money. Thus, a company can limit, or avoid totally, waste disposal costs if it can dump directly into a river or a landfill site. This, however, has become unacceptable to those of us duly alarmed by the needless destruction of our natural resources and by the fact that decisions to pollute our environment imply ever-increasing costs to those next in line to use those resources.

For, in economic terms, pollution is really the imposition of external costs on third parties. The costs, however, cannot be calculated in a counting-house manner. They may involve damage to human health or loss of jobs in other sectors. And, significantly, when environmental pollution crosses national boundaries, the external costs are imposed on whole other jurisdictions and societies.

Acid rain is a prime example of this. Twenty years ago, we experienced local pollution problems with emissions from thermal plants and smelters; so we built ultra-high smokestacks and dispersed those emissions into the atmosphere. The result was acid rain, one of the most transportable and devastating kinds of pollution imaginable, an insidious plague of the biosphere that strikes hundreds of miles from the point of emission. When you examine the plague, you find that no one country can deal with it alone. It is going to take international cooperation on a very large scale.

Acid rain is caused by the release into the atmosphere of sulphur dioxide and oxides of nitrogen. The chief sources of these emissions are thermal generating plants and non-ferrous smelters. The substances go far aloft, undergo complicated chemical changes and come down many days later, and hundreds of miles away, in the form of highly acidic sulphate or nitrate particles which corrode man-made structures and gradually destroy many of nature's treasures.

In Sweden, where acid rain drifts in from continental Europe and Britain, there are now 20 000 dead lakes. Although the Swedish government regularly spreads lime in lakes and on agricultural soils to combat the acid rain plague and keep the lakes and soils productive, the tiny country ends up spending hundreds of millions of dollars a year just to fight the effects of the pollution, most of which is due to industrial emissions from beyond its shores. Meanwhile, hundreds of lakes in Canada and the United States have been rendered so acidic that they are biologically defunct; they can no longer support normal aquatic life, including fish.

These lakes, however, are not my main concern, for the damage there has already run its course and is practically irreversible. The real problem is with hundreds of thousands of lakes in eastern North America facing a similar fate because they have little resistance to acidification. It is really only a matter of time—perhaps no more than a decade —before these sensitive lakes will die if we continue to dump acid rain into them.

The full extent of the aesthetic and economic costs cannot yet be calculated. We know, for example, that the tourism value of sport fishing in Ontario and Quebec is more than $700 million a year; at the same time, we know that the salmon rivers in the nearby Atlantic provinces are already beginning to die.

The impact of acid rain on water systems has been well established; there is no scientific controversy on the essential points. Evidence is mounting that acid rain produces equally damaging effects on land. Important nutrients are being leached from forest soils by acid deposition; the natural decay of forest litter is inhibited as a result. The effect may be to reduce the productivity of forests themselves, an extremely severe development for Canada where forestry is by far the largest industry. It employs one working Canadian in ten, and the process by which these workers carefully nurture a tree to reach its desired commercial proportions is a long and time-consuming one. Forestry is a $22 billion industry and, as a proportion of the Canadian economy, would be the equivalent in the United States of a $300 billion enterprise.

Nor is acid rain damage confined to wilderness areas. In New York and other cities, airborne pollution is at work corroding building surfaces, monuments and countless other structures. The estimated damage cost, according to American scientists, is more than $2 billion a year. Human health is endangered as well. Acidic particles in the air undoubtedly contribute to the misery of asthmatics and others with respiratory ailments. Moreover, acidity leaches heavy metals from the soil and thus runs the risk of contaminating drinking water supplies.

Canadians are principally worried about acid rain *not* because, as some American legislators have suggested, we are engaged in a plot to undermine the productive capacity of the United States and thus weaken its ability to fight communism; nor because we are attempting to increase the price of energy in the United States and thus facilitate the sale of more Canadian electricity to Americans; nor because we are trying to distract attention from our own controversial energy policies.

Canadians are worried primarily because we see unrestrained acid rain pollution gradually destroying the ecology of the eastern part of our country, eroding the economic strength of some of our major renewable resource industries, and sapping the health of our people.

In a country where you can stir bitter political controversy among French- and English-speaking people over the printing of instructions on a breakfast cereal box, the federal government's acid rain concerns draw the rare unanimous support of every member of the Canadian House of Commons and every provincial government across Canada, as well as that of hundreds of thousands of ordinary Canadians who write constantly to the government and their Members of Parliament about their fears. But, in fact, Americans should be as worried as we are. For acid rain, far from being solely a Canadian problem, is extending its pollution into the eastern half of the United States as well. It is thus our joint problem. We have created it together and, if we are to challenge it successfully, we must do so together.

Let us be clear, however, on certain key principles. Firstly, Canada is not asking the United States for a favour. The Canada–U.S. discussions on acid rain actually began as a request to us initiated by the American Congress. We are not asking the United States to do something contrary to its own interests. We are not trying to make the United States a scapegoat. We are not asking the United States to spend money to bail out Canada. We are asking the United States to do itself a favour. We think we are acting as a good neighbour should, drawing your attention to a common problem that we are prepared to help you tackle, while suggesting that it is in the interests of both our nations to tackle it now.

Secondly, in coming to you, our hands are not entirely spotless. We have to clean up our own act. About half the sulphates falling as acid rain in Canada come from Canadian sources. Because they fall on less sensitive areas, however, they constitute only about 30 per cent of our problem. At the same time, we Canadians have responded to the problem: over the past decade, we have cut our sulphur dioxide emissions by about 25 per cent. Our major source of pollution is smelters; in the United States, it is thermal power plants. So, if the causes differ to a degree, the control technologies may also vary. But where it matters, in those source areas that cause the worst problem, our cutbacks have far outpaced those of the United States. Even so, we must reduce present emissions by much more and we are prepared to do so.

For over two years now, we have been trying to act with the United States to combat the acid rain challenge. We have tried the approach that has been used successfully between our two countries in the past in the Boundary Water Treaty negotiations of 1909 and in the Great Lakes Water Quality Agreement.

The parallels between the Great Lakes Water Quality Agreement and today's acid rain issue are striking. Then, as now, industry strongly questioned the need for action. Nevertheless, our two governments agreed on the seriousness of the problem and determined that a clean-up could not be delayed. We began with a regime of controls based on what we knew at the time, and followed that with a second phase of controls in 1978. There is no question that the Great Lakes would have deteriorated by now into a thoroughly unacceptable condition if Canada and the United States had not signed that agreement.

The American Assistant Secretary of State for European and Canadian Affairs, Lawrence Eagleburger, commended the Great Lakes Water Quality Agreement process as a model for the way in which we should tackle our mutual environmental concerns. Indeed, it is the model that we in Ottawa have been urging on the United States for a joint resolution of the acid rain problem. In negotiating the Great Lakes Agreement we did not wait until every last minuscule piece of research had been contemplated. We recognized that there was an urgent problem, and we proceeded speedily with the job while research continued. We used a staged approach, attempting the best solutions we could initially, improving them in subsequent stages. What mattered most was having the political will to take those first crucial steps.

Some progress has been achieved. In the summer of 1980, Canada and the United States declared their conviction that "the best means to protect the environment from the effects of transboundary air pollution are through the achievement of necessary reductions in pollutant loadings." The two governments committed themselves "to take interim actions available under current authority to combat transboundary air pollution." One specific undertaking the United States made was to "promote vigorous enforcement of existing laws as they require limitations of emissions from new, substantially modified, and existing facilities in a way which is responsive to the problems of transboundary air pollution."

Any fair-minded person would regard the above statements as a commitment to more stringent application of environmental regulations. Yet, conversely, regulations in the United States are being relaxed, with two justifications offered: that ambient air quality standards are being met or improved, even though ambient air quality is by definition local and not the standard relevant to the emission and transport of long-range pollution, and that the existing environmental regulations permit exemptions.

Thus, incredibly, in relaxing their standards, the Americans seem to be arguing that the regulations are really being vigorously applied. That is like a judge saying he is zealously imposing the death penalty every time he commutes a sentence because the law permits it. It is obviously difficult, therefore, for those of us in government to convince our fellow Canadians that the solemn commitments given to us, and quoted above, are being seriously honoured.

The United States had agreed to enter the process of negotiations leading to an agreement to regulate transboundary airborne pollutants. But the progress of these negotiations has been disappointingly slow. It is no secret that the United States has taken the view that more research is needed before we respond to the crisis. That is a little like having to know exactly which mosquitoes are carrying malaria before we clean out the swamp.

We know enough now—and this view is explicitly endorsed by America's own national Academy of Science—to recognize that the acid rain problem is extremely serious, that it is urgent, and that its causes and remedies are detectable. More research will no doubt be helpful, possibly resulting in improvements to the technology, more precise assessment of the causes, cheaper methods of control. Still, we know enough now to determine how we should proceed, and we know enough to conclude that it is imperative that we do so.

Canada is prepared to act and willing to do its part. We are ready to cut sulphur dioxide emissions in Eastern Canada, as well as in Manitoba, by up to 50 per cent by 1990, contingent on parallel action by the United States. Our proposed action, combined with a similar level of effort by the United States, would reduce pollutant loadings to levels which Canadian and American scientists believe would protect moderately sensitive lakes and streams.

The costs will be steep. We estimate that the controls we are asking the United States to accept—a 50 per cent reduction in emissions in thermal plants east of the Mississippi by 1990—would cost about $2.5 to $3 billion a year. This translates into an average increase of utility rates of about 2 per cent. Although these costs are high, we believe new developments in technology could reduce them significantly. The economic costs of not acting, however, are far higher.

Indeed, the costs will be proportionately much higher for Canada: about $1 billion per year by 1990. With the Canadian population only one-tenth the size of America's, that means the burden for

Canadians individually would be three to four times as great as for Americans. Clearly, we are not requesting burdens for Americans that we are unwilling to assume for ourselves.

Acid rain is the most serious environmental question we face. As far as Canadians are concerned, it is also the most important foreign policy issue between Canada and the United States.

When President Reagan visited Canada, he declared to Parliament that he would work to control the air pollution flowing between our two countries. His reported words to Prime Minister Trudeau were: "We are not going to export pollution." Canadians believe the President means what he says. So, we count on action; and if it is not forthcoming, the disappointment will be deep and the reaction bitter. Canadians will not understand how a great country can disregard the interests of its friend and neighbour, while at the same time neglecting its own environmental interests.

I believe—I know—Americans want to preserve the magnificent physical heritage of their country for their children. I know that, when they understand the threat which acid rain poses to that heritage, they will wish to act. I assure you that Canadians stand fully ready to fight that good fight with you.

Anthony Westell

The Case for Closer Economic Integration with the United States

In a seminal article, published in 1972, reviewing the history of Canada's relationship with the United States and looking to the future, Mitchell Sharp, then Secretary of State for External Affairs, wrote:

> The real question facing Canada is one of direction. In practice, three broad options are open to us:
>
> (a) we can seek to maintain more or less our present relationship with the United States with a minimum of policy adjustments;
>
> (b) we can move deliberately toward closer integration with the United States;
>
> (c) we can pursue a comprehensive long-term strategy to develop and strengthen the Canadian economy and other aspects of our national life and in the process to reduce the present Canadian vulnerability.

Sharp clearly preferred (c) which he called the "third option," a phrase that was soon capitalized and accepted into the language of political discussion in Canada. Although it seems never to have been formally adopted by the Cabinet, the Third Option became the strategy of the government in the 1970s and into the early 1980s.

The goal of reducing "the present Canadian vulnerability" was, on the face of it, modest. The means by which the goal was to be reached were hardly controversial. The government would seek over time to strengthen the national economy and to diversify trade, build national unity and encourage the growth of Canadian culture. As that is about what any Canadian government would claim to be doing at any given time, the significance of the Third Option has to be found in its context, in the underlying purpose of the strategy. That purpose was to set a "direction" for Canada in the development of its relationship with the United States. As Sharp rejected both the status quo (First Option) and a deliberate move to closer integration (Second Option), the Third Option was clearly intended to steer Canada away from further involvement with the United States and towards greater national independence. As Sharp wrote, the Third Option "assumes that the continental tide can be stemmed to some extent." It would be an exaggeration to describe the strategy as outright nationalism, but it certainly inclined the government in that direction.

A dozen years later, it is obvious that the strategy did not achieve its goal. The trend of economic and of cultural affairs through the 1970s was towards increasing integration of the Canadian and American societies. The flows across the border of trade, capital and ideas all expanded, despite the efforts of politicians. This reality was obscured from time to time by nationalist and protectionist backlashes in both countries, but the underlying trend was clear. The driving force was not a conspiracy by continentalists, or a lack of nationalist zeal on the part of Liberal governments, or treason in the business community. It was the new technologies that were eroding the national borders established in simpler times. The technologies created new opportunities to increase wealth or to enjoy a broader range of entertainment, and the private impulse to take advantage of those opportunities overrode the attempts of governments, prompted by nationalists, to protect sovereignty and identity.

We seem now to be in a new stage of accelerating technological change. Satellites and computers are again transforming the processes of communication without much regard for political boundaries. The means of production and distribution are changing, the international economy is being restructured. In the developed democracies, governments, business and perhaps labour are looking for a new relationship so that they can better manage what may be called post-industrial capitalism. And governments, recognizing the limits of national sovereignty, are attempting to discuss their differences and coordinate their policies in all sorts of international organizations. In such circumstances, it is a dangerous delusion to pretend that Canada can somehow disentangle itself from the United States, achieve greater economic independence and develop a distinctly different culture and way of life.

The Third Option strategy failed not merely to reduce the vulnerability of Canada to economic events in the United States; it left Canada more vulnerable at a time of particular danger. Canada continues to be heavily dependent on the American market for its exports, but it has endangered much of the goodwill it used to enjoy in Washington, at a time when Congress is discussing protectionist measures intended to protect American jobs against foreign competition.

Canada's nationalist policies and its claim to be a wholly independent country with values diverging from those of the United States did not go unheard in Washington. Americans who used to think of Canadians as close cousins are now more inclined to accept the Canadian claim to be quite a different breed. Canadian policies designed to discriminate against American investment have, not unnaturally, strengthened the idea that, if circumstances demand, the United States will be justified in discriminating against Canadian interests. In short, if economic problems persist and the United States attempts a protectionist policy, Canada will not automatically be granted an exemption, or even the courtesy of special consideration. Canada may well be treated as just another foreign competitor seeking access to the American market, and the American government, if it is willing to negotiate at all, will drive a hard bargain. That might be extremely damaging to Canada, even catastrophic.

The Liberal government recognized the danger, quietly shelved the Third Option and accepted the reality of increasing economic interdependence, but it never admitted as much or set out in a careful way an alternative strategy for managing the relationship with the United States. Rather, it drifted towards Sharp's First Option, which was "to maintain more or less our present relationship with the United States with a minimum of policy adjustments." This meant that the government would adapt over time to the private-sector movement towards integration of the two economies and, consequently, of the two societies. There would be no overall strategy or political leadership. The new Conservative government is in danger of following in the same drift.

Far preferable would be the proclamation, in effect, of Sharp's Second Option: to move deliberately towards closer integration with the United States. That would not mean that Canadians would haul down the Maple Leaf and run up the Stars and Stripes. Nor would it mean that they would have to abandon what is best about Canadian society or accept what is worst in the American model. It would mean that Canadians would recognize that the tide of history was moving us towards closer association with the United States, and that the correct response was to seek to manage the process so as to make the most of the economic opportunities while preserving what was important in Canadian society. Accordingly, the Canadian government should state clearly that it recognizes that the country's best future lies in closer association with the United States, and that it wishes to negotiate the terms of a new economic partnership, the updating of the military alliance, and the creation of new bilateral institutions for the discussion of problems and the management of continuing issues.

The basic argument in favour of free trade is that Canadian producers need guaranteed access to the American market in order to compete with large American and foreign companies. The secondary argument is that Canada has already agreed, at the GATT (General Agreement on Tariffs and Trade) conference in Tokyo in 1979, to abolish tariffs on some goods and slash them on others to the point where there will be effective protection for only a few industries by the time the new rates are fully implemented in 1987. And even where high tariffs remain—for example, on textiles, clothing and footwear—the Liberal government saw them as "a bargaining instrument to facilitate the negotiation of improved access to foreign markets for Canadian exports." In other words, the government was prepared to reduce or abolish these remaining tariffs in return for access to the American and other markets, and in fact such negotiations are underway. As the Standing Senate Committee on Foreign Affairs put it,

> The Tokyo Round has, in effect, left Canadian industry in the worst of both possible worlds—with tariffs too low to be effective protection and, at the same time, still without free access to a huge assured market as enjoyed by its competitors, the European Community, Japan, and the United States.

So decisions already made have committed Canada to something close to tariff-free trade with the United States.

But that does not obviate the need for a treaty with the United States in order to deal with such non-tariff barriers as quotas, preferences and regulations designed to protect American producers against competition. In the absence of a free trade agreement, Canada may find itself still excluded from the American market by the non-tariff protective devices.

The argument against free trade has been that it would enable American corporations to close down their Canadian operations and supply the market from their plants south of the border. But this ignores the reality that tariffs are disappearing anyway under the GATT agreement, and it also assumes implicitly that Canadian workers in Canadian plants would not be able to compete successfully with American workers in American plants.

Underlying the arguments about free trade there has always been the fear that economic association would erode Canadian political sovereignty. There is no question that countries participating in a common market, as in Europe for example, do surrender some part of their sovereignty to the central authority in which they have a voice and a vote. It is a matter of paying for the benefits of sharing in a larger association. Supporters of free trade, however, have tended to argue that, unlike a common market, no surrender of sovereignty is involved. They point to the experience of those countries where free trade has existed to illustrate that a country can enjoy the benefits of free trade while carefully preserving its political independence. It is arguable also that free trade would generate a stronger Canadian economy and, therefore, a more confident sense of Canadian identity.

The truth, probably, is that, while free trade would not directly limit the sovereignty of Canada or the United States, it would have indirect effects. Both governments would have to look very carefully before implementing domestic policies that would increase business costs in relation to those of the other country. For example, if the Canadian government raised the rate of corporate tax above that in the United States, Canadian business would be at a disadvantage in free trade competition with American companies; or if the American government imposed on the business sector environmental regulations more stringent than those in Canada, American business might be at a competitive disadvantage in free trade. There would also be pressure on the two governments to harmonize safety regulations and other standards in order to ensure the free movement of goods in the free trade area. So free trade would in some degree limit the freedom of action of national governments.

The essential question about Canadian policy on trade with the United States, therefore, is not whether tariff-free trade would be good or bad in theory, or even whether it would erode political sovereignty. Those questions are being answered by decisions already made under GATT. The essential question is how to deal with *non*-tariff barriers that threaten to deny Canadian exporters the access they need to the American market. The most persuasive answer is to negotiate a free trade treaty with the United States to abolish, over time and with appropriate safeguards for sensitive sectors, both tariff and non-tariff barriers.

Let us recognize at the outset that every form of association limits in some degree the freedom of the participants. This is true in private life—in marriage, in business, in politics when individuals join a party and accept its discipline, and in relations between countries. Canada surrendered some of its freedom of action, for example, when it joined the North Atlantic Treaty Organization (NATO) and committed itself to support a collective security policy; when it accepted GATT and agreed to abide by certain rules of trade; and when it entered into countless other international associations. Canada and other sovereign countries accept the costs of such associations because they are outweighed by the benefits. The advantages of collective security through NATO outweigh the loss of military independence; the benefits of orderly world trade through GATT outweigh the loss of some control over trade policy; and so on. The number of international organizations and arrangements has grown enormously over the past half-century, and most require some surrender of freedom of action by participating countries, providing in return a greater collective benefit.

In recent years, Canada and other countries have been coming to realize that their freedom of action is limited not only by formal agreements, but also by informal associations. They are tied into an international economy by the expansion of trade, the movement of capital and the multinational organization of business activities. Participants have discovered to their cost that, as the Royal Commission on Conditions of Foreign Service put it, economic diseases are contagious. For example, if the American government follows inflationary policies, the prices of American goods imported by Canada will rise, creating inflationary pressures in Canada and probably forcing the Canadian government eventually to introduce anti-inflationary policies. Or if the Bank of Canada puts up interest rates, Europeans will notice that investment funds are flowing out of their countries and across the Atlantic to earn the higher rate of return, and to attract the money back they will have to raise their own rates. Most democratic countries have tried at one time or another to escape from this awkward interdependence by imposing controls and regulations, but such schemes are never fully effective, and the costs of economic insulation can prove to be higher than the supposed benefits of independence.

The alternative policy for democracies has been to try to coordinate their national economic policies with those of their major economic partners. Various organizations have been created for this purpose. Heads of governments, finance ministers, central bankers, government economists and other key policy-makers meet fairly regularly in international forums to review problems and seek common solutions. They do not always succeed because, as Alvin Toffler has written in *The Third Wave*, "At the transnational level we are as politically primitive and underdeveloped today as we were at the national level when the industrial revolution began 300 years ago." In other words, the nations are still trying to reconcile independence with interdependence. They recognize that interdependence limits their national freedom of action, but they have not yet fully accepted the need for international decision-making.

Canada's national independence is undoubtedly limited by its economic and military dependence on the United States. To a much lesser extent, the freedom of action of the United States is limited by its public and private relations with Canada. This is a fact of life,

and the attempt to reduce Canadian dependence by means of the Third
Option strategy has failed. The process of economic integration seems
likely to continue, whatever policies Canadian governments may pursue,
because the initiative is in the hands of private business. By entering
a common market or a free trade arrangement, Canada would not be
agreeing to a new surrender of independence, but recognizing and
formalizing a process of integration already underway. Formalizing the
process in a treaty with the United States would give Canada the opportunity to reserve sensitive areas of the economy, create institutions for
solving bilateral problems and organize programs of transitional assistance to industry—to manage the process rather than to be swept along
by it. A treaty also would give Canada a greater influence in the United
States on the direction of the continental economy.

     Closer economic and military association with the United
States would not necessarily inhibit Canada's ability to make its own
social policies or to continue to place a high priority on the enhancement of the quality of life as a matter of public policy. Canadians must,
however, be willing to accept that there is a trade-off between public
services and private affluence. The United States is inclined to spend
less on public services in order to leave more money in private hands.
For Canada to provide better public services while also trying to match
the American standard of private incomes would result in economic
resources being overstretched to the detriment of the competitive position. In a new association with the United States, there would be no
reason why Canadians should not keep and improve their social services,
their clean cities, their recreational facilities and all the other public amenities that create a way of life better than that available to many Americans,
provided they were prepared to pay for them in taxes that would reduce
their private incomes to below those common in the United States. Nor
would there be any reason why Canadian systems of government, law
and education should change.

     The Canadian national character is supposed by roman-
tics to be shaped by the immensity of the North, the harshness of the
terrain, the severity of the climate and the struggles of the pioneers
merely to survive in such a hostile environment. But what can all that
mean to an immigrant recently arrived from, say, Europe, living in a

high-rise apartment in a brick and cement metropolis, protected from the climate by central heating and air conditioning, working for a multinational corporation, travelling in a few hours across the country for a business meeting, holidaying in Florida, and spending most of his or her leisure hours in a world portrayed by television? Similarly, American myths and values derived from the War of Independence, the Civil War and the settlement of the West can have only a limited relevance for a Puerto Rican struggling to make his way in the urban jungle of New York City. In other words, it is misleading in modern circumstances to think of national cultures and recognizable national types. In every country, some traditions, some folk memories, some particularities remain and no doubt will continue to do so for many years, perhaps centuries, to come. Numerical minority does not mean extinction. As French Canadians have retained an identity within Confederation, Scots within the United Kingdom, Texans within the United States, so Canadians will retain identity however the relationship with the United States may develop. But as Michael Novak, the well-known American conservative writer, has pointed out in a recent article, in the United States the modern pluralistic society produces the pluralistic personality:

> Each individual is, by right and by opportunity, responsible for choosing his or her own identity from among the many materials presented by the contingencies of human life .... Many persons have the opportunity to become involved in many cultural traditions not originally their own, and to appropriate music, ideas, values and even a set of intellectual landmarks not native to their own upbringing.

To adapt this insight to Canadian circumstances, it is not an exaggeration to say that a person may be raised in a Protestant family, take an interest in an Eastern technique of meditation, marry into a Jewish family and in later life become an agnostic; enjoy American television but prefer European movies and English novels; read *Maclean's* magazine, the London *Economist* and the *New York Review of Books*; wear a Canadian parka with jeans and cowboy boots; play amateur hockey, follow American football and watch a Canadian baseball team playing in an American league; admire the work of the Group of Seven, enjoy Chinese food and be active politically in movements protesting against American foreign policy. He or she will still be a Canadian, carrying through life some of the social customs and attitudes that implies and giving allegiance to the Canadian state, but he or she will not easily be identified as a Canadian type, the distinctive product of a national culture. To put it another way, cultural identity depends not so much on *where* one lives as on *how* one chooses to live.

Thus, the concept of national identity rooted in a national culture is being washed away by the technologies of transportation and communication that are producing not the uniform man in a homogenized society, but variety and diversity in an international society. To be a Canadian citizen does not signify a way of life, or a set of values beyond attachment to the community and loyalty to the national state. So, the fear that closer association with the United States will erode a Canadian identity in the making or abort a Canadian culture about to be born is unfounded.

The basic argument being made here is that Canadians, both as individuals and as a political nation, are more likely to prosper and fulfill themselves in free association with Americans than they are by seeking to protect themselves from American competition and influence. The desire to escape from American influence, the desire to put distance between Canada and the United States, arises in large measure from fear of absorption by the United States and from jealousy of American wealth, power and vitality. But fear and jealousy are corrosive in national as in personal life; they feed the Canadian sense of inferiority, encourage parochial attitudes, and give rise in politics to nationalist policies that are bound to fail because they are against the tide of events and against the private aspirations of most Canadians, who wish to enjoy the maximum freedom to trade, invest, travel and exchange ideas. Canadians have no reason to feel inferior to Americans or to be fearful of the United States. They have built an orderly and progressive society that is in some ways an example to the United States, and as workers and producers they are surely equal to Americans. To the extent that size, climate and geography set Canada at a disadvantage in competing with the United States, that can be corrected only by public policy and private effort; protection at the border seeks only to hide such a problem and not to solve it.

Finally, what is required is not so much a change in Canadian policies as a change in Canadian attitudes. Canada, after all, is—through GATT—already committed to the virtual abolition of tariffs on trade with the United States and to the maintenance of the free flow of information and entertainment, which together ensure the continuing integration of the two societies. But instead of regarding this prospect with foreboding, as a defeat for Canadian nationalism and a threat to sovereignty and identity, Canadians should be encouraged to see it as an opportunity to knock down barriers, thereby enlarging their opportunities to compete and to demonstrate the virtues of their society. With a new association with the United States established by a treaty setting out the rules and limits of the relationship, Canada might at last get the ageing monkey of nationalism off its back and be able to turn all its energies to solving the internal problems of economic management, social injustice and political reform.

J. Duncan Edmonds

A Crucial Moment
of Opportunity

Future historians will undoubtedly focus on the current Canadian–American negotiation of an unprecedented comprehensive free trade agreement as a crucial moment of opportunity in the long evolution of an incomparable relationship between two North American allies, already partners in the world's largest and richest bilateral trade relationship.

What some Canadian politicians view as little more than a commercial deal, defining and negotiating a number of thorny details about tariff and non-tariff barriers, may in truth signal the advent of the final stage of economic integration that has been steadily evolving between Canada and the United States over decades. The reality of this will activate in Canada historic political issues related to sovereignty, independence and identity, and the role of market forces as opposed to government intervention, along with a series of fundamental questions regarding the ratification and implementation of the trade treaty and the institutional basis for managing the new relationship in both countries.

If, on the other hand, a bilateral trade agreement is not consummated, Canada will undoubtedly continue to pursue multilateral negotiations through the General Agreement on Tariffs and Trade

(GATT). These, however, are unlikely to solve its continuing problems of economic vulnerability vis-à-vis the United States. Serious negative implications for Canada's standard of living will become all too apparent. Strong pressures will develop for a new industrial strategy, inevitably increasing government intervention in planning and directing Canada's economy, with less reliance on market-driven economics.

Whatever the outcome of the talks, the process we observe over the next few years will significantly shape the Canadian political agenda for the coming decade. One might even suggest that we are about to preview the architectural drawings for the next stage of Canada's national destiny.

Some may fault this as too grandiose and exaggerated a claim. I don't agree, although it is possible that the vision of the political architects and the quality of their handiwork will turn out to be inferior and not meet the test of time. Perspective is the indispensable requirement here. Everything in the architects' plan is interrelated, but it is only their perspective that clarifies the relationships and gives meaning and direction to the outcome. The problem today is that we are far too immersed in short-term considerations.

In January 1911, William S. Fielding, Minister of Finance in the Liberal government of Sir Wilfrid Laurier, concluded an agreement in Washington providing, not for the first time, reciprocity in trade matters between Canada and the United States. An issue that had significantly influenced Canadian politics for most of the preceding fifty years was thus finally joined, it seemed. However, true to form, in the general election a few months later the Laurier government went down to a crashing defeat at the hands of Robert Borden and the Conservatives.

Throughout Canadian history, our relationship with the United States, focused chiefly on trade and economics, has been a preoccupation of Canada's political leadership, closely related to the ongoing struggle for a national identity. Every Canadian Prime Minister from Macdonald to Mulroney has had to face this reality as a central challenge to his governance. Bruce Hutchison defined it in his study of Canadian Prime Ministers:

> All these men, so different as private persons and public figures, have confronted, but seldom dared to utter, the same question that none knew how

to answer. Could a nation conceived in vague compromise and dedicated to the defiance of continental logic long endure? Would Canadians permanently pay the price set by nature for their endurance? Or, rejecting the price— especially the price of biracial toleration between themselves—would they admit defeat, accept the logic, liquidate the national experiment and fall piece- meal into the embrace of their rich American neighbours?

The way in which each Prime Minister treated the American issue reflected his vision of Canada and in large measure domi- nated his period of office. Sir John A. Macdonald, immediately after Confederation in 1867, faced the reality of America terminating the Reci- procity Agreement of 1854, which had brought significant benefits to Canada. Augured, at the time of its birth, by the conspicuous absence of any message of congratulations or even an acknowledgement from the American President, the new Canadian Confederation began life preoccupied by its relationship with the United States, a situation which has continued to the present. Indeed, it was the aggressive presence of the United States, with its tumultuous Civil War ended and "mani- fest destiny" in the offing, that had persuaded Canada to seek safety in its own Confederation.

Macdonald made some efforts in 1869 and again in 1871 to reopen discussions with Washington to put the 1854 agreement back in place, but there was little interest on the American side. Thus, Canada's whole experience with the United States during Macdonald's years in office had a decidedly negative impact on the Prime Minister and led to the development of his national policy, which was unveiled in 1879. That seminal program, with its highly protective trade tariffs, helped lay the foundation for the industrial system we in Canada have today. Even as Macdonald developed his policy, while at the same time building a railroad to unite his vast country, he was in effect creating the frame- work for the modern Canadian nation.

For a few years during the 1870s Macdonald was out of office. In that period, Alexander Mackenzie, the nation's first Liberal Prime Minister, appointed George Brown, founder and publisher of *The Globe* newspaper, to negotiate a reciprocity treaty with the United States. Brown succeeded in negotiating a fairly comprehensive agreement in 1874, but the treaty failed to obtain the American Senate's necessary approval. The historian J.M.S. Careless, analyzing the reasons, noted that "Canadian agreement was not a vital matter to the United States," a telling attitude that we may experience again in our own time. That year, more than a century ago, clearly represented a forfeited initiative, a moment of opportunity lost for both sides.

Macdonald fought his last successful campaign in 1891, accusing the Liberal Party and its new leader, Wilfrid Laurier, of "veiled treason" because of their willingness, in Macdonald's view, to sell out to the United States. Interestingly, an editor of *The Globe*, Edward Farrer, was cast by Macdonald and the Tories as an arch-villain, conspiring with the Americans and the political opposition against Canadian interests, because of a secret pamphlet he had written advising some Americans on how to negotiate with Canada. (Shades of John Diefenbaker seventy years later!) The Liberals were eventually victorious in 1896, Laurier becoming the country's first French-Canadian Prime Minister. His positive attitude towards the United States, combined with the Liberals' traditional free trade policy, led to the Reciprocity Agreement of 1911. That Agreement was to contribute significantly to Laurier's subsequent defeat in the election held later the same year. The Liberal Party was badly split over reciprocity, particularly in the crucial electoral provinces of Ontario and Quebec. The election of 1911, which has been exhaustively studied by historians, is still remembered as one of the most consequential in Canadian history. Most historians agree that the economic aspects of the reciprocity issue were overshadowed by the political and cultural concerns of Canadian voters, who feared the possible loss of their national sovereignty through closer association with the United States.

In 1935, as both nations were emerging from the depths of the Great Depression, a rather successful bilateral trade agreement was forged between Canada and the United States, one that is mentioned now in positive terms by Canadian leaders preparing for the current negotiations. In early 1948, Prime Minister William Lyon Mackenzie King authorized the negotiation of a reciprocity treaty with the United States. This time, the initiative had come from the American government and a treaty was actually drafted. While the Canadian government proceeded privately with cautious discretion, the American side wanted to hasten the treaty through Congress in time for the presidential elections taking place that fall. The matter thus became prematurely public in the United States, leading to a vigorous and negative reaction in Canada, best exemplified by *The Globe and Mail* whose headlines harshly proclaimed of the proposed treaty: "Not on your life." King, disconcerted by the Americans' unseemly haste and unnerved by the reaction in Canada, proceeded no further. The whole matter was simply buried.

This curiously significant event in Canadian history has received little comment over the years, although Ted English, a respected Canadian economist, has referred to it as "probably Canada's most regrettable missed opportunity." King himself must have recalled the lessons of 1911 from his mentor Laurier. In one of King's last entries in his diary, a few weeks before his death in 1950, he wrote: "The more I think over the whole situation, the more I believe . . . that the U.S. foreign policy at bottom is to bring Canada into as many situations affecting themselves as possible with a view to leading ultimately to the annexation of our two countries." Lester Pearson, who at the time was Under Secretary of State for External Affairs, observed years later in the first volume of his memoirs that he was not surprised the treaty proposal never proceeded; had it gone forward, he said, it would not likely have succeeded.

One of the principal negotiators of the 1948 treaty, John Deutsch, noted in a memorandum at the time that it would undoubtedly lead to further integration with the United States. He added, perceptively, that integration would be forced upon Canada in any event by the inexorable pressures of the world economy; Canada's real choice was whether to negotiate from strength or to delay and eventually negotiate as supplicant.

Throughout the 1950s, American investment in Canada greatly expanded and the Canadian standard of living soared accordingly. It was an era presided over by that remarkable Canadian politician, C.D. Howe, and more benignly by Prime Minister Louis St. Laurent, successor to Laurier and King. Donald Creighton, one of our foremost historians, saw this period as a tragic turning point for Canada. In *The Forked Road: Canada 1938–1957*, he argued that, in those years, Canada abandoned the vision of Macdonald and, buffeted by military and economic pressures, succumbed to a perilous reliance on the United States, in effect capping its evolution into North American continentalism.

The storm signals continued through the late fifties and beyond. In his Royal Commission Report of the time, Walter Gordon, one of the great figures of Canadian nationalism, warned of the dangerous implications of increasing American equity investment and ownership in Canada. Between 1958 and 1963, the convolutions of Prime Minister John Diefenbaker once again rendered Americans, particularly President John F. Kennedy, as insensitive saboteurs of Canada's national pride. Diefenbaker even rumbled about diverting 15 per cent of Canada's trade from the United States to the United Kingdom. For a few precious months in 1963, Prime Minister Pearson and President Kennedy had a wonderful relationship, until the shattering of dreams that November.

In 1965, as evidence of the improved Canada–U.S. relationship, came the Automotive Pact, a remarkable agreement and the classic illustration of a highly sensible rationalization of the North American auto industry. The pact has been of enormous benefit to Canada, although it has always caused some disquiet on the American side. However, from the tumultuous Trudeau era through the 1970s and early 1980s, both countries encountered vexing bilateral problems, notably the Foreign Investment Review Act and the National Energy Policy, as well as confusion in the consultative arrangements between the two governments. American frustration was considerable.

So we have arrived at 1986, when numerous factors have converged once again to place the "American" issue squarely on the Canadian political agenda. We have had reports from the Economic Council of Canada, the C.D. Howe Institute, the Senate Committee on Foreign Affairs and various major business organizations, suggesting that Canada negotiate an agreement leading to a free trade zone with the United States. The Macdonald Commission, barely a quarter of a century after the Gordon Commission's cautionary report, recommends with due authority that Canada should immediately enter negotiations with the United States for a free trade agreement. Chairman Donald Macdonald aptly refers to his Commission's recommendation as a "leap of faith."

The lessons of history are clear: free trade and consequent closer economic integration with the United States has been a recurring and contentious issue for Canadians. It ebbs and flows, but it never goes away. The issue reaches far beyond economics and commerce in the Canadian psyche, raising profound questions of sovereignty, identity, survival and national purpose. It is of considerably less importance to Americans, of course, who have seldom exhibited overwhelming interest in trade negotiations with Canada except when such topics as defence or the possibility of unlimited access to Canadian resources have aroused their attention. Finally, whatever the negotiating difficulties, the ultimate process of ratifying and implementing a comprehensive free trade agreement poses fundamental and complex problems in both countries.

Over the years, Canada has developed various policy initiatives to expand its small domestic market and diversify its trade. Diefenbaker's scheme to divert trade to the United Kingdom, Trudeau's "third option," Canadian overtures to the Pacific Rim countries and various other efforts have all been announced with much fanfare and, after a few years, have all yielded only modest results. The sheer size, wealth and attraction of the great American market—with its proximity, common culture and extensive linkages through the private sector —inevitably command centre stage in Canadian thinking. The trade issue goes to the very soul of the nation.

Because of Canada's political structure, the possibilities for conflict in federal–provincial relations, arising out of bilateral trade negotiations, pose a special problem. There has been widespread concern in recent years about the steady devolutionary trend in Canadian federalism. Indeed, Canada has reached the point where its federal government has less far-reaching power than virtually any of the other major federal states in the world today. The increasingly powerful provincial governments, understandably protective of their own interests, present a growing challenge to Canada's federal authority and the government's ability to assert the overall national interest. Provincial regulations affect industry, agriculture, trade, investment, employment and immigration. Many of the non-tariff barriers under discussion in the trade negotiations can only be altered with the direct consent of the Canadian provinces. The premiers of Ontario and Quebec in particular may raise complex objections. Negotiations with the United States are difficult enough without having constantly to look back over one's shoulder to secure the assent of the Canadian provinces. That reality is likely to haunt the federal government throughout the process.

Transcending these concerns is the profound difference in Canadian and American perspectives. Canada, despite its middle-power status and global interests, is preoccupied with its overall relationship with the United States, particularly when it comes to safeguarding Canadian interests and preserving some degree of autonomy for Canadian foreign policy. The United States, as a superpower, tends to regard Canada more in an international context; to a far greater degree, it is concerned with a wide range of world issues. While both countries view their bilateral trade negotiations in the context of the next GATT round, the broader American perspective may prove to be a double-edged sword for Canada. The United States is certainly motivated to conclude an arrangement with its largest trading partner and closest military ally. At the same time, in its negotiations with Canada it will be concerned not to set precedents that could have potentially negative effects on other American negotiations. Canada, like it or not, will therefore be under pressure to broaden its own perspective.

In an essay for the Macdonald Commission, William Diebold of the Council on Foreign Relations notes that what really must be considered in any serious Canada–U.S. talks is "the whole range of economic relations." Diebold queries whether Canadians are really prepared for this. Indeed, he may actually have written the epitaph for the negotiations:

> An historical look at U.S.–Canadian free trade issues reveals that every time there is a new expression of interest in them the same pattern develops. The subject is taken seriously by many people, in Canada very seriously by quite a few. Some good work is done about it. Sometimes nothing happens politically; sometimes some political movement begins. But then, for one reason or another, a strong political reaction cuts off whatever process had begun.

For Canada to enter comprehensive trade negotiations with the United States without a grand or broader design to deal with the implications of increased economic integration will almost certainly lead to a political uproar in Canada that is unlikely to benefit the government or generate the necessary public support for its initiative. Implicit in any trading arrangement with the United States is a significant tilt to reliance on market forces, along with a diminished role for state intervention so favoured by the political left. The Liberals are unlikely to take a firm stand on so divisive an issue; instead, they will seek unity by capitalizing on the apparent incompetence of the government to manage such a complex initiative. In the meantime, Canadian nationalists will campaign vigorously against the proposed agreement. So, too, will special business interests that perceive themselves as threatened, and that will cause serious problems for many of the Mulroney government's supporters, most notably within the Conservative Party's parliamentary caucus. The opinion polls, which currently reflect ambiguous support for a free trade agreement with the United States, will be increasingly linked to the credibility of the Prime Minister.

In the absence of a more firmly articulated commitment, a transcendent vision and purpose, the government of Brian Mulroney risks not only political disaster for itself but tragic consequences for the Canadian nation. What does it mean that Canada and the United States are becoming increasingly integrated? What is required for protecting and enhancing Canada's future within the context of a free trade agreement? These are the fundamental questions troubling thoughtful Canadians.

Integration is already an accepted way of life for many Canadians. The vast increase in Canadian personal and corporate investment in the United States over the past twenty years is only the most visible manifestation of this continental perspective. Our financial markets are essentially integrated. Communications satellites and broadcasting frequencies don't recognize the border. A recent striking example of integration within the American political arena is the Canadian government's decision to engage professional lobbyists to represent Canadian interests in the American Congress. In fact, a substantial majority of the Canadian public has moved ahead of the political establishment in coping with the reality of integration. That, in turn, is a cause of some disquiet and uncertainty. For, as we have been told by the Macdonald Commission and others, Canada has developed into a mature, vigorous nation, occupying a secure position in the world community. It is surely time, therefore, to face up to Canada's North American destiny and begin a systematic development of the framework and machinery for a long-term Canadian–American partnership.

One may sympathize with the politicians grappling with the trade issue today. Their problem encompasses, on the one hand, a process of free trade discussions that, if successful, will lead to significantly increased economic integration. (The social, cultural and political implications of this can be readily perceived even if the Canadian government prefers not to discuss them.) On the other hand, their problem reflects the void of a larger vision of North America's future—the lack of attention in formulating institutional goals and management systems for that future.

Ronald Reagan came closest to expressing a broad vision of North America's future in his 1980 campaign:

> A developing closeness among Canada, Mexico and the United States—a North American Accord—would permit achievement of that potential in each country beyond that which I believe any of them—strong as they are—could accomplish in the absence of such cooperation. In fact, the key to our own future security may lie in both Mexico and Canada becoming much stronger than they are today . . . .
>
> We will also put to rest any doubts of those cynical enough to believe that the United States would seek to dominate any relationship among our three countries, or foolish enough to think that the governments and peoples of Canada and Mexico would ever permit such domination to occur.

The spirit of Reagan's vision is reflected in his Administration's generally positive approach towards bilateral trade negotiations and in the cordial relationship that has developed between the President and Prime Minister Mulroney. This would seem an appropriate time, therefore, for the Canadian government to take the initiative in reviving the President's idea of a North American Accord. Vague though the words may be, they provide a sound base for beginning discussions about the future of North America.

The history of Canada–U.S. relations is replete with formal treaties, notes and a variety of governmental agreements covering hundreds of specific subjects. But there has never been a comprehensive accord establishing an all-encompassing framework for the relationship, one that provides direction, inspiration, purpose and, above all, a symbolic focal point for the electorates and political mandarinates of both countries. The absence of so basic an accord—a so-called Treaty of North America—underscores the indispensability of a collective concept of, and commitment to, a more vibrant North American partnership.

If the negotiations succeed, we will urgently need to establish new bilateral institutions to interpret and manage the agreement and to adjudicate differences. Beyond that, success in the trade talks will inevitably spur both nations to explore more long-range cooperative arrangements in areas like continental defence, water development and the environment, particularly acid rain. Increased trade will doubtless necessitate further agreements in such specific areas as tax treatment, investment flows, labour and immigration, and even currency fluctuations. More coordination, cooperation and consultation in the development of economic policy will be required, as well as the establishment of an implementing mechanism, such as a Joint Economic Commission. That concept has been strongly endorsed by a popular former American Ambassador to Canada, Kenneth Curtis, who, in a recent book co-authored with John Carroll, concluded that "because our economic interdependence is so vital to the welfare of both countries, so potentially disruptive to the relationship, and so tied to future opportunities . . . we believe the uncoordinated ad hoc approach should be replaced."

Maxwell Cohen, distinguished former Canadian Co-chairman.of the International Joint Commission (IJC), has emphasized the importance of both governments fully appreciating the specific requirements for each of the three stages of a comprehensive trade agreement: negotiation, ratification and administration. He warns: "It may be a serious misjudgement of the opportunities and the perils ahead . . . not to prepare for effective administration of the process toward economic 'integration,' whatever the degree, that now seems inexorably underway."

Twenty years ago, Prime Minister Pearson and President Johnson asked two outstanding former Ambassadors to the United States and Canada, Arnold Heeney and Livingston Merchant, to develop the principles that should guide the overall Canada–U.S. relationship. Their report, *Principles for Partnership*, carefully enunciated a set of principles which recognized the constraints on, and obligations of, both governments in the management of their increasingly interdependent relationship, while also reflecting each country's differing national interests and contrasting scale of global responsibilities. With a few notable exceptions, these principles have been followed in practice by succeeding governments of both countries.

Management of Canada–U.S. relations has now evolved into a sophisticated system, presided over by foreign service professionals in Canada's Department of External Affairs and the American State Department and in the respective Ottawa and Washington embassies. Other departments and agencies of the two governments also interact in the process. External Affairs and the State Department find themselves frequently engaged in a feverish role of coordination and consultation. The fact that this extraordinarily complex system works at all is a tribute to the highly qualified officials of both governments. Meetings between Canada's Minister of External Affairs and the American Secretary of State take place four times a year, while various parliamentary and Congressional groups meet regularly. The system understandably has a short-term focus. The players come and go with disconcerting frequency, the result being lapses of institutional memory on both sides. An atmosphere of crisis management is all too apparent at times.

A major weakness has been the unwillingness of either government to commit itself to the development of new transnational institutions to assist in the management process, at the same time as existing institutions have been allowed to atrophy. In the national security area, for example, the Permanent Joint Board of Defense, which has existed since the 1940s, has become largely ceremonial. While the Board provides a modest forum for discussion between senior members of the Canadian and American defence establishments, a gap remains in the overall coordination and forward planning of Canada–U.S. defence relations. The impressive degree of integration that has already occurred under NORAD (the North American Aerospace Defence [Command]), the defence production-sharing agreement and other bilateral security accords should not be minimized. However, it is generally recognized that vitally important opportunities for further integration demand attention.

As for the IJC, a model of bilateral cooperation since

its establishment in 1909, it requires a major infusion of commitment from both governments. Symptomatic of the IJC's current under-utilization is the January 1986 Report on Acid Rain, in which the Canadian and American special envoys, William Davis and Drew Lewis, recommend that their governments establish "a bilateral advisory and consultative group on transboundary air pollution." The recommendation ignores the IJC, the most natural body for dealing with the acid rain issue. Indeed, some feel that an appropriate referral to the IJC, when the issue first surfaced a decade ago, might have prevented a lot of confusion and disagreement between the two countries over definition of the problem.

Any prescription for enhancing the management of the relationship should include the following stages:

First, the Canadian government must take the initiative with the United States in establishing a joint working group that, following the principles of the Heeney–Merchant report, would review and assess the broad conduct of Canada–U.S. relations today. The joint study would provide recommendations for the institutional framework required to direct the increasingly complex Canada–U.S. partnership into the future. The working group should include accomplished private- and public-sector leaders from each country, and its members should work in effective coordination with Parliament and Congress to ensure appropriate legislative and political input.

Second, the Canadian and American trade negotiators must give especially careful consideration to the ratification and implementation process, as well as to the development of specific institutional machinery for administering an agreement. The negotiators may otherwise find themselves lacking the necessary authority to make effective trade policy decisions in the future. Indeed, they could find themselves creating conflicts and tensions with the existing bureaucratic machinery in both governments.

It is clear that many Canadians harbour doubts about their country's future independence vis-à-vis the United States. As their government enters the uncharted waters of trade negotiations, the uneasiness will intensify. The paramount challenge for Prime Minister Mulroney does not lie only in championing his trade policy, which is inevitable and right. It is also in inspiring Canadians with the required sense of purpose and confidence in their nationhood, as Canada accelerates into an ever more integrated relationship with the United States.

Timing, of course, is everything. And the time is now. The current Canadian government has challenged history with its trade policy, although whether it has done so with sufficient wisdom and political courage remains to be determined. For Brian Mulroney, as for each of his predecessors, the Canada–U.S. issue represents the acid test of his leadership.

Studying the memoirs of Jean Monnet and his critical role in the evolution of Europe, one cannot fail to be impressed by his preoccupation with the need, first of all, for institutions and structures, and then for the consummate patience to allow the perception of mutual interests to grow and evolve among peoples. Monnet was an optimist, but he did not believe in miracles. Rather, he understood that "crucial moments of opportunity must never be lost." Towards the end of his memoirs he wrote:

> The main concern of many very remarkable people is to cut a figure and play a role. They are useful to society . . . . But, in general, it is the other kind of people who get things moving, those who spend their time looking for places and opportunities to influence the course of events. Life is made up of nothing but events: what matters is to use them for a given purpose.

History is unforgiving. Those who have not learned its lessons, to paraphrase Santayana, are bound to pay the penalty of planning inadequately for the future. We have the opportunity to guide the direction in which history is inexorably taking us. Only rarely in their evolution do nations have that opportunity. Canada and the United States should waste no more time in exploiting it to their mutual advantage.

William Diebold

America's Stake in the
Free Trade Agreement

Time changes many things, and one that it has changed
is the significance for the United States of a free trade area with Canada.
This is partly because of changes in the United States and the international
economy. Mostly, it is because of changes in Canada.

The basic analysis of the economic advantages Canada
could gain from a free trade agreement with the United States was made
in the 1960s. It showed several things clearly:

(1) the continued expansion of Canada's economy and the
growth of its industrial productivity would require structural shifts toward a larger industrial output than could
be justified by the size of the Canadian market;
consequently,

(2) good access to foreign markets would assume even
greater importance to Canada than it already had;

(3) as a result of continuing international negotiations, Canadian tariffs and other import barriers would have to
come down in order to reduce costs and to meet needs

that could no longer be supplied domestically as production became increasingly specialized;

(4) the resulting import competition might help the difficult processes of structural adjustment;

(5) although Canada would continue to evince strong interest in trading throughout the world, the United States would remain by far its most important market and supplier;

(6) the readjustment in the Canadian economy, required for a free trade area with the United States, would be something like nine-tenths of the adjustment to global free trade.

Cogent as these analyses were, it was hardly surprising that no Canadian government in the sixties showed serious interest in reviving the idea of a free trade agreement with the United States.

The effort had had a troubled history. In 1911, a Canadian government had fallen because it wanted to put through an agreement it had negotiated with Washington for reducing a number of tariffs. In 1948, Mackenzie King reversed his view on the issue and halted the free trade negotiations he had tried to conduct in secret with the Americans. He did so partly for fear of domestic political consequences and partly because he did not want to see a further, abrupt rupture of ties with Great Britain.

At any time, even when no specific proposal was up for debate, the idea of free trade with the Americans was a divisive and emotional issue in Canada. The arguments for it were pragmatic, even prosaic; those against it were intuitional, stoked by fears of the unknown and by imaginative scenarios. Such worries were natural enough in a small country situated next to a giant whose behavior was not always pleasing or dependable.

In the 1960s, there were no compelling economic pressures to force a Canadian government to conclude that it could not continue to get along in the world as it was. Economies were expanding. The Kennedy Round of the General Agreement on Tariffs and Trade (GATT) showed that the multilateral trading system was working well and reducing trade barriers, including those of the United States (although the fact that Canada had reduced its tariffs to a lesser degree than other industrial countries signalled to some observers that there would be more pressure in the future).

The Americans, to be sure, paid less attention to Canada than they had formerly in working out their international economic policies. The dispute over the stationing of missiles in North America created great friction between the Kennedy and Diefenbaker governments. Such trends were hardly conducive to the idea of launching a major initiative toward free trade with the United States. Indeed, it was quite surprising that the two governments should have resolved a threatening trade dispute by negotiating the Automotive Pact of 1965, which created a limited kind of free trade in automobiles and original auto parts. The suggestion, however, that the same approach might be desirable in other industries was soon discouraged.

In the 1970s, things began to change. The world economy became more troubled. Failure to reach multilateral agreement on international monetary reform led to unilateral action by the United States. The Canadian government, accustomed to being exempted from various troublesome American measures, such as the balance of payments restrictions of the sixties, was shocked to find itself treated "like any other country" and faced with a series of demands from Washington.

The energy crisis of the seventies strengthened Canada's economic position in some ways. Its impact on the world economy, however, was disturbing. International financial volatility, the emergence of "stagflation" in the major industrial countries and, by the end of the decade, a menacing international debt problem, all showed their effects in Canada. Although the Tokyo Round of GATT was completed, it did not offer many immediate advantages, and Canadians became increasingly worried about the growth of protectionist pressures in the United States.

A committee of the Canadian Senate held hearings over several years, culminating in a report favorable to the idea of eliminating most barriers to Canadian–American trade. A study by the Economic Council of Canada pointed in the same direction. The Canadian government, however, showed no signs of serious interest in such an idea. Indeed, the National Energy Policy (NEP) and a number of measures concerning investment—often with direct implications for bilateral trade—increased the area of friction between Ottawa and Washington.

During all this time, the United States had not felt the need for a policy on free trade with Canada. Under both Democratic and Republican presidents the basic trade policy had remained what it had been since the end of the Second World War: to foster, largely through GATT, multilateral action that encouraged the selective reduction of trade barriers and the resolution of disputes. Direct negotiations between Ottawa and Washington dealt with most issues; mutual tariff reductions were made in GATT rounds. The American Trade Act of 1979 called for a study of North American free trade, but that was largely in response to the interest of a few legislators. Ideas about a North American common market for energy received some support from Ronald Reagan before he became President, but dissipated in the face of Canadian and Mexican opposition. The matter was prudently put aside once Reagan was in the White House.

The free trade issue was probably not given much thought beyond those small circles in the United States that have a continuing interest in Canadian–American relations. Why should the United States propose free trade with Canada? Certainly there would be some economic gains from such an arrangement, but there would be costs as well. Questions would be raised about the continued allegiance of the United States to the multilateral approach. While these could be answered, doubts would remain, and other countries would find excuses for deviations of their own. Although one could conceive of the American government deploying a given quantum of energy to trade policy, there were other objectives that took priority. Certainly there were no domestic pressures in favor of such a move.

Most serious, however, was the anticipated reaction in Canada. An American proposal for free trade would ring all the alarm bells of history there. American motives would be questioned. The vision of Canada becoming America's fifty-first state would reappear. A threat would be felt not only to Canada's economic interests but also to Canadian institutions, culture and independence. While some of the Canadians who already believed in free trade with the United States might welcome an American proposal, others would see it as reducing their chances to win the argument in Canada. All in all, an American initiative seemed about the least likely way of achieving a free trade area between the two countries; it would probably damage other relations as well.

Suppose, though, the Canadians initiated a proposal to explore the possibilities of a free trade area, or something like it? The matter would then have to be looked at very differently in Washington. The risks and dangers would not disappear, but some would be modified substantially. It could not be taken for granted that a Canadian government would successfully carry through such an initiative, but Washington was in no position to make that judgment or to base a negative response on its skepticism. The issue of free trade between the two countries is, in short, of much greater significance to Canada than to the United States and, to Canadians, carries a far heavier political charge. It would, therefore, be irresponsible for any American government to make light of a Canadian proposal to negotiate about free trade or to refuse to enter into talks and see what could be accomplished.

Whether as the result of good luck, good instincts or good thinking, that was the position of the United States when, in 1983, the Trudeau Administration proposed that the two governments should discuss the possibilities of improving their trade relations in a number of key sectors.

Washington responded favorably. As soon as that happened, Americans had to begin thinking in terms of the national interest in these kinds of arrangements. The first move in this direction was the natural proposal to add certain sectors to the discussions. Then, the United States had to consider what changes to request and what Canadian proposals to accept. Thirdly, if there were progress toward agreement, how many sectors would have to be included to reach a balanced bargain that would be politically acceptable in both countries? Fourthly and not necessarily least importantly, could the agreement be reconciled with the multilateral trade obligations of both countries? The process of addressing these issues began to create an American stake in the free trade calculations that had not existed before.

Though the public record is not all that substantial, there is no reason to disbelieve the conventional view that both sides found the sectoral approach difficult. This was mainly because of problems in striking a balanced bargain and reconciling limited bilateral agreements with existing arrangements within GATT. If, as is generally believed, the Americans made it clear that an examination of broader possibilities would reduce some of the difficulties, it did not follow that the Canadians had no choice (and, indeed, many preferred that alternative). In any case, the 1984 elections in Canada intervened and a long pause followed, during which the new Mulroney government decided whether to move toward a free trade area. Canadian business opinion and the report of the Royal Commission on the Economic Union and Development Prospects for Canada (chaired by Donald S. Macdonald) suggested that Ottawa's subsequent decision to propose that course to Washington had reasonably wide support in Canada, although opponents remained vociferous.

As the talks proceeded, America's equity in the agreement expanded dramatically. The same processes were at work as in the sectoral negotiations, but now the range of issues was greater, more sections of American business and agriculture were involved, and consultations with private groups and Congress were increasing. In the process, more people became conscious of their interests in the agreement, while others pressed for provisions that would take care of their special problems. Links were forged that began to involve Washington in domestic commitments that it would not be so easy to ignore. As time passed, the United States acquired an ever firmer stake in the successful outcome of the negotiations.

Success is something negotiators always claim. But, as the number of people becoming conscious of the issues grew, the harder it became to sell a simple bottle of eyewash.

Along with the domestic and bilateral dimensions of the American stake in the success of the talks, the multilateral dimension assumed increasing importance for several reasons. Firstly, it became clear as the talks progressed that a satisfactory reconciliation of the bilateral agreement with GATT obligations could be worked out; therefore, the possible objections on that score decreased. Secondly, a number of people, American officials prominent among them, believed that, by pursuing the bilateral negotiations, the United States could pressure other countries to stop dragging their heels in initiating the Uruguay Round of multilateral trade negotiations. (A questionable argument, I think.) Thirdly, the inability to reach a bilateral agreement with Canada on important trade issues would, without any doubt, compound the difficulties of persuading other governments to try to work out understandings in a multilateral setting.

It also became important to Washington that the United States should not be responsible for a failure of the bilateral negotiations after the Canadians had taken the major step of accepting the idea of a free trade area. How firmly this conviction was held in Washington it is impossible to say; it is not the sort of thing negotiators or their political superiors can remotely hint at.

Honest people can differ about assigning responsibility or blame when it comes down to insistence on certain provisions in a complex agreement or refusal to give the other side what it wants on a range of issues. Some Canadians subsequently attacked the agreement as a sellout, charging that the Canadian negotiators had been outwitted. It was also said that the Americans forced the Canadians to accept certain provisions as a condition of getting the agreement at all, or refused key Canadian requests on the grounds that Congress would not accept them. Both sides had certain absolutes in their position. There will be no escaping efforts to blame the other party, but outsiders will have little chance to make a firm judgment until the records are opened.

It would require more extensive examination than is possible in an article of this length to determine how fully the free trade agreement serves American interests. This is a matter not only of whether any given point might not have been pushed further, but also of the balance among the many different provisions in this complex accord. The high degree of integration between the American and Canadian economies makes it difficult to trace the real beneficiaries of various changes. Provisions that negotiators press for may not, in the long run, seem to be truly in the national interest. Even in the short run, there are different viewpoints. Not all private interests are identical with the public interest; stipulations laid down by Congress can reflect narrow concepts of what is good for the country. The very vocabulary of trade negotiations—"demands" and "concessions"—suggests a false antagonism and a zero-sum game, whereas the real aim is gain for both sides.

A good case can be made for the view that the agreement was not regarded broadly enough by the American negotiators nor taken seriously enough by the higher reaches of their government for American interests to be as well served as possible. There are clear weaknesses in the pact, some of them the result of holding back on the American side. Some of the unfinished business is recognized by provisions for continuing negotiations, most notably on the crucial matters of subsidies, countervailing duties and the settlement of disputes over what constitutes "fair" trade. The real economic meaning of the agreement, and therefore a full judgment of the extent of America's economic interest in it, will depend on how it is carried out on both sides.

In spite of the uncertainties, there is no real doubt that the signed agreement provides significant economic advantages for the United States. There is also no doubt that the real interests of the United States in the agreement go beyond its specific economic provisions.

The primary advantages are obviously economic ones. Some private interests will be hurt, but these are likely to be few and not extensive. Far more groups will benefit, either as exporters or consumers, from the removal of both Canadian and American tariffs, as well as from the reduction or elimination of other impediments to trade. Americans wishing to invest in Canada will have greater assurance about the rules of the game and how they will be treated once they or their businesses are established there. That is also true of firms and, to some extent, individuals providing services in a number of different fields. Companies that do business on both sides of the border will be freer than before to organize their businesses in the most efficient fashion. American buyers of oil, gas and electricity from Canada are assured that they will not have to pay higher prices than Canadian customers as the result of government actions. In times of shortage, the United States will be entitled to a share of Canadian energy production proportionate to the amount it bought in times of plenty. In short, the American economy stands to benefit from freer and easier trade and investment with its most important foreign market and supplier.

The second set of advantages, not widely recognized, stems from the fact that the agreement gives the United States an opportunity for improving its own fair trade laws, especially those concerning the use of countervailing duties to offset foreign subsidies. One of Canada's main objectives in negotiating the accord was to get some assurance as to how these laws would apply to Canada. The results are in many ways unsatisfactory. The agreement entails some improved arrangements, notably a provision for binational panels to investigate cases, with better opportunities than before to settle trade disputes before final, damaging action is taken by one party. However, the full effect of these rather complicated measures is difficult to assess in advance; clearly, much depends on how both governments deal with them. The American government does not have an altogether free hand because of the rights its laws give to private parties. At the same time, the negotiators failed to reach agreement on the kinds of subsidies that would and would not be exempt from countervailing duties or on the means by which such determinations should be made.

The agreement calls for the two governments to try to negotiate better arrangements over the next seven years. In my judgment, it would be very much in the interest of the United States if that process led to a more general revision of American fair trade laws. As they stand, those laws, and the administration of them, are most unsatisfactory. The laws rarely come even close to providing the level playing field they are supposed to; they virtually invite protectionist abuse. They have frequently led to restrictive trade arrangements between the United States and one or more foreign countries; often, they do not provide domestic producers with the protection to which they are entitled. At the same time, the fair trade laws seem bound to lead to a continuing series of disputes with major American trade partners.

Not the least of the difficulties is the divergence between the criteria of the American laws and the larger role of government in economic life that is accepted as sensible in much of the rest of the world. (That was, and will continue to be, one of the main sources of difficulty in the Canadian–American negotiations.) The changes that have been incorporated in trade law over the last decade or so, along with others that have been proposed, have mostly made matters worse. Of course, Americans should look after these things in their own interest. But experience shows that, in trade policy, governments usually fare better when they have to strike bargains with other governments than when they act unilaterally. That is what made it possible to reduce tariffs so extensively in the post-war period. The best course would be to improve the GATT code on subsidies, but there are only limited prospects of making much progress in that area during the Uruguay Round. By pursuing further negotiations on fair trade laws within the context of the bilateral free trade accord, Canada could help the United States live up to its own best standards and accomplish things that are in its own national interest.

The third American stake in the free trade agreement also relates to the multilateral trading system. Many observers hoped that the bilateral accord would be a model for what could be attempted on a multilateral basis, especially in such "new" fields as services, intellectual property, trade-related investment rules and some high technology industries. An improved method of settling disputes, especially those related to subsidies, also seemed possible. In the event, the agreement falls so far short of the ideal in most of these areas that it cannot be claimed as strong evidence of what could be accomplished if governments would only go about their trade policies in the right way. The accord does, however, break enough new ground to be treated as an example of what ought to be undertaken multilaterally. It also recognizes the common interests of the two countries in certain issues under consideration in the Uruguay Round, thus suggesting the possibility of some joint action on their part. In these respects, the agreement creates yet another American stake.

There is also a stake in avoiding failure. American aspirations for the multilateral negotiations would suffer a setback if the agreement were to collapse at a later date, become a dead letter, or provide few benefits or lopsided advantages to only one of the countries. Two great risks were overcome in 1988: in the United States, a protectionist-inclined Congress approved the work of the executive branch's negotiators; in Canada, a close election returned to office the only party committed to putting the agreement into effect. But further risks lie ahead. Much has to be done by both governments to carry out the agreement. If, at some point in the implementation process, the agreement begins to look like a failure, for whatever reason, it will be all too easy for people elsewhere to argue that it is fatuous to expect substantive agreement among a large number of trading nations on matters that could not even be dealt with by two countries as close in their trading ties as the United States and Canada.

The logic of that argument will be less than impeccable. Still, there are enough people in Europe and the developing countries, reluctant to move toward greater trade liberalization in many fields, to leave no doubt that such conclusions would be drawn. It follows that, to the extent that the deficiencies in the agreement are traceable to the American government's unwillingness to be more daring—or to indications that it has held back from dealing effectively with the unfinished business of the agreement—the United States will have failed to serve its own interests well.

The final stake, or cluster of stakes, that the United States has in the free trade agreement concerns its relations with Canada.

Just as it was right and proper for the United States to make no proposals about a free trade area until after the Canadians had taken the initiative, so it is impossible for the United States to regard the free trade arrangement as simply a commercial pact. Not only does the agreement represent a very substantial change in trading relations, which are a major and integral part of the total bilateral relationship, but it also reflects a set of telling decisions about the Canadian economy and therefore other aspects of Canadian life as well. The economic and social readjustments necessary under the new freer trading relationship are many times greater for Canada than for the United States, as are the potential gains.

Just as the United States could not afford to be negative about any reasonable agreement, so it cannot be careless about how the implementation of the agreement affects the broader bilateral relationship. Although the United States has a keen economic interest in the free trade area, its interest in a continuing strong and independent Canada is even greater. Both those interests could be seriously affected by the agreement and how it is applied.

If the United States has these complex lasting interests in the free trade agreement with Canada, how should it pursue and safeguard them in the future? To a degree, the answer depends on what happens in the next few years. But the general prescription for policy seems clear.

To start with, the United States should take the agreement and its implementation seriously. That may seem obvious, but it is only too easy for the higher levels in Washington to display a narrow attention span, especially when trouble is not highly visible, and to move on to the "next" problem, treating the first one as settled (especially if Congress has dealt with the matter).

The agreement with Canada, for example, could be treated henceforth as a fait accompli, while America's attention in trade matters increasingly focuses on the Uruguay Round, Europe's moves toward 1992 and the perennial problems with Japan. That would not be so bad if it meant that, on the working level, officials could move ahead to make the agreement a workaday reality, putting the new mechanisms for consultation and disputes settlement in working order and constructively exploring the implications of the complex changes in law and administration necessary in both countries to carry out the accord. It will be necessary to staff the new bodies, national and binational, with competent people who are strong enough to withstand the pressures to treat every issue as if it were a matter of bargaining in the American national interest, no matter how limited the groups affected or how weak their case. Those things should be done, as far as it is in the power of officials to do them. It is the way, by and large, that Canadian–American relations were carried out for many years.

Unfortunately, the task will not be easy. On both sides of the border, business interests, worried about new competition, will try to block or delay the removal of trade barriers. Uncertain about the impact of the new rules, private groups will invoke existing fair trade laws to see how far they can get. Government measures to ease the adjustment to the new situation in one country will sometimes seem to the other country like subsidies or illegitimate forms of assistance. As Canada and the United States negotiate with third countries in the Uruguay Round, each may view the other as giving away some of the privileges gained in the bilateral agreement. Troubling problems will arise as general statements in the agreement are converted into concrete arrangements and the devils who live in the details reveal their faces. All these matters will require more than routine attention in Washington and will, from time to time, involve Congress as well as the executive branch.

A central set of issues concerns subsidies and countervailing duties. The agreement's provisions dealing with these matters are quite deficient and are to be replaced in five or seven years. The same political and economic pressures that made for the deficiencies will be obstacles to any improvement. There are technical, legal and administrative problems to be solved as well. Simple solutions will not be acceptable: the United States will not make blanket exceptions to its fair trade laws; Canada will not surrender those subsidies it has judged basic to its welfare and equity. There are promising approaches to matters of wide compromise, but they will not be easy for either country to work out. At best, the parties will leave some problems unresolved.

There will be other difficulties. Some of the most promising provisions in the agreement concern new ways of settling disputes over trade. What kinds of results the innovative but complicated procedures produce depend to an important degree on the spirit in which the two countries approach them. If they fulfill the aim of dealing with one another on a new basis, extracting the greatest common benefit from their changed economic relation, the new instruments will serve them well. It is only too easy, however, to envisage a time when one or the other, or both, governments will act in ways that stultify the new arrangements. If that happens on any scale, the agreement will deteriorate or collapse, even if neither country formally renounces it. The difference in circumstances of the two countries makes it especially important for Americans to take care of their own behavior in these matters.

Simply because it involves trade—with all its references to the grubby and the selfish—the agreement ought not to be regarded as strictly a commercial convenience. It is that, but it is much more, because trade is so vital to Canada and because the history and geography of its relationship with the United States make the issue of bilateral economic relations a matter of high national, even existential, importance to Canadians.

Americans are seldom as acutely aware of these matters as Canadians are. Consequently, America's handling of the free trade agreement needs to be informed by a clear grasp of two sets of propositions. Firstly, the free trade area, by its nature, is a commitment to the idea that the public welfare is enhanced by the liberalization of trade, not by the many forces that encompass protectionism nor by the short-run mercantilism that normally characterizes trade negotiations. Secondly, Americans should be far more sensitive to the implications of the immense discrepancies between the two countries: the difference in the size of their economies; Canada's far heavier dependence on foreign trade; the difference in the proportion of mutual trading; the significantly greater number of Canadian business enterprises that are controlled by companies in the United States.

If they keep these facts in mind and adopt a broad approach to the free trade area, Americans will have a much better chance of realizing their true national interests than if they take a conventional approach to trade negotiations and assume that their relationship with Canada is like that with any other country. It will not always be easy to avoid exploiting America's superior power or the intractability of a given Congress at a given moment to settle issues, regardless of their merits. The temptations of realpolitik may cloud the perception of true national interest, especially since the high degree of integration of the Canadian and American economies can make it difficult to trace out the full impact of economic measures. A narrow approach will make it difficult to grasp the implications of the fact that each country, Canada and the United States, has compelling interests in the well-being and political satisfaction of the other.

To allow the free trade area to deteriorate or become a dead letter would, in my judgment, result in economic loss for both countries. Each, now, has an interest in the implementation of the new arrangement that can only be satisfied if the other permits it to be. That point was demonstrated for Americans when they realized that a different outcome of the Canadian election would have deprived the United States of its stake in the free trade area.

For Canadians, the question of what kinds of lasting economic arrangements with the United States would best serve their interests has long been of paramount importance. As always, the policies and practices of either country can help, or create difficulties for, the other. In the new circumstances, however, neither country can alone obtain the principal benefits of the free trade area, but either one can deprive the other of them. For both, more is at stake than simply commercial advantage. In the United States, that oft neglected point needs to be underlined.

Both countries would do well to let themselves be guided by two principles. "What we want," said the late John Holmes, speaking for Canadians, "is an equitable relationship, intricate and complex, of two disparate states." And it was John Dickey who observed that the United States has "a stake in not permitting the concept of a genuinely independent Canada, as a realistic American national interest, to languish in the dustbins of idle rhetoric."

John Meisel

Broadcast Regulation
in Canada:
An Audible Squeak

Lightning strikes at odd times in the most unexpected places. The week I began collecting my thoughts for this article, *First Choice*, one of Canada's two national pay-television programmers, and *Playboy Enterprises* in the United States announced they would jointly produce "adult" programming in Canada worth $30 million. The programs would be shown late at night on the *First Choice* pay-TV channel.

A storm of anger erupted in Canada. Within forty-eight hours, nationwide demonstrations were underway. Thousands of people in a score of communities—from Victoria, British Columbia to St. John's, Newfoundland—marched in protest. More than 400 demonstrators gathered on Parliament Hill in bitterly cold weather. Newspapers and television flooded the nation with stories on the issue. The Canadian Radio-Television and Telecommunications Commission (CRTC) was buried in an avalanche of more than 7 000 letters and petitions. We are still digging ourselves out.

I was immediately struck by the fact that the public outburst seemed more revealing than the proposed programs. So-called "adult" programming has been available in the United States for some time. In that fabled land of plenty, there are at least three national adult services (*Playboy, Eros,* and *Penthouse*'s electronic annex), as well as more raunchy fare, available on STV or MDS Systems in various metropolitan areas, such as the "Night Owl" programs in Los Angeles. Yet, I recall hearing no American protest in any way comparable to the frenzy in Canada. *Playboy*'s Senior Vice President reported that the corporation was stunned by the response there, and *Playboy* consequently agreed not to organize a promotion campaign for the programming.

One cause for concern in Canada sprang from the fact that the proposal might violate the spirit of Canadian content regulations imposed on pay-TV licensees. A more important part of the protest originated with feminist groups fearful that, once again, women would be symbolically demeaned. The major stream of criticism, however, derived from those holders of traditional moral values who saw the programming as yet another slip in the long, seductive slide into national depravity.

What was really telling about the public response to the *Playboy* affair was the eminently Canadian assumption that broadcasting—even the explicitly commercial medium of pay television—is a matter of collective national concern. Those who objected to the proposed programming were not for a moment satisfied with the option of *not* buying the offending service. Television programming is more to them than simply a consumer good to be provided to individual purchasers by unrestricted programmers, in accordance with the free play of market forces. The incident shows that this assumption, which has been the basis of Canadian government policy for more than half a century, still holds.

All this leads to a key observation: the context of broadcast regulation in Canada is fundamentally different from the context of regulation in the United States. For that reason, the substance and scope of regulation are bound to be distinct.

It is easy to overlook the difference between the two countries when we review their many similarities in language, political traditions, work habits, and economic structures. Our interrelatedness in the communications field is vividly symbolized by the arrangements approved last year for two American pay-television services to be carried on a Canadian broadcasting satellite, and by Canada's most recently launched satellite being dropped into orbit by the National Aeronautic and Space Agency's space shuttle. For a considerable time, moreover, our traditions in broadcast regulation followed a similar evolution: the judgements of the American Federal Communications Commission (FCC), as well as those of the CRTC and its predecessors, revealed a common concern for standards of service to the public in news and public affairs; in the free expression of differing points of view; in balance and variety of programming; and in limitations on the amount of commercial advertising over the airwaves.

Nevertheless, there have also been significant differences, chief of which is the presence of the Canadian Broadcasting Corporation (CBC) as the cornerstone of Canadian broadcasting, and the existence of several provincially funded educational networks. Canadians have also gone to extraordinary lengths to ensure that their main public and private networks are available in remote and sparsely settled areas. In recent years, too, there have been increasingly sharp disparities between the two countries with respect to broadcast regulation.

We have witnessed a strong trend in the United States towards dismantling regulatory restrictions in favour of reliance on market forces to achieve the goals of broadcasting policy. We have seen measures to loosen federal restrictions on cable television to allow it to compete with broadcasters. We have observed the steps taken to license hundreds of low-power TV stations to enhance competition. In an op-ed article in the *New York Times*, FCC chairman Mark Fowler listed the restrictions and requirements he wished to see removed. He had previously argued his position in a *U.S. News and World Report* article, the sum of which was:

> In broadcasting, consumers, through the marketplace, subject the broadcaster every hour to a national plebiscite. When you turn that dial, advertisers and broadcasters get the message. Those programs that most people want to watch will be supported by advertising; those they don't want to watch generally will not be.

There is no mystery about the appeal of reliance on market forces. Economists can enlighten us in a twinkling about the sensitivity of the marketplace to consumer preferences, about its capacity for quickly and effectively exploiting the implications of technical innovation, translating them into products and services that benefit everyone.

We are all familiar, too, with the contention that the free operation of market incentives will yield the best match between scarce resources and individual tastes, creating the greatest possible wealth for the economy as a whole. And for industry, of course, there is great attraction in tossing off the iron glove of government intervention in favour of the silken caress of Adam Smith's invisible hand.

The broadcasting industry in particular has been the subject of vigorous arguments for turning over more of its decision-making to the open market. Technological developments of the past decade, it is said, have so multiplied the channels for public communication that old assumptions about the limited number of frequencies are no longer valid. Hence, it is argued, there is no longer any basis for regarding the use of broadcast frequencies as a public trust, subject to the requirements of public service; the fundamental need in a democracy for the expression of widely diverse viewpoints on matters of public concern will be met through a multiplicity of broadcast outlets. In the words of Walter Block, a Canadian economist, the answer is to allow free competition to create "a tower of Babel of different voices . . . a sort of Hyde Park Corner of the airwaves." Under this approach, it is claimed, the dangers of state intervention in the broadcast media are avoided, democracy's needs are met, and the consumers get what they want.

I confess to a certain scepticism about this line of thought. I question the assumption that free markets lead inevitably to unrestricted choice. We have all seen how heavily financed advertising campaigns can influence consumer preferences and how this can be used to justify the producer's prior selection of items for mass production. We have all seen, too, examples of how the efficiencies of mass production are achieved at the price of reducing consumer choice. Markets may be appropriate mechanisms for allocating luxuries and resources that are in ample supply, but in a caring society, where individuals are seen to have an intrinsic worth, markets alone cannot be allowed to determine how rich the rich shall be, how poor the poor. Nor can they alone be allowed to determine the levels of health care or education available to the public. Or, to probe another aspect of the same issue, would the United States snuff out domestic production of oil and gas even if it knew that, in economic terms, all its requirements could be purchased more cheaply from the Soviet Union?

The routine anomalies of the marketplace are particularly important in the field of broadcasting, which is so sensitively linked to the requirements of a democratic society. Can we really expect broadcasters to address the needs and tastes of minority audiences rather than compete for domination of the mass audience? Genuine program choices are not made by audiences in a free market, but by network executives responding to their advertising strategies. History has shown them to be notoriously cautious, imitative, and unwilling to select programs that address issues in a manner which avoids stereotyping. No less a figure than former FCC chairman Newton Minow, in a celebrated speech, characterized the result as "a wasteland." It seems to me, therefore, that a multiplicity of broadcasting sources will not lead to a broadening of the scope of public debate, and that the market mechanism, so deft at incorporating technological innovations, will prove less receptive to innovations in political and social thought. A Hyde Park Corner of the airwaves, where you can speak only if you lease the property at going commercial rates, will lead to a tower of Babel where all the voices are clamouring to say essentially the same things.

I claim no novelty of insight in these observations. Benjamin Barber, writing in *Channels* magazine recently, warned that the heterogeneity and pluralism of communications technologies may not enhance, nor even permit, an informed public consideration of national issues. Other writers and speakers have expressed concern over the move towards dramatic reductions in regulation. Even the FCC's Fowler acknowledged in his *New York Times* article that certain program needs might not be met in an unregulated broadcast marketplace. Specifically, he noted that children's programs, in-depth radio news, and serious cultural fare might not be provided by the free-enterprise broadcasters. He suggested that fees, charged by government for spectrum use, might support a public broadcasting effort to meet those needs.

Nevertheless, whatever the merits of the arguments about broadcast content regulation, they are unlikely to lead to the same resolution north of the border as in the United States.

The arguments have found a resounding echo in Canada, where the impetus for deregulation is also palpable. On the official level, several major studies have addressed the problems of regulation: the reports of a joint Standing Committee of the House of Commons and

the Senate; of the Lambert Royal Commission on Financial Management and Accountability; of the Law Reform Commission; of the Special
Parliamentary Task Force on Regulatory Reform; and of the Economic
Council of Canada. The emphasis, however, has been on *regulatory
reform* rather than on *deregulation*. In the area of broadcasting, pressures
to lighten the regulatory load have been generated most notably in public
positions adopted by the Canadian Cable Television Association and the
Canadian Association of Broadcasters, as well as in the direct actions
of consumers, especially those in remote and northern areas, who have
circumvented the regulated broadcasting system by installing their own
satellite TV receiving "dishes."

There are, however, important differences in the context surrounding the debate in Canada. For one thing, Canadians have
not developed the finely honed suspicion of government that marks
the attitude of most Americans. Social scientists have found the reasons
for this difference a titillating subject of speculation. Why did the forces
of law and order, symbolized by the Royal Canadian Mounted Police
and its predecessors, play such a prominent role in settling Canada's
West, while the taming of America's frontier was left largely to freewheeling entrepreneurs and the railroad barons? Why does Canada's
Constitution speak of "peace, order and good government," while Americans are urged to seek "life, liberty and the pursuit of happiness"? Why,
in short, do Canadian responses to attitudinal surveys consistently reveal
higher levels of trust and confidence in government?

Various explanations have been suggested: the absence
of a revolutionary past; the dispersion of our small population over vast
distances; a sense of society as a community, enhanced perhaps by the
presence of a self-conscious and distinctive French-Canadian population
in our midst. But Canadian attitudes entail more than an absence of
distrust. Canadians, far more than Americans, have seen fit to use the
state positively as an instrument for common purposes. Our use of public
enterprises spans a long period—from the building of the Canadian Pacific
Railway, through the establishment of public electrical utilities and the
founding of Trans-Canada Airlines, to the formation of Petro-Canada,
the Crown (or government) corporation engaged in oil and gas exploration. In the broadcasting sector, this proclivity for public enterprise is

reflected not only in the broad outreach services of the CBC, one of the world's largest communication networks, but in the emergence of an array of public broadcasting services at the provincial level. Massive involvement by the government in the building of Canada's railways was largely prompted by the need of a vast, sparsely inhabited country for an effective and unifying transportation system. Similarly, broadcasting and telecommunications are seen as vital in forging and maintaining links among the various regions and demographically diverse groups that constitute Canada. The extension of broadcast services to remote, under-served areas has therefore been the goal of public policy, one pursued resolutely in the face of unfavourable market conditions.

Canadian attitudes and traditions, then, suggest that our solutions to the regulation versus deregulation dilemma will differ marked-ly from those in the United States. It may turn out that, left to the operation of market forces, America's less regulated broadcast media will serve the public effectively. But it is inconceivable that market forces could address the central concern of Canadian broadcast regulation: the need to promote a Canadian presence on the airwaves. For the Canadian mouse must not only sleep beside the American elephant; it must also grow and find self-expression in the elephant's looming shadow. This elemental fact has oriented Canadian policy towards broadcast regulation. In the United States, the legislative framework for communications regu-lation sets out its purpose as "to make available ... a rapid, efficient, nationwide and world-wide ... service with adequate facilities and reason-able charges." The Canadian Broadcasting Act, by contrast, speaks of the need "to safeguard, enrich and strengthen the cultural, political, social and economic fabric of Canada." The United States and its markets are big enough and strong enough to support an indigenous, unthreat-ened broadcasting system. Canada and its markets are only one-tenth as strong. So, we must seek means that the United States does not even contemplate to ensure that we can continue being ourselves.

In introducing the first Broadcasting Act in 1932, Prime Minister R.B. Bennett told Parliament that Canada "must be assured of complete control of broadcasting from Canadian sources, free from foreign interference or influence." Without such control, he argued, "radio broadcasting can never become a great agency ... by which national consciousness may be fostered and sustained, and national unity further strengthened . . . ." That theme remains paramount in considerations of Canadian broadcasting policy. If we want to have Canadian voices on our airwaves, we cannot rely on market forces. Indeed, market forces pull entirely the other way. Canadian broadcasters can purchase expensively produced American programs for a fraction of the cost of creating comparable original programs. Moreover, they can derive higher advertising revenues from airing these tried-and-true American products, so that the economic incentives to buy American are reinforced. One can argue that Canadian products, if they are any good, will find their way into the American and world markets. And, in fact, we have seen instances of this, as the explosion of programming services in the United States and elsewhere has created demands for more and more material. However, the overriding fact remains that the path of least risk for a Canadian broadcaster is to buy American. Put more emphatically: rational, exclusively economic decision-making may dictate a virtually total reliance by our broadcasters on American entertainment programming.

The statistics show that, while America imports only a minuscule amount of its TV programming (the figure for the networks in 1978 was 2 per cent), Canadian private TV programmers provide, on the whole, only the minimum required amounts of Canadian programming. In the peak viewing hours, between 7:30 and 10:30 in the evening, only about 30 per cent of the programs on these stations is Canadian in origin; only 5 per cent of the drama shown in this time slot is Canadian-produced. These figures reflect programming by Canadian broadcasters; they do not reveal the massive influx of American broadcast services available directly in areas along the Canada–U.S. border, or via cable from elsewhere.

The history of television regulation in Canada has been one of attempting to reconcile the national cultural objective of strong indigenous programming with the desire of Canadian viewers for an ever greater variety of programming and the need of Canadian commercial broadcasters to make ends meet. The tension between these imperatives has suffused every major television issue that has come before the CRTC in recent years: the expansion of cable television; the extension of TV services to remote areas; and the introduction of pay television.

There is no doubt that the technological environment is changing rapidly in Canada as well as in the United States. There is no doubt, either, that regulation comes at a price in terms of flexibility, innovation, and simplicity. The CRTC is attempting in various ways to reduce the regulatory load on its broadcast licensees. It is also experimenting, in the context of its pay-TV licensing decision, with the incorporation of some of the competitive benefits associated with a free-market system. In that decision, the Commission deliberately rejected the notion of a monopoly pay-TV service, although the option enjoyed widespread support, in favour of a competitive market structure. Our expectation, soon to be put to the test, is that competition in this domain of discretionary services will enhance the prospects for high-quality programming, both Canadian and foreign, and will provide greater variety for consumers.

The Commission has recently taken other initiatives to lighten the regulatory burden—with respect to FM radio, for example. In the Canadian context, however, these moves cannot aspire to wholesale deregulation, but rather to better regulation. One of the consequences of our geographic and demographic singularity is the necessity of devising political institutions and procedures that differ from America's, despite the many seeming similarities between our two countries. It is an often noted irony that these similarities sometimes ill prepare us for dealing with our differences.

As long as Canada aspires to preserve its political and cultural distinctiveness—which is not only in its own interest but in America's as well—and as long as it continues to regard TV broadcasting as an integral part of this effort, there will be a place for active government involvement in the regulation of broadcasts and broadcast content. Canada may not want to be known as the mouse that roared but, amidst the thunderous trumpeting of the American elephant, we still like to hear ourselves squeak.

Mavor Moore

Northern Renaissance:
The Saga of Canada's Theatre

The arts and sciences ... have a common origin in social
concern. In proportion, as they follow their own inner
structures, they become specialized and pluralistic. This is
simply a condition of civilized life: they have to do this,
and the degree to which an art is allowed to follow its
own line of development is of immense importance in
determining the level of a society's culture and, ultimately,
the level of life of its citizens.

Northrop Frye

How does one dissect a nation's culture, particularly one
as seemingly amorphous as Canada's, without succumbing to clichéd
comparisons or parallels? Is there a key to the history and development
of Canadian culture? Or is the term, as its critics would sniff, oxymoronic?

One can make easy but misleading assumptions about
art and society, and the relationship between them. Aristocracy inevitably
fosters aristocratic art; anarchy breeds aesthetic chaos; planned economies
ensure well-planned paintings or novels or symphonies; democracies
encourage freedom for the artist to do what he or she likes. These are
cases of what the grammarians call "transferred epithets."

There is, of course, a connection between a society's
political system and its arts; both are facets of the same social unit. But
the connection is seldom one of cause and effect. The film-maker John
Grierson explains the truer sequence: "First comes the need, then the
art, then the theory." It is precisely the *need* that varies in each society,
and thus the art through which it meets that need.

How difficult it is, then, to draw informed conclusions
about the state of the arts in those societies about which the observer

has only a limited knowledge. One is dealing after all with not only cultures, but with sub-cultures and counter-cultures for which a conceptual grid is lacking. This is especially true in cases like that of the United States and Canada, where the observer can be beguiled by obvious similarities into overlooking significant differences.

The consequence, as American art historian Sheldon Nodelman points out, is that

> not only is the whole matrix of assumptions, values and usages initially unknown to the outside observer, but . . . his spontaneous interpretations are founded, consciously or unconsciously, on patterns of behavior and attitude proper to his own culture, and must almost always be wrong.

Such warnings prepare us to examine carefully our own preconceptions before pre-emptively judging an entire society's culture. All of us require a house for our cultural home, but we have obviously different notions of the kind of house we need. In this respect, despite their neighbourliness, the Canadian experience is necessarily different from that of the United States.

It is a difference of perspective that has been fortified by history. Canadian and American histories have been intertwined from the beginning, but their threads and texture have assumed quite different patterns. To mix the metaphor abjectly, America became a melting-pot while Canada was formed more like a grand salad in which the ingredients have been encouraged to retain their own savour. It is this (call it perverse) social laissez faire that has held Canadians together when every shred of common sense suggests that the continent has been carved up the wrong way.

Canada has always been an improbable nation, born not out of triumphant revolution like the United States, but out of consensus among a bunch of losers: the Indians lost to the French, the French to the British, and the British to the Americans.

When Canada was born, not a shot was fired, not a single malcontent thrown into jail. A passel of colonial politicians got drunk together one night in 1861 and decided, in the rapture of bonhomie, that they loved each other enough to start a nation. At the outset, there were only four provinces. As the country grew to the west and east, the transcendent challenge for Canadians, then as now, became one of establishing and maintaining communications with each other across differing civilizations, across water, tundra, prairie and mountain.

If survival, as some say, is Canadians' common preoccupation, the ability to reach out to one another—to preserve our sense of unity—through a shared communications mode has always been Canadians' deepest, most commanding need. Even today, Canadians are probably the world's champion talkers on the telephone.

To build their first railway and telegraph lines, linking the nation from east to west, private enterprise and government had to work together, setting a pattern of government–private sector cooperation that has markedly distinguished Canada's society from that of the United States, with its general distrust of government intervention in people's lives and in the economy. Canadian business and government cooperated in establishing the first national airline. They collaborated as well in founding Canada's radio and television networks, the most extensive in the world, which happen to consume more than 60 per cent of all expenditures by the federal government on culture. In 1967, Canada's centennial year, the federal, provincial and municipal governments combined to give the nation a special cultural birthday gift—its first complete chain of theatres and art centres across the land.

All this had little to do with political ideology or precepts about government and private enterprise. It simply constituted a national need to unify a vast but fledgling nation of disparate regions. Collective action was dictated by circumstance. Despite Canada's relatively small population, the nation lacked the communicative advantage of those larger European societies that managed to congregate around thriving cultural centres in their countries—London, Paris and Rome, for example.

Canadians, just to keep in touch with each other, had to endure all the centrifugal headaches of countries as large in population as China, India or America. It is surely no accident that the two most influential communications philosophers of modern times, Harold Innes and Marshall McLuhan, were Canadians; or that Canada's most renowned thinker, Northrop Frye, should find it entirely natural to sit as a member on the federal Canadian Radio and Telecommunications Commission. (Can one envision John Kenneth Galbraith, that displaced Canadian, gracing the Federal Communications Commission in Washington?)

Without this background, one cannot begin to understand the state of the arts in Canada, especially such problems as the distribution of the works of our publishers and film-makers; the touring of our performing arts programs and art exhibitions; or the launching of our artists and the sustaining of national associations to lend them professional support. We simply have, as the novelist Margaret Atwood remarked, "too much geography and not enough demography."

Nor can one ignore the fact that history has placed us, culturally, cheek by jowl with the greatest arts, entertainment and education factory the world has ever known. No other country can cite this salutary, if occasionally unsettling, condition except Mexico, which does not, as we do in the main, share a common language with America. In many ways, this cultural bonanza from across the border is something to be grateful for; Canadians are among the world's luckiest consumers. Yet, as Christopher Lasch has observed, the freedom to consume is a pseudo-freedom: there is no real freedom where the choices do not include your own brand.

Canadians have only themselves to blame in this regard if they have been less enterprising, less imaginative, less innovative than Americans. At the same time, Americans, recalling the early part of this century when artists and writers in their country were trying to shed the influences of European art as they sought to find their own voices, can appreciate what Canadians have been going through in recent decades, living in the shadow of the American cultural factory.

Nationalism, as a concept, has different connotations depending on where one sits. Highly developed societies sometimes invoke the term "nationalism" pejoratively to belittle attempts at self-realization by others; they label the spread of their own artistic styles "internationalism." There can be no "international" exchange, however, unless there is something to be exchanged. The true internationalist encourages variety in art as he or she invites others to contribute to the exchange. The false internationalist seeks to homogenize everything, to reduce art to common forms judged by a single standard, preferably his or her own.

What is genuinely universal is neither the forms of art, nor those too often ephemeral standards thrust on us by leaders of fashion, but the *impulse* to create art, to give something lasting to the world. And you cannot do this if you have nothing original or distinctive to give.

Canada's experience in the theatrical arts is as good an exemplar as any of the special challenges our culture confronts.

In most British or American histories of the theatre, even in those chapters on the development of theatre in North America, you will find no mention of Canadian accomplishments in this genre. Canadian theatre does not appear on the historians' radar screens and must therefore be assumed not to exist. It seems not to have occurred to them to check out the screen even when, on occasion, it blipped over the relatively insignificant francophone theatre in New Orleans while ignoring the far more salient francophone theatre in Montreal.

Some of this is due, no doubt, to what Louis Kronen-berger, the New York drama critic, called the "Mediterranean Complex," a reference to a form of pre-Copernican cosmology in which the world appeared more flat than round, with all civilization clustered about a mediterranean body of water that was otherwise surrounded by arid land. Such was the cultural cosmology of those for whom Europe alone represented for so long the *ne plus ultra* of the arts world. Indeed, as recently as 1957, the *Oxford Companion to the Theatre* described Canadian dramatic efforts as "probably no more amateur than were the first plays of medieval Europe."

In fact, by 1957 Canada's professional theatre was already 200 years old, with a respectable if mercurial record. But even illusions have their causes, and there are solid reasons for the historic invisibility of Canadian theatre.

For longer than one cares to recall, the most promising Canadian dramatic talent left our country to practise acts of sublimation in foreign theatre climes. Canadian actors emigrated to New York, London or Paris, and, chameleon-like, turned into Americans, Britons or French. "America's Sweetheart," Mary Pickford, hailed from Canada,

as did Mack Sennett of Keystone Cops fame, the Warner Brothers and
Louis B. Mayer. Before them had come a royal procession of stage stars—
Clara Morris, Julia Arthur, Walter Huston—all of whom were Canadian
exports. They, in turn, were followed by the likes of Bea Lillie, Lorne
Greene, Walter Pidgeon, Raymond Burr, Donald Sutherland and
Christopher Plummer, all of them Canucks masquerading as Yanks.

Until recently, even Canadian playwrights either wrote
directly in English or "Americanese," or allowed their Canada-set works
to be "translated" for larger American audiences. The process was not
unlike the way in which many of today's films, actually shot in Canada,
go to considerable lengths to disguise their provenance. Film-makers have
been known to distribute garbage and refuse on the set, when filming
street scenes in, say, Toronto, to lend the sort of verisimilitude American
audiences expect to see in shots of an American city.

One of North America's most prolific and widely performed melodramatists before the First World War was W.A. Tremayne
of Montreal, yet not a single one of his fifty-odd plays was set in Canada.
When Mazo de la Roche's *Whiteoaks* was performed in London in 1936,
its Ontario family turned out to be impeccably British; when Ethel
Barrymore starred in the Broadway version, the play was unmistakably
set in New England. The same fate awaited John Herbert's *Fortune and
Men's Eyes*, which started as a play about a Canadian prison; by the
time the play reached Paris audiences, the prison had been transformed
into a French jail. Until not long ago, a Canadian playwright's work,
when published, was listed among "American Plays"; to this day, New
York's Grove Press (Herbert's American publisher) will not allow Herbert's
play to be included in any anthology of Canadian plays. It goes without
saying that, whenever a Canadian play or novel has been made into
a movie, the locale has usually been changed to the United States.

In short, until a mere fifteen years ago, a Canadian actor
or playwright abroad was somebody else, while at home he was a
nobody. This was in keeping with the assumption that if a Canadian
performer or writer was any good he would leave his country, and if
he returned it must be because he had failed abroad. Anonymity was
the price of an artist's versatility. Small wonder that Canadian theatre
was thought not to exist.

As Canadians are now beginning to appreciate, their cultural history has in fact been marked by a series of pratfalls—promising starts unfulfilled, collapsed renaissances—feeding the illusion that the most recent slip is the first. We grow old, we Canadians, slipping back from the verge of maturity.

Canada's original native peoples had at one time a rich civilization, especially on the west coast where the totemic culture of the Haida Indians flourished. The European settlers desecrated that civilization because they assumed that culture was something you imported. When Captain Cook landed in 1778 in what is now Vancouver, he found in that primitive setting a theatrical tradition of remarkable vibrancy: a stage bearing a striking physical resemblance to that of Shakespeare's Elizabethans, and performers of obvious skill. But since there existed no written texts, no literary drama of the sort the newcomers were accustomed to, the native theatre was dismissed as non-existent.

On the other side of Canada, the first French settlers quickly developed a sophisticated culture of their own. Montreal spawned gifted composers and professional orchestras while New York was still in its infancy. Corneille's great epic, *Le Cid*, was performed in Montreal only four years after its Paris première. Most of this cultural ferment collapsed, however, with the ascendancy of British rule in Canada.

The new cities and towns under the British developed, in turn, their own theatres and troupes. All too soon, though, these Canadian communities became merely stops on the American concert-and-theatre circuit. An exception was Winnipeg, where an entrepreneur named C.P. Walker turned the tables on the Yanks and ran the midwestern American theatre circuit out of his Canadian base. But in the main, Canadians had to sit and turn a blind eye as their best theatrical talent sought more hospitable auspices elsewhere. For their cultural divertissement they relied increasingly on travelling theatre companies from America as well as, for a time, from Britain and France.

One reason was simply that most of the theatres were owned by Americans. In the early 1900s, while great theatres, opera houses, art galleries and museums were being erected in the United States through the philanthropy of families with legendary fortunes,

Canada, lacking such private wealth, permitted the New York (and, later, Hollywood) syndicates to build theatres for it and fill them with their own shows.

The Royal Alexandra Theatre in Toronto, for example, was built in 1905 largely with money from the Shubert organization; the theatre did not house a Canadian production of a Canadian play until 1949, almost half a century later. Yet during the 1920s, in the same city, there were six full-time theatrical stock companies operating— usually under American management, with English stars and Canadian spear carriers who had to go to New York to get themselves hired. At the same time, Hart House Theatre at the University of Toronto launched a series of Canadian plays that promised a renaissance in Canada like the one spearheaded by the Art theatres of America. It was a short-lived promise: with the advent in 1929 of the Depression and the "talkies," the Hart House venture came to an abrupt end. This time, the illusion was almost complete: there was indeed no such thing as Canadian theatre, and most people refused to believe there ever had been.

The 1930s ushered in tidal changes for Canada. Industry was replacing agriculture as the majority occupation; people moved from the countryside to the cities. National politics, business and labour took on increasing importance. There was a palpable need for stronger communication among different constituencies and a yearning for some identifiable national self-image.

In other times and places, one might have expected the theatre or films to provide that self-image, as they did in Europe and the United States. But Canada's theatre was moribund and its film industry, after several false starts, almost non-existent. So the job was assumed by radio, a medium that in retrospect seemed tailor-made for Canada's eternal problem of too few people strung out too thinly across its vast dominion. Canadian radio drama, especially during its zenith under the producer-director Andrew Allan, not only succeeded in linking Canadians through a shared experience on the airwaves; also, for the first time it achieved front-rank international status for Canadian actors and playwrights. At the same time, Canadian public affairs programs were broadcast to some of the largest organized listening groups in the world.

Then, however, radio gradually saw its light in the firmament dim as it was displaced over the years by a new and extraordinarily powerful medium: television.

The next renaissance in Canada occurred just after the Second World War. The critical mass needed to energize a reborn professional theatre was assembled from three sources: the skilled craftsmen of radio drama; war veterans returning home from years of performing in service shows and determined to pursue careers in the theatre; and the corps of old theatre veterans who had managed to survive the drought. By the late forties, professional companies were again active in Toronto, Montreal, Ottawa, Calgary and Vancouver; *inter alia*, they were producing and staging new plays by Canadian writers.

In 1949, the Massey Commission (a Royal Commission on the Arts, Letters and Sciences, established by the Canadian government, under the chairmanship of Vincent Massey) recommended federal funding for the arts and letters, as well as the entry of the government-backed Canadian Broadcasting Corporation (CBC) into television. The proposals were made less to prime the pump than to cope with a mounting flood of artistic endeavours across the country. Toronto and Winnipeg already boasted ballet companies; symphony orchestras were proliferating, as were opera performances; new plays were opening, and extending into longer and longer runs. In addition, Canadians had found an extremely successful theatrical vein to mine: the topical satire. Ironically, that development occurred at the same time as Americans, in the shadow of rampant McCarthyism, were seeing their own satire constricted.

If Canadians were unsure, collectively, of who and what they were, they began to sense en masse who and what they were *not*. It dawned on them that fate had handed them a licence to mock their betters. Without worldwide political clout and, hence, responsibility, they found themselves in a perfect position to harry those peoples blessed with both. It was a role akin to the court-jester function of the Irish vis-à-vis the English. French and English Canada enjoyed some very successful homegrown revues; and the tradition has extended to the present, when Canadians have masterminded such satirical television shows as "Laugh-In," "Saturday Night Live" and now the "Second City Show." Nobody can carve up the family as well as the family, or the family's next-door neighbours.

Within two years of the Massey Commission's report, Canada was the proud possessor of the following: its own National Ballet Company; Le Théâtre du Nouveau Monde, now the leading theatre in Quebec; Les Grands Ballets Canadiens, also in Quebec; the Canadian Opera Company (which featured a young Jon Vickers in its opening production); and the Stratford Shakespearean Festival in Ontario. Shortly, too, the nation had spawned the National Theatre School and the Canadian Council for the Encouragement of the Arts, as well as many more theatre groups dispersed across the country.

The Stratford Festival became, at long last, the hoped-for breakthrough of the Canadian theatre onto the world stage. It has often been mistakenly thought of as the commencement of our theatre, but indeed the vision that brought Stratford's director, Tyrone Guthrie, to Canada belies that assumption. Guthrie came to Canada, he said, not to re-create the tired old traditions from elsewhere, but to build new ones; and in Canada, precisely because of its long, if discontinuous, theatrical history, he saw the opportunity for innovation, but innovation created on an existing base of trained artists and sophisticated audiences.

Within a few more years, other arts festivals had sprung up: the Shaw Festival at Niagara; the Vancouver International Festival; the Charlottetown Festival of Prince Edward Island, with its Canadian musicals; and a host of new Canadian ballets, operas and plays. As the nation celebrated its centenary in 1967, it seemed as if nothing could stop the momentum of the arts in Canada.

But pride goeth before a fall; or perhaps, more accurately, the nation's artistic ambitions exceeded its economic grasp.

The building spree by Canadian governments in the 1960s had been welcomed by a theatre community convinced that proper halls to house stage productions constituted the necessary step towards a Canadian theatre that could compete on even terms with the rest of the world. But a decade later, it became apparent that theatre companies, saddled with huge operating costs, could not be maintained in the style to which they had so recently become accustomed. The established theatre groups prudently began shelving their plans for more ambitious and expansive Canadian works, falling back instead on relatively "safe" productions, the old reliable diet of classics and fashionable European and American hits.

That left the path clear for those production companies with the least to lose, the shoestring theatres. While the major regional theatres provided mostly Canadian productions of plays from abroad, the pocket-sized theatres now found their true mission: the mounting of original plays by Canadians. As a consequence, we now enjoy at last a considerable number of Canadian plays, in both French and English, that have been produced in Canada. The question is, will they play in Peoria? Or make it on Broadway? This leads back, in the end, to the preconceptions that Canadians and Americans have of each other's arts.

I first became aware of these in 1949 when Gratien Gélinas' play, *Ti-Coq*, following its unprecedented success in both French- and English-speaking Canada, opened in New York. What bothered me was not that the critics did not care for it, or even that they failed to recognize what, to me, were the play's virtues; it was that they turned its virtues into vices. What I knew, in watching the play, to be deadly accurate about life in my country, the American critics assumed to be theatrically contrived, as if they were all convincing themselves that "People don't *do* such things." Next, I noticed that a good many Canadian playgoers came to believe that they must have made a mistake in liking *Ti-Coq* in the first place because, after all, New Yorkers must know a theatrical contrivance when they see one.

A decade later, having duly established its theatrical competence, the Stratford Festival travelled, first, to New York, then to Britain. In both places, the productions drew admirable notices. At the same time, I observed that the American critics praised our actors for their "style" (in which they felt American actors were then lacking), while the British critics praised the Canadians for their "vitality" (a quality in which it pleased them to think British actors were then deficient). The compliment in either case did no damage, of course, to the amour-propre of the givers. Still, I deduced from this that, if Canada's theatre was to be judged abroad by its compatibility with forms approved according to a sort of "Good Housekeeping" standard, then any attempt to be original in concept or performance forever ran the risk of being viewed as an assault by provincials on the reigning orthodoxy—a lamentable state of affairs.

For there is, after all, not *one* universal set of values or practices in art, but many. We would be not richer, but infinitely poorer were the Peking Opera to duplicate the repertoire of the Met. Canadian theatre's most valuable contribution may well turn out to be its *dis*-similarity from American theatre, its offering to the world of not only an alternative North American theatre but a model for greater diversity in general. For Canada is, and always has been, a pluralistic society in which no "national" theatre can flourish, nor should be expected to. As always, we are united by our differences.

Canada today is in the midst of its latest theatrical renaissance. There is more theatre ferment and productivity in Toronto and Montreal than in any North American cities with the exception of New York, although it remains as difficult as ever to find common denominators in the work going on in both countries. Last year (1981), Canada hosted a huge International Theatre Festival, along with, incidentally, the world's largest film festival. From Alberta to Newfoundland, Canadians these days are the blessed recipients of plays and productions that really do manage to present us to ourselves truly, and in original ways. We can only hope that they may be of interest to others.

Part III

Canadian–American
Comparative Perspectives

Nothing can shatter more effectively the illusion of Americans that Canadians are but extensions of themselves than the discovery of how much the two peoples differ in their outlook, traditions and, more often than suspected, their approach to the ordinaries of life.

Canadians' and Americans' view of the world and of what constitutes the priority issues of our time are frequently at odds. Canadians are by tradition a more cautious and modest race than their bumptious neighbors to the south. Americans prize the traits of aggressiveness and risk-taking that have made them a world economic and military force to be reckoned with. Canadians are more inclined to consider the collective in their social and political life; Americans venerate the rights of the individual.

The character and psyche of the two peoples have evolved out of divergent histories, reflected in Canadians' emphasis on order, constraint and deference to authority versus Americans' faith in the virtues of unfettered free enterprise and their impatience with rules and bureaucracy. Nowhere is this attitudinal cleavage more apparent than in the folkways of urban living in the two countries. Who is freer? The American who happily thumbs his nose at bothersome traffic signals, "keep off the grass" signs and "don't litter" warnings? Or the Canadian who can more likely walk her city without fear of being mugged, run down by errant speeders or having her way blocked by mounds of sidewalk garbage?

The way in which the two societies govern themselves also provides a lesson in contrasts. Federally, Canada operates on a far more centralized basis than America with its three-way system of checks and balances. Regionally, Canada is less cohesive, a victim of geography. It is at heart a regionalized country in which the provinces rule with far more autonomy and power than America's states. Canada has thus evolved into a more decentralized entity, while overall the United States has become more centralized politically.

On the following pages, two experts present their views of this phenomenon. Charles Doran, an American political economist who heads one of the leading Canadian studies centers in the United States, assesses the contrasts between the two countries in governing at the national level. Gordon Robertson, one of Canada's most esteemed public servants and an authority on federalism, clarifies the unique status and prerogatives of that country's provinces.

The final essay, a joint effort by two urbanologists, one from the United States and the other from Canada, describes the search by both societies for the Athenian ideal: the livable city. Michael Goldberg of the University of British Columbia and John Mercer of Syracuse University compare their nations' urban cultures, seeking answers to the conundrum of why Canadians appear to have figured out how to make their cities work for them, while Americans seem mostly to work in their cities and live outside them. Hard, cold and isolated rural Canada has driven, proportionately, far more Canadians to live in cities. Americans, on the other hand, reared on the Thoreauvian virtues of rusticity and innately suspicious of cities as effete and decadent, consider making it to the suburbs to be the ultimate goal.

It is this contrast in lifestyle and living preferences that, in modern terms, may best define the core sociological difference between the two peoples.

Charles F. Doran

Contrasts in Governing:
A Tale of Two Democracies

Congressional debate on Capitol Hill tends to be flowery, deferential and conducted according to strict rules. Witty, parochial and adversative, by contrast, Question Period in Canada's Parliament is rated as the best late-night show on Canadian television.

Do the differences in the political institutions of Canada and the United States truly run deep? Or is the contrast more a matter of style and atmosphere? For some, democracy is democracy: all democracies are basically alike. According to this view, only the institutional differences—those, for example, between Soviet communism and American democracy, or between Paraguayan one-party military dictatorship and British democracy—significantly affect foreign policy between nations.

A common misconception is that Canada's government and structure must parallel that of the United States since both countries are democracies with a similar heritage. Another misconception is that, since Canada, like most democracies, has a parliament or legislative body, that must be where various competing interests meet and are reconciled prior to legislation. Each of these misconceptions has in the past encouraged Americans to misread Canadian politics.

The view that no essential difference exists between Canadian and American institutions is not only erroneous, but on a par with the assertion that such differences have little impact on the way Canada and the United States conduct themselves toward one another. In fact, the very difference between their political institutions provides one of the paramount examples of how Canada differentiates itself from the United States.

For Canada *is* different. To a considerable degree, this is because Canada has found itself in dissimilar international political circumstances and because it has chosen to govern itself through differing approaches to democracy. The two countries' contrasting political institutions largely reflect their differing political values. Their separate institutions provide the anchor for those values.

No question of classical political philosophy appears more often in the writings of theorists, from Plato through Rousseau, than "Where does authority lie?" Through their respective political institutions, Canadians and Americans have reached the answer to this question quite differently. Both would agree with Pierre Trudeau that "in the last analysis, any given political authority exists only because men consent to obey it." Authority must ultimately lie with the people. But, in the first analysis, authority rests elsewhere, mostly with elected or appointed officials. Where these officials conduct their work and make their decisions varies greatly. The amounts and the pathways of authority are important to trace.

Confederation in Canada emerged in the last century from the assemblage of powerful and disparate regions like Upper and Lower Canada and Nova Scotia. As it expanded to include Canada's West and finally Newfoundland, the pattern of assertive regionalism was reinforced. Canada's provinces today, though comparatively few in number, are large and powerful political entities. In comparison with the United States, they exercise far more jurisdiction over such important areas of policy as education, immigration, natural resource extraction and health. The provinces also maintain substantial authority to tax and to borrow monies. Even more than their power to tax, they have the authority to distribute. Provincial income can be redistributed across the country, via the federal government, to help equalize revenue and expenditure. Instead of administering this redistribution directly, however, Canada's federal government yields to the provinces the authority to spend funds in those areas of policy for which the provinces have a primary responsibility.

In 1987, Prime Minister Mulroney and the ten provincial premiers met at Meech Lake, a government retreat near Ottawa, where they reached agreement on a number of issues related to the Constitution. The outcome was the Meech Lake Accord. As the debate over this controversial Accord has shown, Canada's bicultural character tends to underscore the cleavage between province and federal government. Meech Lake conferred on Quebec the status of a French-speaking province possessing a "distinctive culture." The Accord also acknowledged that each province reserved certain veto powers over federal decisions. Whatever special prerogatives the Accord conferred on Quebec also had to be shared with the other provinces.

Traditionally, Canada's Liberals have stressed multiculturalism rather than biculturalism, as well as greater centralization than that sought by the Progressive Conservatives (Tories). Indeed, Liberal governments have pursued centralization at the cost of considerable tension between the federal government and the provinces, particularly Quebec. Meech Lake, negotiated under a Tory government, has served to emphasize not only the magnitude of the francophone–anglophone dichotomy, but also the recurring strain of decentralization in the Canadian political system.

The United States, by contrast, has nothing resembling these regional or cultural splits. The Civil War decided once and for all the issue of "states rights." Even the civil rights conflicts of the 1960s stand apart from the Canadian experience. For one thing, those conflicts were violent compared with the campaign in Canada that decided by peaceful referendum the question as to whether Quebec, under Parti Québécois rule, would remain within Confederation. For another, black activists in America were located largely in major cities across the country, rather than in a single area where whites constituted a relatively small minority. Had the blacks been concentrated in a single region, much as most French Canadians are in Quebec, the outcome of the sixties' conflicts might have been chillingly different.

Hispanic Americans, like Quebecers, have sought language rights, but even here the contrasts in approach are greater than the similarities. The Hispanics—divided into Mexican Americans (Chicanos), Cuban Americans, Puerto Ricans and other cultural blocs— have demanded co-equal language rights. Unlike Quebecers, rarely have they demanded exclusive language rights. Moreover, the ethos of the United States, in which English is regarded as the dominant language and the key to success and prosperity, conflicts directly with Canada's multiculturalist ethos. Our political demarcations and institutions, there- fore, reinforce the American tradition of unity and homogeneity.

In short, at the regional level Canada's is a far more decentralized polity than America's. The provinces remain kingdoms unto themselves, run by monarchs in the person of premiers who feel that they own every bit as much legitimacy and power as the federal government in Ottawa. One index of the strong autonomy and political lure of the provinces is that provincial bureaucrats feel that they can pursue a full career at the provincial government level. Many a state governor fixes his or her eye on the White House, but rarely, if ever, does a premier consider office at the federal level. Provincial eyes in Canada remain on things provincial.

At the federal level, however, Canada is highly central- ized in political terms, far more so than the United States. In theory, "responsible" government in Canada means that the federal Cabinet is responsible to Parliament. If the ruling party loses the confidence of Parliament, the government can be thrown out of office. This happened in recent times to the Tory government of Joe Clark, after it had been in power only nine months. But only minority governments or govern- ments with a slim majority are likely to be so vulnerable to dismissal. Thus, one apparent difference between parliamentary and presidential democracy—the continual threat of electoral punishment under the parliamentary system—turns out to be less valid in reality.

Other institutional and procedural differences are of greater consequence, however, leading in a direction that tends to render governments in Canada more durable than those in the United States.

In Ottawa, government is decidedly hierarchic, the Prime Minister being much more than first among equals. He is the effective head of government as well as of the ruling party. This gives the Prime

Minister's Office (PMO) a virtual monopoly of power, especially in situations where the governing party has a solid majority in Parliament. Authority is concentrated in the PMO and within the inner circle of powerful Cabinet ministers. Mackenzie King, at a crucial interval in Canadian history, may have pronounced that "Parliament will decide." But in most cases where Parliament decides, the blueprint for the decision has already been drawn by the Prime Minister, a few trusted aides and a handful of the most influential ministers.

The Prime Minister does have to contend with an occasionally unruly party caucus, as Brian Mulroney has experienced. The entrenched senior bureaucrats can also present a challenge to individual Cabinet ministers, as Flora MacDonald, then Minister of External Affairs, discovered in the Clark interregnum. The Prime Minister may also grant his Cabinet ministers a virtual free rein in their specific areas of competence, as did Mr. Trudeau in his last government. But these amount to matters of choice or, at worst, manageable difficulties compared with the restraints set on American presidential power.

Why does the Prime Minister and his inner Cabinet hold such ascendancy over Parliament compared with the President and Congress? The answer lies in several traditions peculiar to Canadian society and politics.

Firstly, party discipline is extraordinarily strict in Canada, much more so than in most of the leading parliamentary democracies, and particularly than in the American Congress, where discipline is largely a figment of the party leadership's imagination. When a majority government is in power in Ottawa, the Prime Minister, as head of his party, commands enormous loyalty in Parliament. Party discipline flourishes because cross-over voting or changes in party affiliations are considered bad for political careers: a candidate is unlikely to get re-elected without the political and financial help of the party; defectors are punished inside the party and at the polls. Finally, the party counts for something institutionally because through it flow all patronage and benefits for its members.

Secondly, the Prime Minister is dominant, despite being exposed daily to a bruising give-and-take in the parliamentary question period, because of his control over information and because of the tradition of secrecy that frames decision-making in Ottawa. Secrecy is as much a characteristic of Ottawa's behavior as openness is of Washington's governing style. To that can be added the fact that parliamentary committees are weak, small and poorly staffed, and the governing party has no obligation to bring issues before them for review. Therefore, without large staffs and independent research capability, the opposition parties are repeatedly at a disadvantage in parliamentary debate. In short, neither the opposition parties nor dissident back-benchers in the governing party possess enough information at any time to check governmental action effectively.

A third reason facilitating the Prime Minister's dominance is the relative lack of investigative reporting and press opposition that one finds in Japan, West Germany and the United States. The Canadian press is of a high quality, but it does not usually see itself in the role of watchdog and critic in the way that the press does in some other countries.

Finally, the PMO's ascendancy over Parliament has been sustained in part by various bureaucratic reforms over the last fifteen years, the consequence of which has been to remove power from the civil servants and the bureaucracy and to concentrate it at the ministerial level. The increased size of the Cabinet as well as the political ties that bind some of the principal ministers to the Prime Minister inevitably mean that these reforms have given the PMO more control over policy formulation and implementation. Hence, one may conclude that power has become highly concentrated in Ottawa.

As for the Canadian Senate, its role in Parliament more resembles that of the British House of Lords than that of the American Senate. Canadian Senators are appointed by the Prime Minister, not elected. Since the Canadian Senate is not co-equal with the Canadian House of Commons in terms of powers and since Senators do not have to face election, the Senate assumes some of the character of a retirement home. Occasionally, a Senator may ask an inconvenient question or sponsor an illuminating study, but that is about the extent of the Senate's relevance to policy-making.

The effect, once again, is the centralization of authority. Provinces with small populations are not compensated politically through representation in an elected Senate, as they would be in the United

States. A comparable situation there would involve such heavily populated states as California, New York, Texas, Pennsylvania and Florida making policy through their huge Congressional delegations without consulting the rest of the country via the Senate. However, the contrast is even more stark since just two populous provinces (Ontario and Quebec), not five states, carry this disproportionate weight in Canada, and since all the actual political representation occurs in but a single chamber of the Canadian Parliament.

Further institutional differences in the two political systems stem from four sources: a subordinate role for Canada's Supreme Court, despite patriation from London of the Canadian Constitution with its Charter of Rights and Freedoms; a Canadian press that is more deferential than that of the United States while less given to serving as a medium for "leaks" and "trial balloons" from the government in power; a tradition in Canada of limited interest-group participation in policymaking, since for the most part lobbying is considered an indiscretion, if not a genuine perversion; and a strong and dedicated public service in Canada that may tend toward over-government but is nonetheless remarkably committed to "good government."

All these serve to compound the centralization of policymaking and administration in Ottawa. In Washington, there are a thousand entry points politically, a hundred ways to reopen an issue or gain reconsideration of a dismissed viewpoint. In Ottawa, the timing is always clear, the procedures stark and the ultimate locus of decision unambiguous.

The United States, suspicious of centralized power, has established a complex system of separate governing branches and political checks and balances. The activist role of interest groups and the press tends to expand the American political process even further. In Canada, federal decision-making is highly centralized through the ruling party, ultimately in the person of the Prime Minister. In each country, the "people" decide, but they record their will according to markedly different rules of institutional and political behavior.

So where *does* authority lie?

In the United States, the executive branch is the one that most often initiates policy and is solely responsible for implementing it. However, Congress remains the repository of the people's will and, as guardian of the budget, is the government body where compromise and bargaining must ultimately shape national policy. Thus, in any full sense of politics, authority is interpreted by the Courts, but is shared by the President and Congress. This sharing of power at the federal level is the essence of democracy in the United States.

For Canada, questions on the origin of authority must yield a quite different answer. Parliament, unlike Congress, cannot act as the repository of the people's will. It cannot be the forum for bargaining and for achieving consensus. Parliament has usually been far too dominated by the majority party and the Prime Minister. Hence, local interests, the less populated provinces, the regions east and west of Ottawa and those minority communities imbued with special racial or ethnic cultures will all seek representation through the provincial governments. It is these governments that will promote the interests of their own constituencies within the framework of Confederation.

Power and authority in Canada are ultimately deconcentrated because the ten provinces are so large, possess so many constitutional rights and privileges, and are so capable of commanding regional and other loyalties. With authority so centralized at the federal level, the normal democratic functions of representing individual and local interests occur not in Parliament, as in most democracies, but in the provincial legislatures. Because local interest groups seeking representation are unable to penetrate the tightly centralized authority structure in Ottawa and because Parliament does not fulfill their bargaining needs, the provincial governments assume for them this role of advocacy and representation.

Increasingly, policy emerges as the result of bargains struck between the provinces and the federal government or, more explicitly, between the Prime Minister and the premiers. First Ministers' conferences have become more important arbiters of the fate of the nation. With authority shared more and more between the provinces and Ottawa, politics in Canada have become a process of brokered democracy, often noisily contentious. Indeed, the interactions between province and federal government are likely to remain just that. The tumult that other countries experience in their parliaments is experienced in Canada in federal–provincial relations. One should not conclude from this intense and highly visible dialogue that Canada is falling apart, but only that it chooses to conduct its affairs differently. In truth, the Canadian polity is far stronger and more resilient than many observers inside and outside Canada have been willing to recognize.

These patently different styles of democracy are bound to have an impact on how foreign policy is conducted between Canada and the United States. Each government has a principal frustration with the other: Canada disparages the role of Congress; the United States laments the role of the provinces. The role of each institution is well grounded in its country's constitution, and neither role is likely to be altered in the near future in a way that would make Canada–U.S. relations more felicitous.

Canadians do not always fully appreciate how their federal–provincial relations complicate negotiations with, and the extension of commitments to, the United States and other foreign governments. Until Ottawa was able to work out an energy pricing agreement with Alberta, for example, serious negotiations with oil and gas companies and with the American government on a number of energy matters could not take place. Exploration and production of offshore oil and gas fields in Canada's northeast waters by American firms has been held up until the governments in Ottawa and Newfoundland work out their differences. And not until the federal government clearly asserted its primacy in environmental matters did comprehensive negotiation with Ottawa become possible without the prior assent of Ontario and Quebec. Even in the area of military security, progress may be held hostage to memories of the crises over conscription in both world wars that still color thinking in some influential Quebec circles and may therefore affect the federal outlook. While this constraint on Canadian foreign policy conduct is not strictly provincial, the leverage held over the federal government is nonetheless very real and a factor with which all knowledgeable foreign governments in the North Atlantic Treaty Organization (NATO) must contend.

Canada, for its part, has discovered that negotiating with Washington means in practice negotiating with *two* governments, the White House and Congress. Sadly, Ottawa has learned the meaning of the terms "signature" and "ratification": having obtained the President's signature on the East Coast Fisheries Treaty, for example, it was unable to obtain Senate ratification because of the opposition of two powerful New England Senators whose constituencies included the hard-pressed northeast fishing industry. The President can negotiate a treaty in good faith and still not be able to persuade the Senate to accept its terms, as Woodrow Wilson's experience with the Versailles Treaty illustrates.

Canada remains especially sensitive to any foreign agreement—the Canada–U.S. free trade accord being the latest—that might impinge on matters affecting its culture. Quebec has obtained from the government in Ottawa a virtual assurance not only that it will be kept informed on all matters affecting its constituents, but also that, in treaties affecting its jurisdiction, it will play an active role in the negotiations. This is not a bad idea, because keeping the powerful informed, to the extent that their views are incorporated into the treaty provisions *before* the treaty is signed, can be only beneficial to the overall negotiation process. The prospect that Canada might conclude a treaty with the United States and then fail to ensure that all provinces comply with its terms is the nightmare in reverse of what befell the Fisheries Treaty in Congress.

As the author Jack London once observed, neither country's capital is known for its charity. "Ottawa, with one exception," he wrote in 1907, "is the hardest town in the United States and Canada to beg clothes in. The one exception is Washington." Indeed, as increasing world economic pressures force themselves on each nation, public and private interests may be defined ever more narrowly in North America, with charity the loser. The age of the narrow-focus, belt-tightening ethos may take over. Does this mean that Canada and the United States will allow their domestic political institutions—Congress, Parliament, the executive branch and the provinces—to frustrate good relations with each other?

Neither government, I feel, will allow stalemate to replace progress. Each set of governmental processes contains a natural internal political equilibrium. An example of this was provided by the question of how the approval of the free trade agreement on the American side would be handled in Congress. Canada insisted that it did not want a repeat of the East Coast Fisheries debacle. The United States responded by offering a "fast track" procedure: no amendments would be allowed to be attached to the agreement; both Houses of Congress would approve it; the committee route for its consideration would be carefully mapped out in advance. Those arrangements overcame many problems that might otherwise have plagued the approval process in Congress. Similarly, Ottawa may have to offer some guarantees regarding the future implementation of the agreement by the provinces if the United States is expected to negotiate on the same footing with Canada.

Nothing in the Canada–U.S. relationship is immutable. Political institutions on each side of the border will always be disparate, designed as they are to meet domestic needs which themselves differ. Only secondarily will these institutions be shaped to deal with the complexities of foreign relations. But let us never discount the value of the learning process in the march of Canada–U.S. relations. The United States has much to learn from Canada in how to introduce more efficiency and discipline into its decision-making. Canada could learn something from the United States in how to make the political and budgetary processes more responsive and less prone to damaging surprise.

Both nations should develop greater awareness of the impact of their domestic policy initiatives on bilateral relations, and beyond. Two democracies they are, but vastly different in concept and practice. Neither should ever be taken for granted by the other.

Gordon Robertson

Contrasts in Federalism:
The Power of the Provinces

The magnitude of the provincial powers and the provincial rights that are a fact of the Canadian political system may be difficult for American observers to comprehend. They would not, perhaps, have been as incomprehensible to Americans 200 years ago, especially to that small, inspired group of men who designed the United States Constitution. For them, states rights and the protection of the states against possible invasion of their powers and interests by the proposed new central government were among the principal areas of concern. The Constitution was devised to ensure a continued strong place for the states and significant powers for their governments. In a sense, the success of the 1787 design in this respect was one of the factors that made possible a "war between the states"—and against the national government—in 1860. That war was considered by the then British colonies in what is now Canada to be the result of overly great power for the states. When the idea of a federal union was discussed among those colonies in 1864, the Civil War was still raging. The Canadian leaders of the day were determined not to repeat in their union what they thought had been so disastrous a mistake in the American one.

The Fathers of the Canadian federation designed a very centralized system. The central Parliament was given a long list of powers, including residual or unspecified ones. In the United States, it was the states that got all unallocated powers. In addition, the new Canadian government was given many unusual powers, such as that of "disallowing" or annulling any provincial enactment for whatever reason the central government thought fit. No such power existed in the American Constitution. The central government in Canada was to appoint Senators to represent the provinces in Parliament. In 1787, that power in America had been given to the state legislatures. So centralized was the Canadian Constitution, as devised in 1867, that it has been referred to as a "quasi federal" system, not a truly federal one.

It has not worked out that way. Judicial interpretation in the early decades of the Canadian union substantially limited federal powers. While the parliamentary debates about confederation in 1867 made clear the intention to create very limited "local" governments operating in the shadow of a strong central one, what gradually emerged were strong provinces casting their own shadows over many areas.

It is an irony of history, and a demonstration of the potential power of judicial interpretation, that the Constitution of Canada in this respect has been stood on its head. So has that of the United States, although factors other than judicial interpretation played a larger role there. States rights are a much diminished shadow of what they were from 1787 until the Civil War. It is as a result of these evolutionary processes that Canada and the United States find themselves today in such different constitutional and political positions.

The situation in Canada is more the result of accident than of planning. When Canada became a federation in 1867, it was not a fully independent country. It was the first "dominion" created within the British Empire—more than a colony but less than a country. To ensure that the provinces could not frustrate agreements entered into in the conduct of foreign relations, then handled by the British government in London, a clause (Section 132) was inserted in the Constitution of the new dominion. It provided that

the Parliament and Government of Canada shall have all Powers necessary or proper for performing the Obligations of Canada or of any provinces thereof, *as part of the British Empire*, towards Foreign Countries, arising under Treaties *between the Empire* and such Foreign Countries.

By the 1930s, Canada had evolved to independence and was handling its own foreign relations. However, the question remained: if the government of Canada entered into an international obligation, did the constitutional clause give it the power to fulfill it, regardless of provincial jurisdiction, as it had been able to do when it incurred such obligations as a member of the British Empire? Ontario and several other provinces decided to challenge the federal government on the question. They went to court over some international conventions signed by the Canadian government, and the issue came to final judgement in 1937. The court's answer was that the federal Parliament and government had no such power to override the provinces. After considering the new status Canada had achieved, with full capacity to enter into international relations and to incur obligations towards other countries, the judges crushed the federal government's hope that it had the power to fulfill such obligations. The court went on to say:

> It must not be thought that the result of this decision is that Canada is incompetent to legislate in performance of treaty obligations. In totality of legislative powers, Dominion and Provincial together, she is fully equipped.
>
> But *the legislative powers remain distributed* and if in the exercise of her new functions derived from her new international status she incurs obligations they must, so far as legislation be concerned when they deal with provincial classes of subjects, be dealt with by the totality of powers, in other words *by cooperation between the Dominion and the Provinces.*

The law remains as the judges declared it fifty years ago. If a treaty or international agreement entered into by Canada contains obligations in areas of provincial jurisdiction, those obligations can be carried out only by the provinces or with their consent. They cannot be carried out by Parliament or by the federal government alone.

Under the American system, Congress, representing the states, acts as the constitutional brake on too freewheeling an executive branch. Yet, one part of the checks and balances so admirably contrived to protect the freedom of Americans has at times been a source of frustration to Canadian governments in their relations with the United States. No matter how long negotiations to reach agreement on a treaty have taken, no matter what compromises have been made to achieve that agreement, no matter how confident both the Canadian and the American governments are that a mutually advantageous accommodation has been achieved, 34 per cent of the votes in the American Senate can kill it. It takes a two-thirds vote to ratify any treaty binding the United States, and the Administration may have little influence on how the Senators decide.

The world became aware of the significance of this "balance" within the American Constitution when the Treaty of Versailles and the Covenant of the League of Nations went down to defeat in the Senate, despite the leadership of the American government in producing them and the personal commitment of President Woodrow Wilson. Agreements negotiated by Canada with the United States, involving protracted agony and painful concessions, have suffered similar fates. In August 1888, the Senate rejected by a vote of 30 to 27 a fishery treaty that was the culmination of months of work. Nearly a century later, in the 1970s, the same fate overtook the fisheries section of the ocean-boundary agreement between Canada and the United States, a pact that had been negotiated with much difficulty and mutual compromise. It was withdrawn because ratification was clearly impossible in the Senate. The fate of fisheries agreements, it should be added, has been by no means unique in this regard.

In contrast, the parliamentary system of government in Canada does not involve a comparable separation of the powers of the agencies that constitute the national government. There is no system of checks and balances. Any agreement signed by the authorized representative of the Canadian government can be carried through Parliament, if Parliament is consulted at all, or else the government will fall. Indeed, the consultation of Parliament is not constitutionally necessary; it is simply a tradition with respect to important agreements. However, the magnitude of the powers of Canada's provinces, especially in relation to their own economies—coupled with the lack of a "treaty-making power" on the part of the Canadian government—is likely to raise problems similar to those created by the independent American Senate if Canada and the United States finally reach an historic free trade agreement.

At a conference in Halifax between Prime Minister Mulroney and all ten provincial premiers in November 1985, a full day was given to public debate over the desirability of entering into discussions with the United States on a comprehensive trade agreement. The first thing of note is the fact that there was debate at all among the leaders of all eleven Canadian governments. No such meeting and no discussion took place between the President of the United States and the fifty state governors, and nor would it. No meeting was needed. Whatever agreement is negotiated by the American government can be implemented, if it is ratified by the Senate. The powers of the American states cannot stand in the way. The "treaty-making power" of the President, plus two-thirds Senate approval, can legally commit the United States regardless of the views of any number of state governments. The terms of a treaty entered into in this way become part of "the supreme law" of the United States under Article 6 of the Constitution. A treaty is law even if it deals with a matter that would otherwise be within the jurisdiction of the states. In Canada, that is not the situation. *Negotiation and ratification of a treaty by the national government, whether Parliament approves or not, cannot override the powers of the provinces.* The terms of a treaty do not become part of the law of the land. If a law is required to implement any part of a treaty, it must be passed either by Parliament or by a provincial legislature, depending on which has jurisdiction over the issue involved.

The relevance of Canada's constitutional situation to the negotiations for a comprehensive trade agreement with the United States is that, in today's circumstances, such an agreement could hardly fail to include provisions affecting areas of provincial jurisdiction and measures that many provinces either now have in effect or may wish to apply in future.

Most trade between Canada and the United States already moves with very little impediment from tariffs. The C.D. Howe Institute, a prestigious Canadian research organization, estimated that, as of 1987, 80 per cent of Canadian exports of manufactured goods to the United States were subject to tariffs of 5 per cent or less, while 70 per cent of American exports of manufactured goods to Canada moved at the same low level of protection. An agreement to do no more than remove the remaining tariffs would accomplish little. It is *non*-tariff barriers in both countries that are now the most significant factor restricting the freedom with which goods and services move. As the Royal Commission on the Economic Union and Development Prospects for Canada (the Macdonald Commission) put it, international trade relations and discussions "have come to focus more and more on non-tariff barriers such as subsidies, discriminatory purchasing policies and product standards designed to exclude competition."

In Canada, many of the practices of this kind fall within provincial jurisdiction and are implemented under provincial legislation. Provincial liquor commissions control the import of all types of liquor into any province and the terms under which it can be sold within the province. Discriminatory mark-ups are frequently used to give an advantage to wines and other alcoholic beverages produced within the province. Provincial government purchasing, like state government purchasing in the United States, can and does discriminate against non-provincial goods and services. Provinces, with respect to their internal economies, have the power to impose restrictions affecting the private sector as well. For instance, the provincial ownership of extractive resources enables provincial governments to impose conditions for the exploitation of these resources that gives an advantage to local operators providing specific degrees of processing within the province. Many of the provincial measures in Canada can probably find their parallel in the American states. The important difference for international agreements is that, in the United States, a treaty commitment can take precedence over state power or state legislation; in Canada, it cannot.

Because of the provinces' concern over the possible impact of a trade agreement on their economies and because of the stake they have in various non-tariff measures of their own to protect those economies, the premiers at the Halifax Conference demanded "full provincial participation" in any negotiations to be undertaken with the United States. That phrase was agreed on after hours of difficult negotiation, but there was no agreement as to what it means. Premier David Peterson of Ontario affirmed that the provinces want full participation, "not just consultation." In his view, the Canadian negotiating team would take its instructions from the First Ministers—eleven of them—not from Ottawa. Premier William Bennett of British Columbia agreed: eleven governments would establish the mandate of the Canadian negotiators. Premier Donald Getty of Alberta went further. When the negotiations took place, he would not be prepared to have reports from others about what went on between the negotiators: he wanted his own representative "in the room." On the substance of the trade talks, some premiers went still further, suggesting that every province have a veto. If, for example, Ontario did not want the current Canada–U.S. Automotive Pact to be discussed, Ontario would have its way. The veto would apply to other issues objected to by one province or another.

When Prime Minister Mulroney came to power in September 1984, he had committed his government to establishing a new atmosphere of cooperation in federal–provincial relations. At the Halifax Conference, his desire to maintain that cooperative atmosphere was compelling. As a result, the Prime Minister did not argue publicly with the premiers' claims on television about vetoes, mandates and instructions. Conference harmony was achieved by shelving the problems. The provinces were given three months to work out just what "full provincial participation" meant and how it was to operate.

The Macdonald Commission, in its report of August 1985, had foreseen the problem of provincial involvement in international trade negotiations. It rightly felt that the lack of a federal treaty-making power was not likely to be remedied in the near future. Any remedy would require formal amendment of the Canadian Constitution with provincial consent, a less than promising prospect. Its report said:

> Before Canada begins multilateral or bilateral negotiations, there should be close consultation between ministers about provincial, as well as federal, objectives and the binding commitments required to achieve them. During international trade negotiations, provincial representatives should be on hand to counsel the federal delegation. The delegation should also keep provincial governments informed and request their advice on specific proposals advanced during the bargaining process.

The demands made at the Halifax Conference in November 1985, and the continued differences in the months following, made it clear that the Macdonald Commission's proposals would not

be enough for the provinces. Some more active role for provincial governments was going to be necessary.

In fact, a strong provincial presence during treaty negotiations between Canada and the United States was not unprecedented.

Canada's provinces have jurisdiction over natural
resources within their boundaries. Thus, the government of British
Columbia occupied a crucial position when it was decided in 1960 to
explore mutually advantageous arrangements for joint Canada–U.S. development of the waters of the Columbia River. The construction of giant
dams on the river in Canada would help regulate the flows of enormous
quantities of water for the production of power downstream in the
United States. The International Joint Commission (IJC) had worked out
principles for the division of such "downstream benefits" if agreement
on the storages could be reached. Timely operation of the storages in
Canada would also greatly reduce the risk of flooding in the United
States, with its attendant damage to lands and property there. The agreement of the British Columbia government was essential to any joint
plan: the province would have to build and operate these storages and
provide the land to be flooded by them in Canada. To ensure such
agreement at the end of the line, representatives of British Columbia
were included at every stage of the negotiations that began in February
1960. The senior representative of British Columbia sat at the negotiating
.table: four Canadians on one side, three Americans on the other. The
difference in arithmetic reflected the difference in the constitutional
situations. There was no need to have a representative of any American
state.

In September 1960, the delegations reported on the basic
terms to be incorporated in a treaty. The formal report again reflected
the constitutional differences: three American signatures to four Canadian,
one of them the authorized representative of the British Columbia government. However, for external purposes, the unity of Canada and the
solidarity of Canada's voice in negotiation were preserved: the British
Columbia representative was described simply as "Member, Canadian
Delegation."

The Columbia River Treaty was completed and signed
early in 1961, and the American Senate ratified it within months. However,

differences of opinion within Canada were not resolved, despite provincial representation in the negotiations. The government of British Columbia decided that it would not accept its obligations under the treaty without a significant change in the handling of its share of the increased hydroelectric energy produced in the United States—the "downstream benefits." Since British Columbia's cooperation was essential to the whole project, it was a case of "back to the drawing board" for the national governments. After further extended negotiation, a "Protocol of Agreement" was worked out and formally signed in January 1964. Only then was the whole agreement put before the Canadian Parliament under the tradition that has developed for important international agreements. Parliament approved it in May 1964. Ratifications were at last exchanged in September, more than four years after the original negotiations had begun.

The problems of negotiation for a comprehensive trade agreement between Canada and the United States are comparable in some respects to those of the Columbia River Treaty, but different in others. Depending on its terms, a trade agreement could affect all ten Canadian provinces; the Columbia River Treaty affected only one. It was impractical to have the representatives of ten provincial governments present, as part of a Canadian delegation, during the trade negotiations; yet the provinces demanded "full participation, not just consultation." In fact, despite many interprovincial meetings of ministers and a raft of proposals, no solution could be found within the three-month time limit. In the end, another meeting had to be called between the Prime Minister and the provincial premiers for June 1986. The plan that finally emerged from that meeting definitely reflected the intense degree of provincial concern over a new trade arrangement. While there would be no provincial representatives at the table when the Canadian and American negotiators sat down, there would be close and constant consultation with designated provincial representatives. In addition, there would be an unprecedented involvement of the Prime Minister and the premiers personally. They would meet regularly every three months as the trade negotiations proceeded. Even that degree of involvement did not halt the manoeuvring for further influence in the trade drama. The provinces made clear that they would have to participate in some special way in the ratification of whatever agreement emerged between the two countries. Premier Robert Bourassa of Quebec made no bones about the degree of control his government expected to exert. "Quebec wants the power to be able to refuse or accept the treaty in the light of its impact on our economic interests," he declared. The other provinces would insist on no less. For, if there is one thing clear in Canadian federalism, it is that the powers of the provinces are equal. Whatever right is accorded to one is demanded by all.

Quebec is a province with a difference. It is the only province with a French-speaking majority: over 80 per cent of its population have French as their mother tongue. It is scrupulously aware of its role as the cradle and centre of French culture in Canada and sensitive to its place in North America, surrounded as it is by an English-speaking sea. Premier Bourassa made it clear that economics would not be the sole concern of his government. Quebec, he said, favoured free trade with the United States, as long as issues affecting cultural identity and social programs were not included in the negotiations. To ensure that nothing was agreed to that would endanger Quebec culture, Mr. Bourassa insisted on "a decisive role for Quebec" in ratifying any proposed treaty. One possibility was "an outright Quebec veto." Alternatively, ratification might require the approval of the legislatures of all the provinces, as well as that of the federal Parliament. A final possibility was unanimous provincial consent for certain issues, a large provincial majority for others —perhaps seven of the ten provinces, representing 50 per cent of the national population.

The American Administration is well aware of the constitutional situation in Canada and the problems it creates. It is also aware of the varying concerns of the different provinces. In preliminary discussions between the trade negotiators on both sides, the United States made it clear that there would have to be adequate commitment by the provincial governments to ensure that any treaty obligations would be carried out in Canada, whether they involved federal or provincial jurisdiction. That is a legitimate concern. Washington must have confidence that the undertakings of Canada will be met, just as Ottawa must have the same confidence in undertakings made by the United States.

In each case, there will be a degree of doubt until actual ratification has occurred. In the United States, the process by which certainty is achieved is clear: it is laid down in the Constitution and requires a two-thirds vote of the Senate. In Canada, it is not clear. In the case of the Columbia River Treaty, an arrangement was adopted by which the government of the one province concerned, British Columbia, accepted the obligations of the treaty and carried them out. That arrangement will not work with ten provinces. The fact that some uncertainty must exist until the process of ratification has run its course should not be incomprehensible to Americans. It is a situation that is quite familiar to Canadian negotiators in their dealings with the United States. Over the years, they have had to wonder whether an American delegation could deliver—not because of problems with the states per se, but because of uncertainties about ratification by the Senate. That concern will exist on the Canadian side as negotiations for a trade agreement proceed. Each delegation will have to keep a wary eye on the hazards that its national constitution creates for it and will have to guard against them. Each will have to impart confidence to the other that the obligations it accepts are not likely to be rejected at the ratification stage by whatever domestic institution, Senate or province, has the power to do so.

Canada's problem with provincial jurisdiction is more complex for the Canadian side to handle than the problem of the Senate is for the American side. However, there is almost certainly less risk for the American negotiators. In other words, if effective consultations with provincial representatives are maintained by the Canadian side, as has been agreed by the Prime Minister and the premiers, the chances of an agreement being thwarted in Canada after it has been concluded should be less than the risk of an upset by the American Senate. There are no continuing consultations with the Senators as there are with the Canadian provinces. Each Senator has his own views and his own regional interests to protect. There is probably little to choose between the independence of Senators under the American separation of powers and the independence of provinces under the Canadian Constitution. The lack of consultation with the Senators, coupled with the fact that a large number of approving votes must be secured from them, would appear to make insurance against rejection much more problematical in the United States than in Canada.

For the Canadian government and its negotiating team the problem is that the concerns and wishes of the provincial governments tend to differ widely. The Western provinces have generally wanted the widest scope for any treaty and the closest approach to genuinely free trade. At the same time, each has areas of sensitivity and special interests needing protection. The government of Alberta can moderate its zeal for free trade if its budding petrochemical industry appears to be at risk. The Liberal government of Ontario has made ambiguous noises about any trade agreement, given that the province's crucially important manufacturing industries—including automobiles—could suffer disruptions under an agreement, resulting in layoffs and unemployment. In Quebec, another Liberal government has worried over whether a trade treaty might not begin a slide to something more: a customs union or an economic union. It, too, has vulnerable industries, proportionally more that need protection than Ontario. The Atlantic provinces, economically the weakest of Canada, evince special concern for the continuance of regional development programs that guarantee the life of their precarious industries. Non-tariff barriers—against products from other provinces as well as from other countries—are a basic part of the fabric that supports the economy of the Atlantic provinces.

With such widely differing provincial interests, the Canadian government and its trade negotiators have their hands full in achieving agreement on trade-offs regarded as equitable and politically saleable across the country. Federal–provincial meetings are part of the warp and woof of Canadian federalism, though never before in our history have we had a pledge by a Canadian Prime Minister to meet the premiers every three months on a specific problem. These meetings constitute a vital part of the process of reaching a trade agreement that will "sell" at the point when each provincial government and legislature makes its own decision as to whether to accept the obligations of that treaty.

The problems of final acceptance in Canada may be substantial. The period between the making of commitments during negotiation and the acceptance of those commitments by provincial legislatures may be a long one. It will take even longer for passage of provincial legislation to implement any part of the treaty that comes under provincial jurisdiction. Public opinion in support of local interests may be mobilized against a treaty provision; political campaigns may be waged over sensitive issues; governments may change. Given such hazards, it is of paramount importance that the Canadian side does every-thing it reasonably can to ensure as high a level of provincial consensus as possible *before* any treaty is concluded and signed.

There is no aspect of the Canadian situation, then, that should be incomprehensible to Americans. Canada and the United States are federal democracies whose basis is respect for human rights and the protection of freedom. Both countries support these tenets through bills of rights and principles of law designed to protect the individual, and through judicial processes and legislative structures erected to protect state and regional interests. The constitutions of the two countries have succeeded in achieving these objectives. They differ mainly in the methods and the mechanisms by which they do it. If, in the course of negotiating a trade agreement, Americans have become impatient over Canada's difficulties with its provinces, it may be comforting to reflect that the underlying objectives that give rise to such problems are enshrined in their own Constitution. They are indeed basic to the concept of liberty so properly celebrated by the American people on the centenary of the great statue in New York harbour on July 4, 1986. The problem with liberty and individual rights is that they sometimes get in the way of quick, neat action.

Michael A. Goldberg and John Mercer

The Livable City: Comparing the Urban Cultures of Canada and the United States

The idea of the North American City is misleading—a myth. On the contrary, there are but two kinds of cities found across the upper part of the continent: American and Canadian.

The notion of the North American City is part of the larger "continentalist" debate which holds that Canada and the United States are so integrated, socially and economically, that they constitute one homogeneous entity. Though largely reflecting American values and needs, the argument is consistent with the dominant position of the United States on the continent. Historically, certain predominantly American interests sought to create a North American state. Strong economic linkages—the Canada–U.S. Auto Pact, energy grids, the penetration of American corporations into key sectors of the Canadian economy—served to bolster that effort. In the social sphere, the Canada–U.S. border is easily hurdled by telecommunications, by myriad family and social networks and by frequent two-way travel.

In the development of our cities, the continentalist approach tends to minimize the importance of national culture and geography. Most people will recognize the structural similarities of the North American City: the retail and office business core; adjacent high-rise apartment areas; outlying commercial centers and strips; various types of industrial zones and residential areas—all connected by streets, arterial routes and freeways in the typical grid-radial pattern. Regional shopping centers in suburban Toronto and suburban Chicago are essentially similar in location, market orientation and internal layout. Canadian and American cities house equally diversified neighborhoods.

To a large degree, Canadian and American centers are key indicators of, and vehicles for, the tidal changes in their social and economic systems experienced by the two countries. These changes, or challenges, include the transformation of urban economies from industrial- to service-based; the decline of family households and the rise of non-family households, factors in North America's so-called "birth dearth"; the waning flow of European immigrants to the continent and the dramatic rise in immigration from Third World regions; the spread of AIDS, drug abuse and drug-related crime to near-epidemic levels—afflictions that owe their contagiousness in large part to the density of human interactions typifying and defining urban living.

While the cities of Canada and the United States share most of these daunting problems, they must deal with them from quite different perspectives. They are situated, after all, in two distinctive societies that possess common antecedents but have been shaped through sharply divergent social and political histories.

Americans, for example, place great value on being American. This involves: having pride in their system of government; valuing the individual and individual initiative, as well as the competitiveness that attends such values; decrying government involvement in their affairs; viewing the United States as the last bastion of free (private) enterprise; and expressing and exhibiting an assurance about the "American way."

Canadians, by contrast, are less doctrinaire. They view themselves as deferential to authority; they tend to value collective and government action more than individual effort; they are less competitive, and generally far less sure about what constitutes the "Canadian way." In fact, one of the few readily identifiable elements of the Canadian character has been the continuing search for the "Canadian identity" that has so preoccupied scholars and writers. (In classroom discussions about the McCarthy era and the House Un-American Activities Committee, one always evokes chuckles by asking students to consider a House of Commons Un-Canadian Activities Committee: no one can imagine what constitutes Canadian activities and therefore how one could be un-Canadian.)

In the United States, with its strong sense of "American-ness," it is not surprising that the prevailing social myth is that of the melting-pot. Immigrant groups are expected to shed their ethnicity and adopt the ways of the dominant culture. Alternative views may emphasize the durability of social life in which one's ethnicity remains an immutable pillar, or may regard ethnicity as a sort of garment, to be put on or shucked off depending on personal preference and circumstance. In Canada, with its less well-developed national identity, the prevailing social mythology is that of a mosaic. Given Canada's heritage of two founding nations and the absence of a strong sense of "Canadianness," the mosaic parallel is predictable. It is also practical, since a considerably larger proportion of the Canadian population is born outside its borders than that of the United States. Thus, the mosaic mythology helps legitimize the demographic reality of Canada. At the same time, the absence of institutionalized racism in Canada stems from a far different social history, vis-à-vis race relations, than that of the United States.

Canadians are much more tolerant than Americans of ruling élites and oligarchs, including those in government bureaucracies. This "ascriptive" social system, as opposed to the "merit-based" one of the Americans, is consonant with those facets of the Canadian character that underscore deferential and collective behavior. In addition, despite the fact that both nations are English-speaking democracies, rooted in English common-law tradition (Quebec, of course, being the exception here), important differences abound in their political systems and institutions.

Some have linked the greater sense of deference in Canada to those conservative "anti-revolutionaries" who helped to found English Canada, the United Empire Loyalists. Certainly, the founding principles of government in Canada and the United States differed starkly from the very start. From America's declaration of "life, liberty and the pursuit of happiness" and Canada's prescription of "peace, order and good government," two singularly contrasting political systems were to emerge.

The American government operates within a carefully designed system of checks and balances between the legislature, the executive and the judiciary. Rising above all is the Constitution, ultimate arbiter of disputes affecting the commonweal, with the Supreme Court its chosen interpreter. In Canada, Parliament is supreme and its laws constitute "the supreme law" of the land. Indeed, the nation's parliaments, federal and provincial, wield far more power relatively than do Congress and the state legislatures. Even Canada's new Charter of Rights and Freedoms may not necessarily abridge or restrict Parliament's established authority.

This greater power of Canada's Parliament is reinforced by another British legacy, party discipline, whereby members of Parliament are obligated to vote according to the decisions of their party leaders and caucuses. Thus, a party with a clear-cut majority can customarily pass legislation with predictable ease if it merely follows established parliamentary procedures. By contrast, there is a demonstrable lack of strong party discipline in American legislatures, accounting for the brokering nature of Congress and state legislative bodies. In fact, despite the mutually federal nature of the Canadian and American governing systems, things have worked out quite differently.

Initially, America's confederation was seen as comprising a weak central government and strong state governments exercising vital states rights. Yet, over the past two centuries, the American federal system has come to be dominated by the fiscal and legislative power of the central government in Washington, with a more limited scope for independent action granted to the states. In Canada, the reverse has occurred. Conceived as a federation with a commanding central government and clearly subservient provinces, Canada has watched for more than a century as the provinces have gradually achieved essentially equal footing with the federal government in Ottawa through a series of court decisions and the assumption of provincial control in such areas as education, health care and natural resources. Federal–provincial conferences in Canada abound to settle issues that could be solved almost by fiat in the United States by the federal government. This political brokering by the increasingly assertive provinces has brought a contentiousness to those areas where federal and provincial interests collide.

Cities constitute one of the more important of those areas. Today, in contrast to the United States, there is little in the way of a direct federal government presence in Canada's cities and urban affairs.

Of particularly major consequence for urban development are the fundamental differences in the financial structure and capital markets of Canada and the United States.

Since the early 1970s, Canadians have been saving at a rate twice that of Americans. That saving has had a direct impact on the cities because it has provided an enormous pool of mortgage funds. It has also provided needed capital for resource development and the retooling of aging and outmoded manufacturing. The United States has not had the benefit of similar domestic savings pools; instead, it has used foreign borrowings and encouraged direct foreign investment to cover the costs of its restructuring and development projects. At the same time, the two countries have nurtured markedly different financial structures and systems to provide savers with outlets for surplus funds. Canada's national banking system encourages the five largest banks, with thousands of branches in all provinces, to solidly dominate the Canadian banking scene. The American banking system remains largely state-based; it includes some of the world's largest banks, as well as thousands of small local and state banks. Canada's system reflects its society's relative tolerance of élitism and centralization; America's seems consistent with populist notions relating to fears of big-city bankers and the power of centralized institutions.

These striking differences carry with them implications for the ways in which the cities of Canada and the United States are organized and managed at the political and social levels.

For example, the greater acceptance of authority by Canadians, their inclination to look to government for collective solutions, has led to a greater public role in urban development and a stronger exercise of planning powers. One consequence has been Canadians' more stringent control of urban sprawl, resulting in more compact metropolitan areas and higher population densities. By contrast, liberalism, the guiding political philosophy of American society, celebrates the value of the individual and thus finds expression in what the historian Sam Bass Warner has called "the private city." Publicly provided goods and services in urban transportation and recreation are less relied upon in America, while privatism—symbolized by the single detached dwelling unit on its own extensive lot—is more the norm.

Surprisingly, perhaps, America is a society of many governments—one, in fact, for every 2 801 Americans in 1979. This galaxy of governments, however, is largely made up of special-purpose districts and small urban municipalities, which can be viewed as quasi-public extensions of small, well-defined, relatively homogeneous social classes and special-interest groups that in effect promote private concerns. Witness the use of exclusionary land-use practices in American suburbs, for example. In short, the widespread fragmentation of the American metropolis rests on the twin foundations of local autonomy and privatism.

Another set of expectations is attached to the notion of urban livability. Americans strongly prefer to live on the peripheries of cities. Despite the revitalization of the downtown core in certain American cities, Americans tend to display less affection for central city living than Canadians. Underlying these different preferences is the reality of race: racial polarities are embedded in the dual housing markets of urban America, while a dramatically higher incidence of violent crime permeates its metropolitan areas. Canadian cities appear relatively free of racial tensions, although these tensions are becoming more apparent as increasing numbers of racial minorities immigrate to such major centers as Vancouver and Toronto. The generally high level of public safety contributes to a sense of the well-ordered city in Canada: in 1986, a total of 524 murders were recorded in the entire country, a 20 per cent decline from 1985 and less than the total of one year's similar tally for such American cities as Houston and Los Angeles.

Americans' preference for more extensive private space has led to a more decentralized urban scene in the United States, as employment and goods and services have followed the stampede to the suburbs. The trend has been facilitated by massive federal expenditures on freeway systems. With an additional push from ill-considered urban renewal programs, these forces have served to destabilize inner-city housing markets and promote further urban flight.

By contrast, as testimony to the general attractiveness and livability of central cities in Canada, the inner-city housing districts there are in demand as residential locations. Many successfully retain their traditional social status and accessibility in the absence of massive freeway development. Not surprisingly, the demand has led to higher housing and land prices, which in turn have resulted in the profitable redevelopment of high-density housing, with attendant employment and services. Under these circumstances, ironically, there has been little need for the public sector in Canada to subsidize private redevelopment in the central city.

American metropolitan areas have, on the average, much lower population densities in their centers and, for each metropolitan American, there are four times as many miles of urban expressway available as there are for his or her Canadian counterpart. At the same time, Canadian mass transit systems have nearly two and a half times the number of revenue miles per capita than the American systems. Canadian cities, in short, rely much more heavily on a high-volume public transit system and a dense urban population, while American cities depend more on extensive freeway networks to service their more dispersed residents. One-quarter of Canadian commuters use public transportation in contrast with one-eighth of American commuters; 67 per cent of Canadians use automobiles to get to work in contrast with 85 per cent of Americans.

On balance, too, it is clear that, compared with American cities, Canada's central cities retain a higher proportion of such economic activities as retailing, business services and, to a lesser extent, wholesaling and manufacturing. They have also suffered fewer losses in population and households than have the great majority of American urban centers.

A comparison of four Canadian and American cities underscores the validity of these findings.

At first glance, Toronto and New York seem an appealing pair. Formerly overshadowed by Montreal, Toronto has drawn ahead in certain measurable respects, not the least being the sheer size of its population (3.4 million in 1986). Most importantly, the city is now Canada's leading corporate center, a position long held in the United States by New York. Indeed, the actor Peter Ustinov has observed that "Toronto is like New York would be if it were run by the Swiss." Corporate

Toronto, however, is a minor player on the world stage compared to the New York colossus. New York's population is also more than double that of Toronto, while its urban region is about four times larger.

Both cities pride themselves on their highly developed commercial cores, which continue to prosper despite decentralization and the growth of alternative "downtowns" (for example, Stamford, Connecticut, or Scarborough and North York, suburbs of Toronto). The similarities fade, however, as one examines the nature of their inner cities—such as housing conditions, transportation services and mode of government. In these respects, Toronto arguably offers greater livability than New York.

While New York boasts expensive, high-quality housing in certain parts of Manhattan, the specter of abandoned and ravaged residential areas there and in other boroughs of the city looms in contrast to Toronto's relatively vital and violence-spared inner-city neighborhoods. Extremes of wealth and poverty, though evident in Toronto, are neither as acute nor as dramatic as in greater New York. Also, Toronto's transit services have been widely hailed as a model for other North American cities; although New York's services are improving in terms of newly purchased vehicles, reconstructed trackage and tougher actions against graffiti "artistry," they lag behind those of Toronto. Moreover, the majority of Toronto's residents are well served by a cohesive metropolitan form of government. The New York City region sprawls across three states and several counties; even within the city, the boroughs serve on frequent occasions as autonomous political fiefdoms. Problems of coordination and administration are immense, often spawning special-purpose agencies like the Port Authority that paradoxically contribute to further fragmentation of government.

Boston and Montreal are similarly sized metropolitan centers whose systems of government and approach to development have led, however, to dissimilar results. Montreal's commercial core expanded and prospered under the pro-development policies of Mayor Jean Drapeau and his administration. While adopting a generally supportive role, leaving development in private hands, the city's government took an inspired lead in certain public sectors. It initiated (and funded) Montreal's acclaimed subway, "Le Metro," contributing to a successful metropolitan transit system that has served the city core especially well. However, success has had its costs: the city's innermost residential districts have seen their special character eroded under the pressures for development, with no civic support marshalled to preserve them until recently.

In Boston, the city's core also remains vital, more so in the office sector than in retailing and entertainment, which have experienced sharp declines. By contrast, Montreal, with its base of about a million people living in relatively close quarters, enjoys far more sound retailing operations. Boston's considerably smaller city core is economically poorer on a per capita basis and is not, at this time, particularly well served by its public transportation, which has noticeably become less effective. (In the 1980s, barely one-third of all Bostonians travel to work by public transport compared to more than one-half of Montreal's commuters.) The system's difficulties stem at least in part from the fragmentation of local government and from intergovernmental responsibilities for transportation services. Boston has achieved far greater success in protecting and upgrading the residential fabric of its inner-city neighborhoods. Unlike those in Montreal, successive administrations in Boston have vigorously supported planning for this purpose, although an unintended consequence of their success has been increasingly costly housing for city dwellers.

As the suburbanization of America proceeds, a pattern of local government has emerged that is decidedly small-scale—"toy governments," as one urbanist described them. This fragmented pattern of local governments, far more common to American than to Canadian metropolitan areas, has markedly altered the urban landscape in America, and not for the better. Greater "balkanization" of America's local public sector has bred greater differentiation between the nation's rich and poor municipalities. There is evidence to confirm a growing split in the financial capacities of America's cities, as opposed to the generally more robust fiscal health of Canada's central cities.

A final indicator of Canada's comparative success in achieving desirable standards of urban living is the higher proportion of traditional family households populating its central cities. Inner-city neighborhoods, supported by fiscally sound school systems and a prevailing sense of public order, are still regarded as eminently suitable for traditional, children-oriented family life.

For metropolitan America in the 1980s, the economic action has occurred by and large in the outer city. In Canada, conversely, the dominance of the metropolitan regions' central cores has seemed more assured. Large parts of the inner city in urban America have apparently been written off—areas that provide barely adequate shelter for the so-called impoverished "underclass." Yet, in the past, these areas have been important to those who govern the central cities because of their electoral potential. The fact is that central city governments today are chronically short of the resources needed to tackle the multiple problems concentrated in such areas. Canada's inner-city neighborhoods, by contrast, are for the most part attractive, if increasingly expensive, places to live. Renovation and redevelopment there are largely initiated by the private sector, frequently by individuals (many of them recent immigrants using their own savings), in little need of the subsidies and government grant programs that are deemed so essential for investment and change in American inner cities.

As for the unhelpful fragmentation of local government in the United States, it will persist in the absence of any significant federal government or grass-roots action to reduce it. America's central cities will find few friends or allies in a suburban officialdom whose members operate on the basis of their own self-interest. County governments, meanwhile, will continue to play an increasingly important role in American metropolitan regions, but they have not so far shown themselves to be particularly responsive to central city needs. There are, however, growing pressures on the state governments to assist and succor their own municipalities. Such assistance, however, is likely to be disproportionately skewed to the suburban districts, which are favorably represented in the state legislatures, to the continued dismay of the central cities, particularly those older cities in less rapidly growing regions.

In Canada, on the other hand, a completely different situation will prevail: far less local government fragmentation and no strong trend toward large-scale new municipal incorporation, even though suburban development continues at a healthy pace. The numerous metropolitan government structures that, over the last thirty years, were created and fine-tuned in Canada have a reassuring permanence about them, although they will likely evolve further to meet changing circumstances. In terms of direct funding and influence on the future of Canadian cities, the irrelevance of federal initiatives from Ottawa will likely persist.

The contrast between Canadian and American urban lifestyles will remain pronounced, anchored as they are in persistent and deep-seated cultural attitudes. Americans will continue to prefer the small-town, quasi-rural settings of suburbia and the outer reaches of the metropolis; Canadians, although eager enough suburbanites, will continue to display a more positive regard for living within, and actively maintaining, their cities. In sum, the apogee of urban living in the United States (excepting such perceived Edens as San Francisco, Boston–Cambridge or perhaps the penthouses of Manhattan) is most likely a ranch house or Cape Cod clapboard on Honeysuckle Hill, at least an hour, if not an entire mindset, from Wall Street or State Street. Canadians will happily, perhaps dutifully, settle for a comfortable condominium in the greeny innards of Toronto or Edmonton.

For there is a sense of commitment built into the Canadian urban culture—commitment to the maintenance of a fiscally sound central city, with the means to provide quality services and to direct private redevelopment in order to achieve public goals (while permitting maximum profits to accrue to private developers). In the United States, maintaining protected suburban jurisdictions, their amenities and private property rights, is the priority; others are left to deal with the problems of restoring livability to the inner city or of preventing neighborhoods from becoming the domain only of affluent childless households.

America's cities, long noted for racial conflict, may be facing an increase in such tensions if recent, and fatal, incidents in New York and Philadelphia are any indication. Race relations will continue to grow more complex, spawning frictions between various Asian groups and American blacks, between blacks and hispanics, between Asians and whites. However, immigration, curiously, may serve as a calming influence. Immigrant households in America could constitute an effective lobbying force for the "soft" inner-city housing districts that are marked now by the scars of abandonment and arson. Affordable housing and access to jobs with low-skill requirements, plus a stable if low average wage rate, are the critical features of this scenario.

Canadian cities have experienced a rather different racial

history, with violence and institutionalized discrimination confined primarily to specific locales like Vancouver and other parts of British Columbia where Asians were "the problem," or to Halifax where a black slum was permitted to evolve into a ghetto resembling those in some American cities. Immigration has introduced significant numbers of Chinese, Indian, Caribbean and other peoples into more Canadian cities than ever before, so that race has now become a social issue in such areas as housing, schooling and employment. Canadians must confront not just a multilingual or multicultural reality, but one that is increasingly multiracial as well.

The ultimate challenge is how to plan for and manage the future of the cities in Canada and the United States, given their social and economic complexities. The means for social and economic change lie within the private sector. City officials in the United States more often than not react and respond to private developments, the instigators of which greatly influence the elected officials who control the administrators. The same occurs in Canada, but there the local public sector is more active and assertive. Some believe that the Canadian city is over-regulated, stifling in its conformity to the largely middle-class design; others believe that, despite appearances, the private interests of the élites will always prevail. In our view, weighing the subtle contrasts between the two cultures, the likelihood is greater that Canada's cities will be better able than those of the United States to plan for and successfully confront the array of social and economic challenges facing the urban societies of North America in the coming decades.

Part IV

Culture and Conflict in Canada

Canada's regional tensions, a phenomenon little experienced in modern America, derive in part from geography and population disparities. These have created a vast under-inhabited hinterland in the West alongside a heavily populated, industrial zone in the Central–Eastern sector, which embraces the provinces of Quebec and Ontario. History and cultural divergences have done the rest.

The United States still experiences some cultural uneasiness between the North and South (race) and the East and West (establishment versus parvenu). But time and progress have softened these discords, while television and the jet have accelerated the sense of national unity. America, the great assimilator, has become a largely homogeneous political–cultural entity. Canada, by contrast, remains a regionally conscious and regionally driven society.

Populous Ontario and Quebec, which account for some two-thirds of the national Parliament in Ottawa, brandish the powerful political and economic levers. Oil-rich but vote-poor Western Canada resents Ontario's power ("Let the Eastern bastards freeze in the dark" was a memorable Western bumper-sticker from the 1970s energy crisis) as well as Quebec's strident demands for special treatment as a "distinct society." The Ontario–Quebec axis is envious of the energy sufficiency and wealth of the West, resenting as somehow unneighborly the West's attempts to charge Eastern Canada higher international prices for its oil and gas. The absence of an American-style Senate, representing regional interests at the national level, abets the divisiveness and the "every-province-for-itself" mindset.

Language, soul of a society's culture, continues to divide Canadians. Quebecers, feeling their vibrant but isolated culture threatened, insist on the supremacy of French in their province, while other French-speaking communities, surrounded by the alien sounds of anglophones, vigorously pursue their rights under the federal bilingualism law. The current leaders of Quebec belong to a generation that remembers all too well the past humiliations of being made to feel like second-class citizens in their own province. Gerald Godin, architect of Quebec's controversial language law in the early 1980s, recalled for an Americas Society audience how he had come originally from a small town, Trois-Rivières, which was 99.9 per cent French-speaking. Out of a population of 10 000 persons, 22 were English-speaking—"they were the bosses of the local pulp and paper companies, and they imposed their language on our town."

It is the English-speaking minority in Quebec that has now felt the backlash in terms of language rights: the denial, for example, of the right of merchants to hang English-language signs alongside French ones outside their shops. Across Canada, meanwhile, many among the majority of anglophones, particularly those in the far West—people who, separated from Quebec by several thousand miles of prairie and mountain range, seldom in the course of their lives encounter a French-speaking person—bridle at the notion of enforced bilingualism. For some, the inability to master a second language may deny them fulfillment of a career ambition to serve their federal government in a senior post. For others, having bilingualism imposed throughout the country, except in Quebec where anglophones must defer to French's primacy, seems a galling inequity.

Yet, the issue of language may one day fade, overtaken by more compelling economic concerns. In Quebec this trend is already underway with the emergence over the last decade of an aggressive business class of French-speaking entrepreneurs. In Montreal they have gone far to fill the vacuum created by the exodus in the late 1970s of Canadian and multinational corporations, moving into the managerial slots once dominated by anglophone executives. Many of these francophone businesses have expanded across Canada or into the United States, leading some observers to speculate that Quebec's primary political goal in coming years will be to secure its economic, rather than its cultural, base within Canada. This implies a possibly new internal struggle within the province, one pitting its intellectuals, custodians of Quebec's cultural legacy, against members of the business class, champions of more liberated corporate enterprise, to decide which of the two values, cultural or economic, will dominate the Quebec of the future.

Economic concerns, too, are at the core of Western alienation from the rest of Canada and the federal government. The so-called Sagebrush Revolt of the early eighties had its roots in Westerners' resentment that the industrialized East traditionally regarded them as lowly purveyors of crude natural resources that the East would refine and shape for the economic benefit of the region. In the Canadian elections of 1988, similar disaffection also cost the governing Progressive Conservative Party a substantial number of seats in the West. In Alberta alone, the so-called Reform Party, a right-wing movement demanding a stronger Western voice in national affairs, drew an unusual 15 per cent of the popular vote, much of it at the expense of the Tories. East–West friction has always been, in its particulars, largely the result of a debate over the disposition, the sharing, of Canada's resources between Ottawa and the provinces. There is an ongoing struggle between federal and provincial jurisdictions regarding such fiercely coveted perquisites as mineral rights and taxation powers.

  Regional strains are perhaps as endemic a condition of Canada's landscape as environmental pollution is of America's. Neither will disappear soon; each, however, is surmountable. As Jacques Parizeau, one of Quebec's most prominent public figures, eloquently recounts in the following essay, Quebec has managed in remarkable ways to emerge the stronger from the separatist ferment of its recent past. And, as journalist Peter Brimelow argues in a companion piece, Canada's West will survive the economic and cultural skirmishing with its nemeses in the East, becoming an ever more powerful regional political force and, perhaps, out of shared economic and trade concerns, forming with a new Quebec a potent regional coalition that will redefine Canadian politics.

Jacques Parizeau
The Dynamics of Change in Quebec:
A Quarter-Century of Ferment

It is a perilous exercise to analyze the dynamics of change in Quebec over the past twenty-five years—the pace has been so swift, so much has been altered, the winds of politics have blown so tumultuously. To understand much of what happened and is happening now, one needs some idea of Quebec society as it was in the years from the Second World War until the end of the 1950s.

Quebec then was seen as a quaint, rural, priest-ridden society that the twentieth century had bypassed. There was some validity in that perception, but it missed some main points and distorted others. Quebec was never a particularly rural society. As early as the end of the nineteenth century, it was urbanized to the same extent as a number of other industrialized societies. But it was a truncated society. What had bypassed it was not the twentieth century, but capitalism. As this century developed, it became clear that most Quebecers had been convinced, and had been largely encouraged in that belief, that they had been born to a small loaf. The dynamic among them went into politics, controlled the labour unions, expanded the universities, graced the liberal professions, competed as journalists for the minds of the people. But, by and large, Quebec society was closed to business and business was closed to it. One could have imagined that Max Weber's *The Protestant Ethic and the Spirit of Capitalism* has been written by a French Canadian.

Major economic decisions were taken outside the native francophone community. First the British, then an anglophone minority operating largely from Montreal, and later the Americans dominated Quebec's economic world. From natural resources to banking, from shipping to rail, the French community was insignificant. Its only importance was in supplying a rapidly growing, relatively cheap and docile labour force. Thus, at a time when taxes were low and income taxes in particular were inconsequential, at a time when wealth could be rapidly accumulated throughout North America, French-Canadian society was excluded from the process. As time went by, the centres of economic decision-making were increasingly located elsewhere.

Yet, until the late 1950s, no significant socialist pressures were noticeable. The Church in Quebec had been obsessed by the influence on the clergy of the most extreme forms of republicanism in France before the turn of the century, then of the Bolshevik Revolution in Russia, and later still of the Spanish Civil War. In response, the Quebec Church managed with considerable effectiveness to maintain an anti-socialist, indeed an anti-state, attitude among most French Canadians.

In my own experience, Quebec society was in a very real way a stable society. It took me some time to understand the source of that stability beyond the usual clichés. The real source had to do with education. In the early 1960s, Quebec francophones still had the lowest level of secondary education in the Western world, along with Portugal. Under such circumstances, it was not all that difficult to keep things in balance: 20 per cent of the province's population—the anglophones—controlled 80 per cent of the management jobs at all levels, the other 80 per cent of the population being grossly undereducated. But over time, as this enforced stability became less acceptable, the ripples of unrest grew slowly into tidal waves.

With startling suddenness, the waves broke early in the 1960s. The so-called Quiet Revolution was indeed largely quiet. There was violence, but it was short-lived and quickly quelled. But that it was a revolution there could be no doubt. Within a few years, Quebec's

educational system was fundamentally transformed and radically democ-
ratized. Social services were enormously expanded, following a trend
throughout Canada, and were "declericalized" in less than ten years.
But, in a way, the changes were even more profound than such institutional transformations can suggest. The birth rate dropped by nearly
one-half in a decade. Traditional moral values were rejected by a generation that promptly replaced one form of radicalism with another. The
pendulum swung with such speed that it produced a sort of collective
bewilderment that is still noticeable today.

The provincial government, the state, the bureaucracy,
became the central agents of change. They were accepted as the fundamental means for achieving what was necessary. The role of government
was enlarged, deepened, diversified, all the more easily because the transformation was seen as a means of catching up with what has come
to be known in other countries as the welfare state. Modernization
required strong government, a major centre of decision-making and the
only one that French Canadians could truly consider their own. They
rapidly became acquainted with financial and administrative decisions
of a size they had never known before. Inevitably, there appeared an
expanding body of bureaucratic managers who owed nothing to the
private sector, who had never been subjected to the cold wind of competition, but who nevertheless learned quickly to administer billions of
dollars and direct tens of thousands of employees. This new breed
breathed the intoxicating air of social engineering.

It was inevitable that government would be perceived
as the basic instrument for transforming and developing the economy.
A large, powerful public sector was involved in the establishment of
state corporations that specialized in mining exploration, oil and gas
operations, forestry products, food manufacturing, transportation, steel,
asbestos and hydroelectricity. Large pools of capital, available to public
authorities as well as to private investors, were organized. The imprint
of so many agencies and corporations on the economy, while vast, was
not immediately visible. Many of those who managed these new corporations belonged to the same group that managed Quebec's public
services, the educational system and the bureaucracy. That new class
of managers would gradually emerge to place its special stamp on the
province.

All this ferment implied a growing degree of autonomy on the part of the provincial administration in its relations with Canada's federal authorities. Successive Quebec governments would expend ever greater efforts to obtain from Ottawa more money, more taxation powers and substantially more freedom to allocate whatever federal transfers were available. In that sense, Quebec was increasingly responsible for inducing a notable degree of decentralization in Canada, a little-known phenomenon. In fact, no other federation is as decentralized as Canada. Under intense political pressures—stimulated more often than not by Quebec during the 1960s—the federal government agreed to a transformation in provincial responsibilities: the tax base was shifted to the provinces; equalization payments were made on an unconditional basis; most shared-cost programs were replaced by block funding; and all funds collected by the Canada Pension Plan were lent back to the provinces, an arrangement which set the stage for Quebec to set up its own plan.

The sixties were the years when public authorities spoke of the *State* of Quebec, where new concepts in international relations and for economic and industrial policies were being developed and employed. Should Quebec seek special status within Confederation? Or should it aim for the status of an associated state? Intellectuals and artists played a vibrant role in this affirmation of Quebec society: pride and lyrics went well together. The spiritual renewal of French Canadians was refreshingly profound. The people born to a small loaf suddenly discovered that the future might be in their hands after all. Only a strong collective purpose was required.

It is not surprising that, in these turbulent years of the sixties, the idea of independence for Quebec seized hold of a growing number of people. Scattered in the beginning, small in numbers and electoral clout but closely tied to the volatile language issue, the separatist movement started on its fateful course.

In these same years, separation coincided with the drift of English Canadians out of Montreal, as financial activity gravitated towards Toronto and Ontario. There had been such movements in the past. In the financial world, Toronto had already become the metropolis of Canada and, furthermore, due to a variety of circumstances—the opening of the St. Lawrence Seaway; the 1965 Canada–U.S. Auto Pact;

the high concentration of "soft" industrial sectors in Quebec and their lack of attraction for multinational investment—Ontario had gained a marked edge over Quebec in terms of economic development.

The Quiet Revolution generated its own economic breakthroughs, which in turn generated strenuous philosophical and sectoral struggles over the future of the province. Anglophone financial and economic power in Montreal fought the Revolution with everything it could muster. The idea that government could act as the main economic lever of francophones was anathema. The nationalization of hydroelectric companies; the creation of an industrial holding, the Société Générale de Financement; the establishment of the Caisse de Dépôt et Placement du Québec, which was to become the largest stock portfolio in Canada—these were the battlegrounds where the old power and the new fought it out. And in 1967, the first of the so-called flights of capital occurred with appreciable effect on those Quebec politicians who still had much to learn where financial markets were concerned. Ordinary English Canadians, meanwhile, could read the writing on the wall: the natives had become restless and were obviously after real power. Some of these anglophones, whose families had been responsible for the building of the Canadian economy and who were deeply conscious of their historical role in the life of the nation and the province, asked themselves what future their children might have in Quebec. The occasional bombing only added to their conviction that more serene skies existed elsewhere. Thus, the anglophone diaspora picked up speed.

French Canadians, meanwhile, became increasingly conscious of the significance of what they were doing. Some, horrified by the prospect of independence—finding it difficult to sustain confidence in a democratic process of self-fulfillment and being wary of what they felt were deep reactionary strains in old Quebec society—flocked to Ottawa to preserve the federal link. Others, operating within the existing framework of provincial parties, tried to fight the rising tide of separatism. Still others organized themselves to try to give the idea of an independent Quebec effective political expression.

In October 1970, a wave of terrorism struck Quebec. It profoundly shocked a population that had become divided over the idea of an independent Quebec but that was deeply opposed, as it had

always been, to any form of violence. The terrorism was quickly sup-
pressed, but inevitably it remained the strongest and most vivid image
in many Quebec minds in the early seventies. At the same time, the
harsh War Measures Act, imposed by the national government, left the
impression that the real aim of federalists in both Ottawa and Quebec
had been to destroy the Parti Québécois (PQ). This eventually helped
to give the PQ the status of the underdog, reinforcing the impression
that the native francophones probably had a point if the "system" could
seem to brutalize them in such a way.

Yet, it is hard to escape the impression that, from 1970
to 1976, it was the combination of the federal "French power" bloc in
Ottawa and the anti-federal financial interests in Quebec, rather than
the War Measures Act or any other factor, that was most instrumental
in bringing the PQ to power.

The federalist forces in Quebec could not stifle the
dreams, the power, the expectations of so many people. The issue of
Quebec and the future of French Canadians dominated the political
scene in Canada. Problems of immense consequence, such as the first
major shocks on the international oil markets, seemed to pale by comparison. Ontario and the West might be at loggerheads over the price
of domestic oil, but a solution would be found expeditiously so as not
to distract attention from what had become the central issue: the fight
within Canada for its very existence.

In the meantime, the PQ had forged ahead, employing
a dual offensive that seemed clear at the time, but bore the germs of
a fundamental ambiguity. It wanted to be not only the party of Quebec's
sovereignty, but also the party of those who held the small loaf.

Logically, therefore, the PQ should have approached the
workings of society from a social democratic viewpoint. Social democracy,
however, had been until then the domain of the labour unions. Furthermore, as the welfare state in Quebec had reached its limits, other special
groups were taking the lead in social consciousness, a prospect they
found exciting until the real costs became known. Yet, electorally, the
combination of the PQ's two objectives proved remarkably successful.
Few people realized then that it might be prohibitively difficult to attain
political sovereignty, through a democratic process, against the kind of

systematic opposition that indigenous business interests were bound to mount against the party's social democratic objective. Strategically, the obstacle did not seem all that formidable: after all, wasn't indigenous business in Quebec relatively insignificant? The real business bosses were English-speaking.

The PQ came to power in 1976. In its campaign it had promised not to embark on the process of sovereignty before receiving a mandate to do so through a referendum. However, the PQ was correctly perceived as a separatist party with specific ideas as to how it intended to change Quebec society. For many, it was the true inheritor of the Quiet Revolution. For some, it was the Quiet Revolution run wild. In any event, it was brought to power on a wave of popular enthusiasm. The victory represented revenge for the defeat of 1760; the assurance of a French society now master of its own fate on an Anglo-Saxon continent; the hopes of the small-loaf holders for their children; the pride of a persistent if sometimes innocuous history. The party of the real Quebecers was triumphant at the polls and now in charge.

The battle started right away with the introduction of Bill 101, the charter for the protection of the French language. The bill was a bombshell, but it quickly brought peace among francophones. Montreal would be French, as Toronto was English. It would at last be possible to work freely in French, to earn one's income in French and to spend it in French. The psychological impact was startling.

At the same time, the government moved to show that it was on the side of the small-loaf holder: Quebec's tax structure was reorganized. Legislation was introduced to benefit the farmer, that remnant of the fabled rural society of old. The province's labour laws became among the most advanced on the continent. Small businesses and the cooperatives, traditional pillars of the Quebec economic structure, were singled out to receive special incentives. Steps were taken to prepare the public for the referendum on the sovereignty issue.

On the opposition side, efforts to derail the PQ's agenda gathered momentum. The economic dangers of separatism had to be revealed in all their dramatic impact. To this end, everything was exploitable. At about the time of the PQ's election, the Canadian dollar had collapsed. Any observer knew that this development had been rendered inevitable by recent wage settlements in Canada, yet the coincidence was too remarkable not to be used by the opposition. At the time of the Olympic Games, a huge wave of construction had taken place in Montreal, with a resulting increase in prime office space and hotel facilities. The subsequent decline in construction was additional fodder for the PQ's political enemies. To compound the situation, the exodus to Ontario had accelerated and head offices were moving out of Quebec. Separatism was seen as a threat to their standard of living by people who, unsympathetic to the goals of so many countries that had become independent since the Second World War, had a great deal to lose.

Yet, oddly, until the early 1980s the annual rate of growth of Quebec's economy was quite good on the whole, in comparison to that of its eternal competitor, Ontario. Serious doubt had been shed, however, on the economy's resilience in the face of major political change. Coupled with a very aggressive federal policy of selling Canada and the merits of confederation to Quebecers, the economic issue contributed in casting doubt on the capability of the PQ government.

It need not have done. In the vacuum created by the departure of anglophone businesses, a phenomenon was occurring that was as potent in some ways as the most profound developments of the Quiet Revolution. Francophone entrepreneurship was coming of age. It had been long in maturing. Often undercapitalized, unsure of its ability to adapt to modern management, hindered in its expansion by an overvalued exchange rate and accustomed to being on the periphery of the action, it suddenly bloomed. It learned to work with the public sector and to obtain from it the support it required when necessary. Aggressive, imaginative, now fully aware of the technical requirements of the times, Quebec entrepreneurship has in the past fifteen years acquired impressive strength. In the ferment of recent Quebec history, this fact has taken some time to win recognition. Likewise, the extent to which the public sector, the cooperative movement and the entrepreneurs have moved to support each other, rather than to be mutually exclusive, has only lately been realized. An economic structure has emerged in Quebec, the like of which does not really exist elsewhere in North America.

In the years preceding the sovereignty referendum in 1980, the PQ government found it difficult to understand the changes taking place. Yet, economic issues were at the very centre of the sovereignty debate. The provincial business community was creating 80 to 90 per cent of all jobs. Dynamic new forces were flowing through Quebec society, but were not recognized soon enough for what they were. And so the referendum was lost. Francophones were divided. Half of them, true believers, clung to the issue they had always regarded as the party's raison d'être. The other half, weary of the fight and fearful of the impact of sovereignty on the economic health of their society, spurned the notion with their vote. In the end, it was the anglophone minority, voting en masse against sovereignty, that made the difference.

A new attempt to resurrect the sovereignty issue would have been a reasonable course to follow, after an appropriate lapse of time and after some calm had been restored. But calm turned out to be elusive. Though re-elected in 1981, thanks to the personal magnetism of its leader René Lévesque and the ineptitude of the opposition Liberals, the PQ was shortly faced with the worst recession that Quebec had known since the 1930s. The gross domestic product fell by 6 per cent and employment by 8 per cent. The overall statistics across Canada were not all that better and some provinces fared worse. Quebec, as a province, could not follow the federal path of letting its deficit increase massively. As in other provinces, expenditures had to be substantially cut, wage growth in the public sector curtailed and taxes raised. Pitched battles were fought with the unions. Social groups, in the habit of getting what they wanted, could not fathom the meaning of austerity. Corporate interests, which had thrived easily in a growing economy, found themselves suddenly curtailed.

The welfare state was being reassessed everywhere. Social enthusiasm was being replaced by concern over abuses. The managers of the sixties were faced with the tough realities of the eighties. The real managerial stars were now in the private sector. After eight years in power, the PQ, which had so polarized the issue of sovereignty, did not wish to jeopardize its chances of reaching that goal as it sought to cope with the austere realities of unemployment, slow growth and budget management.

The PQ government fought its battles well, however. The recovery from recession was rapid, in some ways even spectacular. The investment recovery in Quebec, engineered by the government, was without parallel in Canada. What emerged as a peculiarly Quebec economy, responsive to stimuli of a different sort from that of Ontario, for example, reacted positively to the government's policies. The province's mixed-enterprise system showed an aptitude to adapt and be competitive.

Yet, somehow, a spring had been broken in the engine of political dynamism. The recession had underscored the difficulties facing young people in the labour market. The economic facts of life moved them away from political enthusiasm. In a sense, the very success of the PQ in so many areas of government militated against its original objective: sovereignty. Why become independent when so much could be done as a province? The federal government's repatriation of Canada's Constitution, with its various controlling amendments, in fact reduced the powers of the Quebec government. Yet even that did not cause the furor one would have expected. When real power is actually exercised, battles over jurisdiction seem of lesser importance. So, weariness slowly permeated the political field. Poets and singers were subdued. The collective goal diminished in importance as personal ambition and success became an activating and popular force within the province.

At this juncture, the PQ broke apart. The pressures had been too great; the challenges seemed impossible.

The PQ government's renunciation of its objective of political sovereignty implies far-reaching repercussions for the dynamics of change over the coming years. The decision has come at a time when the new federal government in Ottawa is attempting to avoid confrontations and to improve the poisoned atmosphere of federal–provincial relations. But Ottawa faces budgetary problems of enormous proportions that will prevent it from proposing financial "sweeteners" that might harmonize its relations with Quebec. Indeed, if the federal deficit is to be cut, Ottawa will have to practise an infinitely difficult balancing act to avoid penalizing some regions of Canada more than others. It can move on the constitutional front to repair the damage done to Quebec's jurisdiction by the previous federal government. But the balancing act will again be delicate: it is not at all clear that the other provinces are ready to reopen this Pandora's box.

We may, in the end, be entering a period of relative political calm in Quebec. This would, in part, be due to sheer psychological exhaustion after so many years of tension. It might also be due to some instinctual urge to consolidate the effects of the massive strides Quebecers have made in the last twenty-five years. In any event, the shift in social–economic values and objectives that has occurred over the last few years must run its course.

The equilibrium of social, economic and political forces will be a fragile one, however. By ceasing to be a truncated society and gradually becoming a completely rounded one, by establishing an open economy exposed to the world but distinct in its workings from other provincial economies, by keeping an unalienated but proud sense of specialness as a tightly woven French-Canadian community, Quebec will remain highly sensitive to the actions of the federal government and the nation as a whole for a long while to come.

Having rejected independence for now, Quebecers should not be viewed as having renounced the spirit of nationalism that has sustained them over the centuries. That spirit adopts various shades and forms. For generations it was largely defensive. I suspect that, lately, it has become more aggressive in a diffuse sort of way. Quebecers now tend to feel there is little they cannot do to change their destinies. A people's whole mentality has obviously undergone a sea change in that regard. A lot of sail has been added to the mast, perhaps somewhat more than is warranted by the keel. Any attempt to slow down the ship, though, may well be a perilous exercise. Calm is the sea for now.

Peter Brimelow

Regional Strains and Canada's West: The Politics of Alienation

When a large, cohesive minority believes it can transfer its allegiance to a neighboring state, or make a go of total independence, it will be inclined to disassociate itself from a consensus the terms of which have been altered in its disfavor.

Pierre Trudeau

Western Canada, like Quebec (although to a lesser extent) is a separate state within a state.

Pierre Berton

The thesis of this essay is that the governing institutions of the Canadian confederation are badly designed and seriously misrepresent the country's political and cultural reality.

What is, in effect, a British-style unitary system has been imposed upon a continental-sized polity that is riven by acute sectional and absolutely irrepressible ethnic division. In the short run, this has meant an illusory stability in Canada, although arguably at the price of various unpleasant side effects such as the relative impoverishment of periphery regions and a persistent overall economic underperformance compared to that of the United States. But in the long run, this condition could well render Ottawa unable to respond to submerged but steadily accumulating grievances.

The most publicized such problem is, of course, the gradual emergence of Quebec, under a succession of governments, as a French-speaking nation-state on the European model. My focus here, however, is more upon the costs inflicted by the present version of confederation upon Western Canada—the area north and west of the Ontario line. Western Canada is often treated as peripheral both by

Canadian politicians and by students of Canada. But, as a result of the prolonged post-war economic expansion, the population of Western Canada now exceeds that of Quebec. And there are signs that it is waking up to its plight.

Geography is still destiny in Canada, just as much as when Goldwin Smith wrote his classic *Canada and the Canadian Question* in 1891. "Whoever wishes to know what Canada is, and to understand the Canadian Question," he wrote, "should begin by turning from the political to the natural map."

It is worth emphasizing that, even by North American standards, Canada is breathtakingly vast. With 3.8 million square miles, it constitutes the second-largest country in the world, compared with 8.6 million square miles for the Soviet Union and a mere 3.0 million square miles for the continental United States (which has an additional half a million square miles in Alaska).

Sheer size poses a more serious political problem for Canada than is generally recognized. Human communities tend to be centrifugal. It has been the exception rather than the rule for the great overseas possessions of the European imperial powers to retain political unity after independence. The Spanish-speaking area of Central and South America is only slightly larger than Canada at 4.4 million square miles, but it has fragmented into seventeen separate, sometimes warring, regimes. Australia suffered a secession crisis in the 1930s. And in the United States, regional or "sectional" rivalries have been a notoriously important and often dominant political theme. A similar torsion is continuously if quietly at work in Canadian politics.

Goldwin Smith's point was that the different parts of Canada—the Maritimes, Central Canada, the Prairies, British Columbia— were sharply divided from each other ("by great barriers of nature, wild and irreclaimable wildernesses or manifold chains of mountains") but closely connected ("by nature, physically and economically") with the American states immediately to their south. In the United States, of course, since the eclipse of Frederick Jackson Turner and his "Frontier Thesis" school of American historiography, the study of sectionalism has largely been superseded by an interest in class or race. But it is significant that, when the *Washington Post* writer Joel Garreau recently redrew the map of the continent for his ingenious update on contemporary American sectionalism, *The Nine Nations of North America*, he ignored the 49th parallel altogether and assigned English Canada to the regions immediately to their south. Quebec, even more significantly, was treated as a "nation" unto itself, the only place where political and "national" boundaries coincided.

Goldwin Smith thought that north–south ties predominated in North America and that English-Canadian and American societies were in a state of what he called "practical fusion." Echoing his diagnosis nearly a century later (in *The Patriot Game: Canada and the Canadian Question Revisited*), I argued that English Canada should properly be viewed as a component part of the greater English-speaking "supernation" of North America. It comprises a distinct section, or group of sections, like the South or the Midwest. It differs in nuance from the other sections, but it shares a core of common values, like a facet of a diamond or a petal of a rose.

This concept, apparently hard to grasp, merits another metaphor. The answer to the hoary debate about English Canada's identity is that Canada does indeed have an identity of its own, but it is also a member of the English-speaking North American family, whose common heritage is manifest in its every feature. Quebec, of course, does not belong to this family at all, unless as a distant relative like every other First World country. It is clearly a "distinct society," to use the terminology of Prime Minister Brian Mulroney's Meech Lake Accord.

Just as a glass can be perceived as half full or half empty, so the sectional nature of North America often misleads observers, particularly those preoccupied with their own section or unmindful of international comparisons. The *New York Times*' Ottawa bureau chief Michael T. Kaufman once wrote an influential article about the differences between Canadian and American values, beginning with the remarkable tendency of Canadian pedestrians to stop at red lights when no cars were in sight:

> Like most Americans, I had assumed that an all-embracing North American civilization radiated from New York to Toronto and on to Yellowknife and Hudson Bay, and the discovery of just how different Canadian values are from our own came as quite a surprise . . . .

This surprise would be natural for a New Yorker, coming from one of the few cities in the world where automobiles are in danger of being run down by pedestrians. But just an hour away, via the Eastern Airlines shuttle, pedestrians regularly stop at red lights in Washington, D.C., and are actually ticketed by the police if they don't. This is also true in supposedly car-crazed Los Angeles. Canadians may not act like New Yorkers, but neither do most Americans, particularly those from the upper Midwest or the Pacific Northwest, the two sections perhaps closest in attitude to English Canada. North American civilization simply does not "radiate" from New York; hence Saul Bellow's quip that "New York is the capital of a nation that does not exist."

The example may seem frivolous, but the issue is serious. Any student of Canadian–American relations is accustomed to being told that the two countries differ profoundly: in their respective levels of violent crime, for example. But statistics in the United States aggregate many heterogeneous communities, such as those of its central cities, which are really extensions of the Third World. The more appropriate comparison is between specific sections and even between both countries' core populations, still basically a similar British–German–Italian blend. Similarly, Canadian statistics often compound the problem by aggregating anglophone and francophone communities, thus suppressing any systematic differences.

Another reason for widespread misunderstanding of Canada, and particularly of its sectional nature, is that much of what is conventionally attributed to the country's unique (that is, non-American) politico-economic "culture" or "values" is, in fact, the accidental by-product of its peculiar institutions. Canada's parliamentary system was imported more or less uncritically from Britain by politicians, many of them British immigrants with no experience of the difficulty in ruling a continental-sized polity and with no pressing necessity to consider it. Indeed, only Ontario, Quebec and some Atlantic provinces participated in the Confederation negotiations more than a century ago.

By contrast, the American Founding Fathers were acutely aware of the problem posed by geography. They consciously rejected a head-counting view of democracy and tried to design a constitution in which the separate communities and interests would be represented rather than repressed. Their concern had many consequences, probably the most important of which was the provision of a Senate to which each state, regardless of size, was entitled to send two members. In Canada, the "Fathers of Confederation" responded only reluctantly to the reality of sectional divergence. They treated it variously as a glorified problem of local government (hence, Canadian provinces that in some respects have more power over their internal affairs than American states) or as a symbolic issue (hence, appointments to the federal Cabinet and to Canada's moribund Senate that are supposed to be by region). The crucial difference is that the Canadian sections have no institutionalized say on what goes on in the federal capital.

In recent years, Canadian federal and provincial political bodies have both been simultaneously grabbing at power. This has resulted in a tug-of-war to which those notoriously endless federal–provincial conferences are little more than an *ad hoc* and, ultimately, unsatisfactory response. But in America, paradoxically, the states have tended to be more willing to cede power to Washington in time of economic crisis or war precisely because they have some institutionalized influence in the capital. In contrast to this flexibility, Canada's constitutional system, to cite Stephen Leacock's famous line, has behaved like the man who throws himself on a horse and rides off in all directions.

A prototypical case of misinterpreting Canada out of ignorance of this institutional dimension occurred in 1980. It was widely claimed that the outcome of the American and Canadian federal elections that year, when a conservative American President replaced a liberal and a liberal Canadian Prime Minister replaced a conservative, indicated that the two countries were "polarizing." But the simple truth was that, if the American election had been held under the same rules as Canada's, Thomas "Tip" O'Neill, not Ronald Reagan, would have emerged as American Prime Minister. O'Neill, a decidedly liberal Democrat, was Speaker of the House of Representatives because he led the party that won most seats in that body, which is elected on the same basis of equal-sized, single-member, winner-takes-all districts as is the House of Commons. Under this system, the populous cities of the East dominate the spaces (and arguably different societies) of the West. O'Neill's Democratic Party retained control of the House in 1984, so he would have been able to continue as Prime Minister in the year when Canada depolarized itself, this time without fanfare, and Brian Mulroney came to power.

The consequences of the parliamentary system for Canada and its regions are even more subtle and pervasive, as two examples suggest.

First, the parliamentary system's characteristically tighter party discipline has enabled Quebec to pyramid its national influence through its domination of the Liberal Party. Although the Liberals have been conventionally described as Canada's natural party of government, English Canada has actually voted Tory in every election but one since 1953. Despite this clear evidence of majority discontent, however, Ottawa was, throughout this period, almost wholly preoccupied by Quebec issues—above all, the perceived need, an absolute necessity from the point of view of the Liberal electoral coalition, to appease francophone separatism.

Second, the greater power which the parliamentary system gives the executive branch has, in the words of Queen's University professor C.E.S. Franks, "enabled the executive branch to express a public interest beyond party and interest group . . . and, as an institutional feature, has permitted Canadian governments to be more activist and welfare-oriented than the American . . . ." Put less glowingly, this means that Canada's parliamentary system greatly strengthens the position of its political class, which includes both professional politicians and civil servants. With less fear of voter revolt, Canadian governments can intervene more ambitiously in society and, in particular, appropriate directly and indirectly some 55 per cent of the gross national product, twenty percentage points higher than what the American governments appropriate and significantly closer to Western European social democratic norms. This burden is arguably responsible for Canada's chronic shortfall in per capita gross national product compared to the United States.

At this point, a key concept in my analysis of the "Canadian Question" can be introduced: the "Public Choice" concept of rent-seeking, that is, the use of political power to extract subsidies (called "rent" by economists) from society.

Canada's political system makes rent-seeking fatally easy; above all, it allows the dominant region of Central Canada to extract rents from the peripheral regions. The separate sectional communities of Canada have been the principal toad beneath the parliamentary system's harrow. The remainder of this essay will be devoted to their discontents. (Except, that is, for the discontents of Quebec, which are addressed elsewhere in this section. Quebec's grievances are not so much regional as cultural and national. They follow a clear cyclical pattern: upsurges every generation or so, succeeded by periods of quiescence and renewed anglophone complacency, although each upsurge has left the francophones progressively more in control of Quebec's institutions. As the Canadian political system has allowed Quebec to occupy a pivotal position, it may be that any major constitutional reform must await the next cycle of francophone nationalism.)

The dynamic process by which Canada's constitutional system would disadvantage the country's sections became clear directly after Confederation in 1867.

The Maritime provinces, strategically located on the Great Circle route between the United States and Europe, had built what the historian David G. Alexander described as

> one of the world's foremost shipbuilding industries, the third or fourth largest merchant marine, financial institutions which were the core of many central Canadian giants, and an industrial structure growing as fast as Central Canada.

Confederation, however, threatened to forcibly reorient the Maritime economy towards Central Canada. Most importantly, the end of free trade and the imposition of tariffs meant that the Maritimes would be retarding their own growth by having to pay higher prices for imports, while the industries implicitly subsidized by those tariffs were all located in Central Canada.

Nova Scotia, in particular, was not easily reconciled to its fate. It elected separatist majorities provincially and federally in 1867, and again provincially in 1886. Ottawa's response was to become its standard policy towards troublesome frontiersmen. Firstly, it simply ignored the separatists; this was institutionally possible because they were powerless both as a provincial government and as a small non-disruptive minority in the federal House of Commons. Secondly, Ottawa tried to buy the separatists off; the Nova Scotia leader, Joseph Howe, eventually entered Sir John A. Macdonald's Cabinet in 1869 and new financial terms were negotiated. Thirdly, Ottawa out-manoeuvred the troublemakers by making a specific election appeal in 1888 to monarchic and British imperial sentiment. The Maritimes remained in Confederation, but their status has steadily declined to a peripheral one relative to Central Canada, requiring ever greater subsidies.

A similar scenario is now being played out in the island province of Newfoundland. Culturally a unique brew of Irish and West Country English, quite distinct from the rest of Canada, Newfoundland was only narrowly induced to enter Confederation in 1949, after much bitter and arguably manipulated debate. Since then, despite massive subsidies, Newfoundland has steadily lost ground. Its declining economy contrasts with the comparable, but more vigorous, economy of Iceland, which has been independent since the Second World War.

Here, a specific disadvantage of the Canadian system becomes apparent. Newfoundland was in large part a fishing economy. Yet, Ottawa strongly opposed the extension of its territorial waters beyond the three-mile limit. Iceland, by contrast, practically went to war with Britain over the issue. Newfoundland not only had no authority to take action on its own; it had no effective institutional mode of expression in Ottawa, which accordingly placed a higher priority on other problems. Similarly, Newfoundland has been unable to prevent the Mulroney government from proposing fishing concessions, at its expense, in negotiations with France over the claims of the French-owned islands of St. Pierre and Miquelon. In the American system, of course, the executive branch simply cannot implement treaties without the consent of the Senate, and Senators from fishing states have been notoriously hard to please.

The problems of the Maritimes in Confederation were a sort of prologue to the potentially far-reaching difficulties experienced by Canada's Western provinces in more recent times.

Canadians' alleged special relationship with their landscape is a popular theme of their political mythology. So, it is worth noting that the West is different—dominated not by the Canadian Shield, but by the northern extensions of the Great Plains and the Western

Cordilleras. The people are different too: the British component has been augmented by heavy Eastern European and American immigration dating back to the early years of the century. This perhaps accounts for the hesitation with which Central Canadian publicists and politicians some-times view the West. In 1945, Prime Minister Mackenzie King actually confided to his diary his fear that the United States

> could take peaceful possession of part of Canada with a welcome from the people of B.C., Alta. and Saskatchewan . . . I felt perfectly sure that once the Western provinces became alarmed in the matter of security, they would look to the United States for protection, not to Canada or to the Commonwealth.

The feeling is mutual. Western Canadians have voted against Ottawa with a persistence so stubborn that it is hard to avoid the impression they are trying to send some kind of message. From Progressive Conservative John Diefenbaker's election in 1958 to Brian Mulroney's sweep in 1984, the West consistently elected a majority of opposition Members of Parliament except during the brief interregnum of Joe Clark in 1979. For Western voters the governing party, the Liberals, virtually ceased to exist. The West has also persistently experimented with minor parties. (Both these trends were evident in the 1988 federal election: despite the dominant issue of free trade, historically a vital Western concern, Prime Minister Mulroney's new Quebec-oriented version of the Tory Party actually lost seats in the region, to a large degree because right-wing groups like the Reform Party and the Christian Heritage Party drew off enough votes to elect New Democrats and Liberals.)

The reasons for this estrangement are historical. Western Canada, unlike Quebec, has been indisputably an economic loser in Con-federation. As Harold Innis, the pioneer of Canadian economic history, wrote as far back as 1923, "Western Canada has paid for the develop-ment of Canadian nationality, and it would appear that it must continue to pay."

The West has been a colony of Central Canada in a purely mercantilist sense. Its development has been channelled by polit-ical power in directions that are contrary to natural economic forces but concordant with the perceived interests of a distant metropolis. Historically, the West has never been allowed to buy freely where it wished, but has had to pay the Canadian tariff on imports, thus implicitly subsidizing Central Canadian industry. In the modern era, federal government intervention also prevented the West from selling its principal products, oil and gas, where it wished—in the world market. Instead, Western energy was compulsorily diverted to the Canadian market, where it could only be sold at prices that Ottawa fixed well below prevailing world levels. In effect, it was expropriated. Ottawa also intervened to inhibit the import of foreign capital, making the West more dependent on expensive Central Canadian capital and various government concessions. Ottawa created and favoured its own agency, Petro-Canada, to take increasing areas of the industry directly into its own hands.

It is true, of course, that in former days, when the international oil companies controlled production and held prices low, Ottawa, like Washington, fostered domestic production by reserving part of the home market for it. The implicit transfers involved, however, were of entirely different orders of magnitude. Ottawa's implementation of the policy offered a telling insight into the political economy of Canada. When prices were low, Western oilmen were denied protection in the Montreal market, then Canada's largest. But when the Organization of Petroleum-Exporting Countries (OPEC) boosted prices, Montreal was immediately given access to Western oil's controlled lower price, except that, because an actual transfer of Western oil was technically infeasible, foreign oil was imported and subsidized. The only common thread in this tangle has been Ottawa's sedulous attention to Quebec, the sort of thing that explains why many Westerners seem to react to francophone power in Canada as a symbol and symptom of their own dispossession.

In the case of energy, Ottawa's interventionism reached its apotheosis with the National Energy Program (NEP), enacted by Trudeau's Liberal government after its return to power in 1980. The NEP was justified as a measure designed to increase Canadian ownership and ensure energy self-sufficiency. But Professor Charles Doran is probably right to argue, in his *Forgotten Partnership: U.S.–Canada Today*, that a possibility not entirely to be discounted is that Ottawa never really was much interested in petroleum self-sufficiency . . . . [In reality, it] needed to defend the interests of Central Canadian consumers and industrial users, a defense Ottawa pursued under the disguise of "equity."

The NEP dramatically demonstrated the cost to the West of the absence in Canada's political system of institutionalized regional representation. Ottawa undertook to subsidize Central Canada by holding oil prices below world levels and, in addition, expropriating through taxation the windfall profits which the West would otherwise have reaped as world prices soared. This sort of despoliation of a politically weak region is precisely what an effective Senate would prevent. In fact, the Australian Senate, which is elected, blocked a similar grab at Western Australia's mineral windfall profits by the national Labour government of Gough Whitlam, forcing an election that Whitlam lost.

As it happened, of course, Pierre Trudeau's Liberal government was attempting to patriate the Canadian Constitution, and amend it in the process, during the very same period as the NEP controversy. So why didn't the Western premiers refuse to go along with any constitutional accord unless it allowed for an elected Senate? "Brutal stupidity," according to one prominent Tory Senator, himself a former Western leader. There could be no clearer demonstration of the importance of ideas in politics. The Western premiers are learning slowly: during the Meech Lake negotiations, they at least raised the question of an elected Senate, but were persuaded to defer discussions of it until after Quebec's constitutional concerns had been satisfied.

Perhaps the most fascinating example of a policy generated by Canada's flawed system has been the imposition of institutional bilingualism not only within the federal government (Canada's largest single employer), but as far out into the reaches of Canadian society as its writ can be made to run.

Official bilingualism was central to Trudeau's post-1968 overhaul of Canada's institutions, an overhaul so radical that modern Canada in a real sense may be said to be a Trudeauvian state. But, at that time and ever since, for reasons of their own, Canada's major political parties have fought desperately to keep the issue of bilingualism out of politics. This process was well described by the *Toronto Star*'s

Ottawa columnist Richard Gwyn in his biography of Trudeau, *The Northern Magus*:

> Bilingualism, in truth, was nothing less than a social revolution. Like the introduction of the postwar welfare state, like the counter-cultural revolution of the 1960s, it was a development that effected fundamental changes in the character of the country. But in contrast to those transformational phenomena, no one in authority in Ottawa in the late 1960s and early 1970s let on that massive change was about to happen . . . .

So successful has this virtual conspiracy of silence been that some foreign Canada-watchers have totally missed the policy's significance. Only two references are carried in the index of *The Canadians*, the 1985 book by the *New York Times* Toronto correspondent Andrew H. Malcolm: that the federal government is "officially bilingual," and that the national anthem is sung in both languages at baseball games.

It is vital to note that the discussion of Canada's official bilingualism is *not* about the alleged virtues of any individual being able to speak two languages. Rather, it is about the mandatory requirement that the institutions of the Canadian federal government operate in both languages, something that absolutely requires those institutions to be run by people who are themselves bilingual.

The plain fact is that in Canada there are few such people, particularly within the anglophone community and, above all, in the West. Only 15.3 per cent of the Canadian population, or about 3.7 million people, reported to the 1981 census-takers that they could "conduct a conversation" in both languages. And this almost certainly exaggerates the number of Canadians who are sufficiently bilingual to operate professionally in either language, a much more difficult achievement than being able to order dinner or exchange a few goodwill "bonjours." Despite overwhelming enthusiasm among the élite for bilingualism, the proportion of bilingual citizens nationwide has remained fairly stable over time. As far back as 1931, it was 12.7 per cent, and some demographers think any recent increase can be attributed largely to Canada's falling birthrate, which reduces the proportion of children, a group less likely than adults to speak a second language. (At the time of writing, preliminary results from the 1986 census suggest the proportion of bilingual Canadians has risen to 16 per cent.)

Nor is the proportion of bilingual Canadians likely to change dramatically any time soon. The upper-middle-class phenomenon of "French immersion" schooling, though much celebrated, involves relatively small numbers of children and is, in any case, restricted to anglophones, for reasons that are perhaps suggestive of bilingualism's underlying premise. Even more indicative is the fact that the Meech Lake Accord, by recognizing Quebec as a "distinct society," has essentially endorsed that province's official French-only unilingualism as implemented by both the Liberal and Parti Québécois provincial governments. This automatically makes English less necessary in Quebec, at a time when there is some evidence that bilingualism has already begun declining among younger francophones. Nevertheless, the federal government under Mulroney has continued to press the expansion of institutional bilingualism in English Canada.

The distribution of Canadians claiming to be bilingual is sharply skewed. In 1981, substantially more than half reported French as their mother tongue: some 2.2 million, compared to 1.1 million who reported English. (The balance was mostly either immigrants or native peoples, referred to in Ottawa as "allophones.") That still meant that, for every francophone who could speak English, nearly two could speak only French. But, for every bilingual anglophone, there were nearly fifteen who could speak only English.

Moreover, nearly all bilingual Canadians are located in or near the province of Quebec. In 1981, 56.1 per cent lived in Quebec itself, 25.1 per cent in Ontario (which, of course, includes the federal capital). New Brunswick, on Quebec's eastern flank, had 5 per cent. This geographical skew is hardly surprising given the even more unequal distribution of Canada's 6 million francophones. All but a half-million or so live in Quebec. In the whole of Canada west of the Ontario line where, according to the 1981 census, more than 7 million people live, a mere 86 665 individuals used French in their homes—as opposed, say, to 95 070 who spoke German. Just over half a million Westerners said they spoke both French and English.

There is, thus, little demographic foundation for the bilingualism policy, and there is less with every passing year: the number of francophones outside Quebec, and of anglophones inside Quebec,

has been declining both relatively and absolutely. Whatever their government may say about the efficacy of the policy in allowing the two communities to live together, the people of Canada have been quietly voting
against it with their U-Haul trucks.

Indeed, the form of bilingualism that has been imposed
on Canada is more demanding than in societies where it truly reflects
a cultural reality. In Belgium, where 60 per cent of the population speak
Flemish, 40 per cent speak French and about half speak both languages,
only Brussels is officially bilingual. Nine out of ten Belgians live in unilingual regions where either French or Flemish is used exclusively for
government and education—this in a country with less than one-third
of one per cent of Canada's land area, and one-half its population. Yet,
in Canada, in defiance of all the facts and any pretence of administrative
practicality, the established policy basically assumes that francophones
and anglophones are coextensive and coterminous throughout the Canadian state, and it undertakes to offer them federal services in both languages everywhere. Thus, signs and announcements in Alberta airports
are duplicated in French, although few, if any, in the airport crowds
may understand it. It reminds one of the bowls of milk left by Irish
peasants on their doorsteps to propitiate the phantom nation of Little
People with whom they believed they shared their land.

To a certain extent, this extraordinary policy may be
attributed to the false consciousness of the Canadian political élite. In
Montreal and Ottawa, though not in Toronto, it is possible for a determined doctrinaire to imagine that Canada is in some sense bilingual
and bicultural. According to Margaret Trudeau (of the Vancouver
Sinclairs), her husband-to-be simply assumed she was bilingual until social
disaster occurred in the form of a dinner party hosted by anglophone
civil servants but conducted entirely in French. Even after that, according
to other observers, Trudeau continued to converse in French at social
events despite his wife's incomprehension.

One symptom of this false consciousness is a persistent
tendency to overestimate the numbers of francophones outside Quebec.
In 1983, for example, at the height of the pitched battle in Manitoba
over plans to make the provincial government officially bilingual, Marc
Roy, president of a British Columbia organization said to represent 45 000

francophones, urged that his province adopt the same policy. "Sooner or later, each province will have to recognize that the price to pay for a united Canada is the recognition of French language minority rights," Roy told the Victoria *Times-Colonist*. His public relations director predicted that "the 45 000 French-speaking British Columbians could easily increase tenfold to 500 000 in the next decade . . . ." Roy went on to say that, despite British Columbia's strong anglophone tradition, French education should be "made the right of all British Columbians" and they should have "the right to correspond with the provincial government in French as Francophones do now with the federal government."

However innocently offered, the numbers cited by Roy and his organization were ludicrously unrealistic. According to the 1981 census, only 154 170 persons or 5.7 per cent of British Columbians were bilingual; only 15 125 reported speaking French in the home; only an infinitesimal 1 445 were unilingual francophones. Roy's claim to represent 45 000 "French speakers" was presumably based on the census report of 45 000 respondents giving French as their "mother tongue"; in Canadian usage, that is essentially an ethnic designation rather than a measure of language practice. This cultural goading of Westerners goes some way to explain why, in 1984, in one of the very few votes ever held on the issue, Manitobans overwhelmingly rejected proposals to extend official bilingualism to their provincial government.

Beyond this, however, the enthusiasm for and the opposition to bilingualism must be attributed to an entirely realistic understanding of its effects. As Richard Gwyn acknowledged, the policy meant that unilingual Canadians "would be disadvantaged for life, through no fault of their own . . . . The central fact of bilingualism was becoming clear: it means loss of power for unilingual English Canadians." Gwyn detailed the meaning:

> Initially these "rewarding" jobs (for which bilingualism was required) meant just the top ones at Ottawa; inevitably though, it would soon mean all the middle-rank jobs that fed the top; then jobs in "para-government," all the way from the Canadian Manufacturers' Association to the Canadian Labor Congress, on down the line to jobs in all companies which had dealings with Francophones, and to some government positions. Eventually, unilingualism could mean a life sentence to job immobility.

Trudeau knew this all along. He fibbed about it as a necessary means to an end.

Canada's bilingual experiment has been, above everything else, a supreme exercise in social engineering. Its immediate effects have been intensely regressive. It has acted as a rent-seeking device, benefitting precisely those disproportionately bilingual groups from whom power in Canadian society has been slipping: the francophones, whose relative proportion of Canada's population has been declining; the Montreal anglophones, whose city is being eclipsed by Toronto and the West; the established upper-middle classes, whose financial and social status is threatened by the new wealth of the oil fields and industrial estates. Ultimately, of course, the policy has benefitted Central Canada, where most bilingual Canadians live.

Official bilingualism has committed Ottawa to a course that will increasingly collide with the political culture of English-speaking North American society: minimal class distinctions, high social mobility, the determination of status by private activity rather than public prescription. It inevitably tends to create, through government coercion, what is in effect a system of first-class and second-class citizens. Increasingly, public life is restricted to the former.

Thus, in the Progressive Conservative leadership contest of 1983, bilingualism and its demands reportedly kept the strongest Western candidate, Premier Peter Lougheed of Alberta, out of the race altogether. It derailed the campaign of John Crosbie of Newfoundland. And it enabled Brian Mulroney, a bilingual Quebecer who had never sought elected office, to gain control of an essentially Western party.

Conventional wisdom in Canada increasingly asserts that no unilingual person can ever again head a major party or even, apparently, occupy such a prominent position as that of Speaker of the House of Commons. This means that Western Canadians cannot replicate a typical American political career, whereby a successful person may enter politics in mid-life, like George Bush or Jimmy Carter. Only the atypical few who have learned French will be eligible. These will tend to be apparatchiks like Joe Clark, co-opted by the Ottawa establishment. "The Canada that Mr. [René] Lévesque wants to separate from no longer exists," Joe Clark told Quebecers during the 1980 campaign on the Parti Québécois referendum. But what happened to the Canada to which the West wished to belong?

In reorienting national politics towards Quebec, a response partly dictated by the peculiar operation of Canadian political institutions, Canada's élite have risked making Westerners the "large, cohesive minority" alienated from "a consensus the terms of which have been altered in its disfavor"—the very force that Pierre Trudeau identified in his *Federalism and the French Canadians* as underlying Quebec separatism.

The parliamentary system, with its permanent party leadership, its absence of primaries, and its infrequent elections, severely inhibits democratic insurgencies of the type that, in the United States, produced a Goldwater, a McGovern, or a Reagan. Nevertheless, Western alienation has become an important trace element in Canadian politics. Just as Quebec did in the 1950s, so the West in the 1980s has seen a proliferation of particularist and separatist splinter groups, some of which have occasionally achieved not insignificant electoral results, including the brief occupation of a seat in the Alberta legislature. These groups are, of course, ignored in Central Canada, but they worry Western politicians, who are uneasily aware of the region's long tradition of prairie fires that suddenly immolate established political dynasties.

Its alienation and political vagaries aside, the West will inexorably assume a more important role in Canadian politics. The reason is demographic. In 1901, the four Western provinces constituted only about 10 per cent of Canada's population. Ontario claimed 40 per cent, Quebec 30 per cent, and the Maritimes 20 per cent. By 1981, the West had risen to 27 per cent of the population, for the first time exceeding Quebec (26 per cent). Ontario claimed nearly 37 per cent, and the Maritimes had declined into insignificance with only 10 per cent.

What this means is that Canadian politics is becoming a three-actor system. The long Liberal hegemony has been based on an alliance between the provinces of Ontario and Quebec, which between them could dominate Canada. In the future, it will be increasingly possible for either to break away and govern Canada in alliance with the West. Paradoxically, this new system is already visible in the coalition underlying the Mulroney government's decision to seek a free trade agreement with the United States: the West and the Quebec élite strongly favoured free trade; the Ontario provincial government and much of the Toronto élite did not. The coalition increased its visibility as a determining force in the 1988 election triumph of Mulroney and the Tories.

Thus, it is possible that the West may be able to force fundamental change in the Canadian system. In the end, Canadians may have to do the bedrock thinking about federalism that Americans did two centuries ago. They may yet have a chance to shake off the insidious dream of a unitary state and create a loosely organized polity dedicated to individual freedom and the arts of peace—what Ronald Reagan invariably used to call "a city on a hill."

Part V

Canada and the World

For a nation that seems so absorbed with its regional problems or, equally, obsessed with every twitch of its elephantine American neighbor, Canada expends a surprising amount of effort working the corridors of international diplomacy, burnishing its image as a modest peace-seeker (and frequently peacekeeper) on the world scene. While others brandish the bomb, Canada dispenses balm.

With minimal moral posturing, Canada manages, through the pragmatic ways of its diplomats, to stay in the forefront of the handful of middle powers that spend their time calming the viler tempers in the world, trying behind the scenes to separate argumentative adversaries before the blood flows. Canadians, quite capable of destabilizing their own communities over language or other cultural disputes, are unusually adept at spreading coolness and good sense through the councils of the world. Released from their own confining provincialism and the paternal tether of the United States, they appear to thrive in international and multilateral settings.

Canada sees itself not only as honest broker of the superpowers' conflicting interests, but as a judicious and dispassionate counsel in East–West disputes. As NATO ally and northern neighbor, Canada is careful not to ruffle unduly the eagle's feathers over strategic and nuclear arms issues between the United States and Russia. But neither does it share the paranoia that often colors the superpowers' perceptions of one another, a point that Canada's former Ambassador to Moscow, Geoffrey Pearson, made in a talk several years ago to the Americas Society.

While it positions itself solidly in the Western camp, Canada promotes its own arms control and disarmament agenda, not all parts of which are consonant with those of the Administration in Washington. As Canada's Ambassador for Disarmament, Douglas Roche, observed in a 1985 Americas Society speech, his country has attached much more importance to maintaining the integrity of the 1972 Anti-Ballistic Missile (ABM) Treaty between the superpowers—so much so that, while Ottawa quietly acquiesced in the Reagan Administration's decision to forge ahead with the Strategic Defense Initiative (SDI), it eschewed any government-to-government effort in support of SDI research.

In this section, six Canadian and American contributors appraise Canada's role and policies as a middle power; the special influence it brings to bear in helping defuse international conflicts; and the limits and potential, the success and failure Canada has experienced as hemispheric neighbor, strategic ally, United Nations peacekeeper and diplomatic conscience to the world.

Gérard Pelletier

The Multilateralist Role
of the Middle Power

Defining a middle power—and Canada, for better or worse, has inherited that role in current world affairs—is as difficult as trying to define middle age. Canadians are in the habit of describing their country as "la plus petite des grandes puissances ou la plus grande des petites": the smallest of the large powers or the largest of the small ones.

Middle should not be confused with middling; nor is Canada by any stretch of the imagination a superpower on the scale of the United States or the Soviet Union. It has probably not yet achieved status in that category of major powers which lies between the super- and middle powers: France, West Germany, Japan, China and the United Kingdom. We Canadians are too modest to place ourselves in the same league with those countries whose economies, military might and populations are at least twice our own, even if our territory and natural resources may be equal to theirs.

Thus we have the four categories of power—super, major, middle, small—that comprise the international structure in strategic terms. But what factors determine which category applies to a nation of, say, Canada's dimension and experience?

Initial determining factors are territory, population and economic viability, including natural resources, scientific and technological capabilities, and military power, including the possession of nuclear weapons. At the same time, a country's relative importance depends on factors that are not as easily quantified as gross national product or army divisions. There is a nation's culture and traditions to consider. As our Secretary of State, Mark MacGuigan, recently observed,

> The capacity of nations to survive and prosper is conditioned in large part by their understanding of conditions and events in the world beyond their borders; and by their flexibility in fashioning their institutions and policies to make survival possible in the world at large.

Such understanding depends to a certain extent not only on the number of computers a country possesses and the general quality of its communications, but more so on the quality of its schools and universities, the scope and creativity of its artists.

In light of those considerations, it is right, I think, to describe Canada as a middle power, a title shared with such countries as Australia, Brazil, India, Italy, Mexico and others, despite the many considerable differences that exist within that group. What makes Canada's participation in world affairs so different from that of other middle powers is largely due to the unique conditions of Canada's place in the international firmament. The application of Canadian foreign policy by successive governments has been largely an exercise in skillful exploitation of the possibilities and constraints inherent in Canada's special situation.

We have, in common with other middle powers, a deep commitment to multilateral institutions. This is principally because our limited influence makes it often uncomfortable and frustrating to deal on a bilateral basis with super- and major powers. A tête-à-tête with one of those "big brothers" is not always a pleasant experience. As Woody Allen once said, paraphrasing the Biblical passage, "The lion will share the lamb's bed, but the lamb won't sleep very well." Middle powers show a distinct preference for multilateral fora in which numerous countries of varying size and influence can make their voices heard. While they are not about to substitute multilateral for bilateral relations, they regard multilateralism as an additional and indispensable dimension to their foreign policy, one to which they attach far more importance than do the major or the superpowers.

Canada is no exception. The commitment we have made to the United Nations (UN) from its inception, the constant support we have provided to this institution, have their roots in our status as a middle power. We prefer to think of ourselves as idealists, patient listeners and negotiators. No doubt, we would exhibit less idealism, a lesser disposition to listen to others and less patience in international negotiations if we were a super- or a major power. Nations like the Soviet Union or the United States have a tremendous capacity to lead, to make others react to their policies and actions while, at the other end of the scale, the small powers find themselves in a position that is totally defensive and reactive. The middle powers are far from helpless, but neither can they afford to operate independently or in isolation. They need the association with others in order to play a more influential role. They entertain no illusions about their capacity to change the course of human events, just as they require no explanation of the course of interdependence among nations. They feel all this in their bones.

How then does a middle power like Canada pursue its interests, given the opportunities and constraints of international diplomacy and power play? The term "honest broker," which has been applied to Canada, may suffer from overuse, but it remains valid in terms of the role Canada has actively played over the past quarter-century in the UN. Since the days of the first UN peacekeeping force in the Middle East, an initiative for which Canadian Prime Minister Lester B. Pearson won the Nobel Peace Prize in 1957, Canada has been perceived as the quintessential middle power. It has never borne the burden or onus of having been a colonial power; it enjoys sound political relations with virtually every nation in the world; its economic interests and predilections are not seen as a particular threat or challenge to other states or blocs. Canada is, instead, regarded as a country that can be relied on to play an intermediary role on a broad number of issues, a role that might be best described as catalytic.

Canada's ability to perform with distinction in multilateral settings is a reflection of the totality of its foreign policy. The influence it manages to exert is a function of the consistently judicious positions it has taken over time on political and economic issues, multilaterally and bilaterally; of the policy and operation of its foreign aid program; and of the personalities, interests and reputations of its political leaders, and the expertise of its officials.

Canada has neither the pretence nor the power for world leadership. Canadians believe they approach international relations with an appreciation for the interests of all the parties in any negotiation, and that they do so with sound principles and common sense. There seems to be widespread recognition of this Canadian approach within multilateral institutions and, thus, it provides an avenue of influence for Canada. As the late mayor of New York, Fiorello H. LaGuardia, said in 1946, while urging the UN Social and Humanitarian Affairs Commission to resolve a thorny issue before it: "We've got to bring this thing to a head. I will take sight unseen any resolution which the Canadian delegate will propose."

The times and Canada have changed since then, but Canadians' view of their contribution and esteem in the world is still captured in that quotation. Lest you believe, however, that Canadians are the ultimate altruists in diplomacy, oblivious to their own national interests, be reminded of Lester Pearson's classic aphorism. "Diplomacy," he once said, "is letting someone else have your way."

Aside from the opportunities and constraints common to middle powers in general, Canada has its own special reasons for performing multilateral arrangements. There are four in particular that no Canadian government or statesman can ignore.

The first is Canada's proximity to the United States and the fact that Canada is the foremost trading partner of America, the world's largest economy. That circumstance alone would make Canada's position in the world unduly special. People may assume Japan is a more important trading partner of the United States, but the fact remains that Canada constitutes the United States' largest supplier and customer. Nor can Canadians ignore the fact that American corporate interests own a lion's share of Canada's economy and that Canadian foreign trade would be modest in the extreme if the United States were to stop buying from us. Canadians know that they owe an exceedingly large part of their prosperity and high standard of living to commercial exchanges across their southern border.

Canadians may thank God that the principal foreign owner of their assets is the United States, a nation with which they share so many values and interests. At the same time, they cannot help wondering at what point a society loses the freedom of its political decision-making when so many economic decisions are made for it from abroad. There is also the danger that Canada risks being identified in the minds of other countries as possessing no distinct identity or policies of its own. Our Secretary of State for External Affairs, speaking in the House of Commons, observed that, "For Canadians, the art of conducting relations with the United States is to cooperate in the development of what is in most ways a fruitful and mutually beneficial relationship, while safeguarding Canada's paramount national interests." An irony of the relationship, he added, is that "the very similarities which exist between Canadians and Americans can make the inevitable problems which arise more difficult to resolve." To Americans, that last may seem contradictory, but to Canadians it makes a lot of sense.

A second reason for Canada's affinity for collective arrangements lies with our nation's peculiar problems of national security. Geographically situated between the two superpowers, endowed with the second-largest national territory on earth and therefore the second-longest borders to protect, Canada can neither remain neutral nor rely on its relatively small population to mount a plausible defence against a potential attacker. Collective security, through participation in the North Atlantic Treaty Organization (NATO) and the North American Aerospace Defence (Command) (NORAD) is the only solution. Otherwise, Canada would be either desperately exposed or almost totally dependent on the United States for its defence.

There was a time when a significant section of Canadian public opinion was bitterly opposed to NATO, but over the years the realities of our national security requirements came to be recognized by the vast majority of Canadians. Opposition to NATO or NORAD was replaced by a realization that, within such mutual defence alliances, Canada can exert an influence not only on matters directly concerning its own security, but also on issues crucial to world peace. Canada is not, of course, a military power of great consequence. However, its military role in peacekeeping operations, its early decision *not* to become a nuclear-weapons state when it had that capability after the Second World War, and its militant advocacy of disarmament have, I believe, given the nation a distinct image.

Thirdly, Canadian history and the bilingual composition of our country have led us to further involvements of a multilateral nature, specifically Canada's membership and prominence in both the British Commonwealth and la Francophonie, the union of French-speaking nations of the world.

When the British Empire was replaced after the war by the Commonwealth, that association of newly independent nations formerly governed by Great Britain, Canada itself was coming of age and seeking to play a transforming role in the international sphere. It was only natural that it should turn to countries like India and Pakistan, so lately under British rule, since it shared with them a belief in democracy as well as similar political institutions. The result was the advent of the Colombo plan, Canada's first major venture in the field of foreign aid and development. Next came the blossoming of relations with the Commonwealth countries of the Caribbean Basin, where Canadians had been doing business since the dawn of the century, then with East Africa and, eventually, most of the developing member-states of the Common-wealth with which Canada became engaged in diplomatic relations as well as development projects.

At about this time, too, francophone Canada responded to the need to reach out beyond the confines of Quebec to those coun-tries with which it shared a common language and culture. As a linguistic minority within Canada and the North American continent, French Cana-dians were vitally aware of the new francophone institutions being devel-oped throughout the world, following peace in 1945—institutions designed to promote a culture shared by French Canadians, as well as to utilize that common heritage for cooperation, development and exchanges between the emerging francophone nations. Thus, the dual nature of Canada's origins, the bicultural and bilingual makeup of its population, account for its special ties with the Commonwealth and la Francophonie. The member-states of both institutions are located on four or more continents. Together, they constitute for Canada still further evidence that, in such international fora, a middle power tends to carry more weight, performs more usefully for others and pursues its own national interest with more vigour and efficiency.

In an article he wrote for the French quarterly *Politique internationale*, Prime Minister Trudeau explained why Canada attached so high a priority to the Commonwealth and la Francophonie: in both associations, Canada constituted the largest non-European developed country among the members. That, in turn, afforded Canadians an unusual opportunity to further the North–South dialogue within both groups. This leads to the fourth and concluding reason for Canada's multi-lateralist posture.

One of the main thrusts of Canadian foreign policy is to champion the concept of global negotiations. At various conferences, Canada has given ample evidence of that preoccupation. We are a middle power of contrasts and contradictions that render us strangely vulnerable, yet also sympathetic to the problems of other countries. Canada shares the advantages and inconveniences of being simultaneously a developed and developing society, highly industrialized and affluent, yet largely foreign-owned and dependent on foreign capital to develop its enormous resources. Because of that, we feel we enjoy a privileged position, better able than most to understand the issues and feelings of the "have" and "have-not" nations of both the North and South, and to play a significant role in that dialogue at this crucial juncture.

A final warning with regard to the deceptively modest stand that Canadians take in world affairs: if we are careful to claim nothing less but nothing more for the influence that goes with our middle-power status, it is because we believe that bidding for more would expose us to ridicule, while being satisfied with less would be cheating ourselves as well as our allies. Scratch the superficial modesty of most Canadians, however, and you will uncover sizable ambitions. It is just a matter of time and patience. Within ourselves we feel confident that, in a couple of centuries or so, all this foolish talk about Canada as the typical middle power will be, well, passé.

McGeorge Bundy

Canada, the Exceptionally Favored: An American Perspective

Americans, at once too close and too far removed, may not be the best qualified of people to render accurate perceptions of Canada. My own experience—I once approved a White House communiqué that led to the downfall of a Canadian Prime Minister, John Diefenbaker—has been one of some distance from the kind of understanding of Canada one ought to have before engaging in so challenging a subject. The fact is, Americans, unlike Canadians, tend to trip around the world seeking popular benediction in the vein of a well-known New York mayor who perennially queried, "How'm I doing?" Among Canadians, particularly within the circle of their coolly expert diplomats, one seldom hears that refrain.

A visitor from outer space, equipped with even the most elementary indices of this planet's leading nations, would halt in his tracks when he reached Canada, stunned by the combination of statistics indicating that country's extraordinary dimensions: immense size physically, with a relatively small population; large gross national product per capita; low expenditure on military operations and defense; relatively generous programs of development assistance to less endowed countries;

relatively low levels of internal tension compared to those of other societies; a highly stable form of government.

The visitor would also express astonishment that, in a world of fiercely separate nation-states, here is one that, by all the ordinary criteria, appears to comprise not one but at least two nations, and yet, remarkably, holds together. It would be surprising if the visitor did not mark this country as both exceptional and exceptionally favored.

Yet, this is not, of course, the only way of perceiving Canada.

Stalin, explaining his view of Germany to President Roosevelt's aide, Harry Hopkins, is said to have remarked: "You Americans are very lucky—you have weak neighbors." There is a certain brutal truth in that analysis by a leader who was totally obsessed with his own power, the security of the Soviet state, and the question of how to extend both. His is a profoundly erroneous analysis for reasons I will explain shortly, but it is certainly not an improbable inference, even today, of how the leadership in the Kremlin regards America's northern neighbor.

Canada is also naturally perceived as a fast friend and ally of America's, although the bilateral relationship has seen a marked shift over the long term toward a greater degree of distancing and the exercise of independent judgment on Canada's part. Canadians with far greater frequency now render self-determined opinions on matters in which we Americans are considered to have a predominant interest. Yet, it is still as a close continental ally and supporter of America and its ideals that Canada continues to exert an impressive intermediary role in many parts of the world. It was not that long ago, for example, that Canada served, relatively speaking, as the pro-American member of the International Control Commission, which worked valiantly but in vain to maintain the fragile peace that had been established in Indo-China in the 1950s.

Throughout recent history, Canadians have managed to grace the world scene as diplomats blessed with special access to the American power structure. During the Korean War, they played this role skillfully, if at times to the irritation of our then Secretary of State, Dean Acheson. Similar circumstances are bound to recur. Were I an adversary of the Americans, bearing a message I wanted those wretched people in Washington to understand, I would find it opportune for my purposes to put that communication on the Canadian diplomatic channel, for the singular professionalism and accuracy of Canadian diplomatic reporting are legendary. The Canadians have the capacity to communicate a level of understanding of the American position that is as balanced as it is fairly nuanced; it is hardly the kind of reporting that would have characterized the transmissions, say, of Krishna Menon, India's foreign minister, during the Korean War years. Canadians are exceedingly well positioned not only to transmit the message accurately, but to gloss it both ways.

Another observation about the Canadians' impact on the world scene is that they belong to everything. There is hardly an international agency extant that does not have a Canadian presence. Many an agency has experienced Canadian leadership over the years; many more probably would have, had Canada not become so closely identified with the United States and, to a degree, American aspirations. One is reminded of that post-war period when many influential Americans favored the appointment of Canada's Lester Pearson as the first Secretary-General of the North Atlantic Treaty Organization (NATO). It did not happen. At the same time, Pearson and Canada figured prominently in the formation of the United Nations (UN) following the war. Canada was also one of the trio of nations that made the fateful (and not entirely correct) decision in November 1945 to place the effort for international control of atomic energy under the aegis of the UN.

The capacity of Canadians for participating in these kinds of international fora is highly developed, thanks to decades of practice along with what appears to be a consensus of support, or at least benign neglect, on the part of Canadian public opinion. In the area of development aid to other countries, particularly, Canada's efforts have achieved a scale that is remarkable. The Canadian contribution has been characterized by exceptional professional performance and an ability to maintain programs of technical assistance and cooperation that is the envy of those in Washington who struggle to keep these kinds of programs alive and kicking on the American foreign policy agenda. Why two societies, Canadian and American, which are so similar in many ways, diverge so markedly in their approach to foreign aid, requires too long an explanation. The fact remains that, in the world of development assistance, Canada's performance has shone.

The Canadians have also played a significant intermediary role of sorts in the affairs of the Commonwealth. There was a time, for example, when the government in Ottawa performed important services in keeping Washington and London from misunderstanding each other out of a false assumption that both were speaking the same language. Mike Pearson, who deservedly won the Nobel award for his successful efforts in the aftermath of the Suez crisis in the late 1950s, later recalled the stakes that were in play during his operations then. A primary motive was not only the restoration of peace—the ending of an adventure that Pearson regarded as enormously self-destructive for Britain and France, the twin parents of Canada in political and cultural terms. It was critically important as well, he felt, to repair the breach which the ill-fated Suez operation had opened between Britain and the United States.

Seen from afar, then, Canada has played a disproportionately large and active participatory role in world affairs. Why this should be, the outsider can only speculate. Perhaps the cause relates to Canada's having endured so much trouble and strife of its own, having had to learn so much the hard way as it struggled to maintain a peaceable kingdom within its own borders. The diversity of Canada's political-cultural origins, the historical and ongoing attempt to preserve national unity in the face of differing regional attitudes and separatist tendencies—these have contributed to Canada's long experience in learning to reconcile apparently irreconcilable positions. They have admirably equipped Canada with a pragmatism, unencumbered by impeding principle, to participate effectively in all kinds of international endeavors. Canada's constructive impact on the world scene has been amply demonstrated through nearly two generations since the Second World War.

No small part of this success is attributable to the fact that Canadians, broadly speaking, are trusted. In bilateral relations, where they are no better or worse than anyone else, their diplomacy has tended to lack tact; in international relations, however, they have shown how persuasive a role subtle mediation can play.

Nations defending their own interests, particularly democratic societies, tend to behave very much alike. But, in international operations, where more than one interest is represented, the mediating talent assumes special distinction. Experience has disposed many of us to see in Canadian representatives the character and skills of the honest broker. Even in bilateral matters, on those economic issues that create conflict within our relationship, we have found Canadians good people to bargain with. They lack the insecurity which so often breeds misunderstanding and deception. Indeed, that is precisely why Diefenbaker was exceptional. It was *our* failure to understand how exceptional he was that led us to overreact. The fact that he was exceptional also led the Canadian democratic process in the end to disown him: first, from within Diefenbaker's own Progressive Conservative Party, then in the federal election of 1963.

Henry Kissinger, Secretary of State under President Nixon and one of my successors as National Security Adviser at the White House, remarked quite accurately that Canada has played a far greater role in international economic and political affairs than her size or the engagement of her public opinion at home would have led one to expect. Overall, it has been a self-reinforcing process, one that on balance is regarded with respect by other countries.

Despite its affinity for international fora, Canada has not sought to establish its presence universally. Indeed, Canada's attachment to some associations has been wary, to say the least, beginning with the Commonwealth itself. It is no secret that Prime Minister Mackenzie King spent much of his time maneuvering to stay just beyond the grasp of Her Majesty's first government in the new United Kingdom. Nor has Canada's association with the southern part of this hemisphere advanced significantly, despite its noteworthy inclusion in the Americas Society's Center for Inter-American Relations.

The Kennedy Administration should not have preached the Alliance for Progress to Canada as it did in the early 1960s. It may be one of our relatively milder perpetrations, but it is still annoying to others when Americans assume that what is good for them has to be good for everyone else on the continent. Thus, when President Kennedy, in his address to Canada's House of Commons, raised the topic of Canadian participation in the Alliance for Progress, we were disappointed at the tepid response. There appeared to be little corresponding

Canadian interest in our concern for, or entanglements with, our Latin American neighbors. In the intervening years, of course, we have seen a marked increase in Canadian attention to Latin America, most especially in the Caribbean where Canadian government assistance and the commercial expertise of Canada's private sector have been jointly, and effectively, applied toward a host of development projects.

One may ponder the kind of evolution Canada faces in the future. How will the world perceive it?

Normally not a newsmaker, Canada has received substantial press attention in recent years due to the issue of Quebec and the specter of its separation from the Canadian union. That story, if anything, has been overplayed. Grounds for optimism about a successful outcome seem firmer than the prognoses of the doomsayers. Canadian commentator Bruce Hutchinson came closer to being correct when he concluded that the forces holding Canada together are considerably stronger than those fostering the notion that an independent or sovereign Quebec is ordained. The world may yet come to think otherwise. Still, one hopes that exaggerated concerns by Americans on this issue are misplaced.

Among Canada's considerable strengths are its Western tradition of self-government and the tremendous resilience of its society as a whole. The abiding belief of that society is that wrongs should be redressed—be they the social injustices inflicted on French-speaking Quebecers in the past or the economic inequities that Western Canadians complain of—rather than the structure torn down and refashioned. Canada has no tradition of revolution, unlike France, one of the two nations from which Canada was formed. Rather, there is in Canada an expectation of political resolution, a sense of continuity in all kinds of traditions.

Thus, it would not occur to a Canadian, any more than to an American, that those associations within his or her country, many of which may now be celebrating their centenaries, will not be enjoying their bicentenaries in time to come; that universities entering their second century will not sooner or later enter their third; that the professions, the unions, and the other operational elements of a pluralistic society will not, on the whole, be recognizably themselves in another fifty years, instead of having metamorphosed into oblivion. Canadians, in short, inhabit a buoyant society, one that possesses an internal coherence as well as the binding energy derived from a distaste for contemplating something radically different.

The key to Canada's future conduct in world affairs may be to expect no dramatic shifts, but rather an evolution of attitude, a movement away from the currently pervasive sense that, most of the time, it is wise not to stray too far from established American positions on a range of international issues. That may not always turn out to be the right or judicious course, because most of the issues that divide America and Canada, leaving aside those of a strictly economic cast, also tend to create divisions within our respective countries. It is a curious facet of Canada–U.S. relations that on so many controversial international issues—arms control, nuclear-weapons policy, NATO strength levels, economic-trade tensions between the industrialized powers, and North–South relations—one recognizes not only differences between our two governments that may change in shape from one administration to another in both capitals, but also differences inside the opinion circles of both countries.

Canada, it seems to me, is moving inexorably toward a more visible autonomy in its foreign policy, a larger willingness to be critical of the United States. My own experience tells me that this change can be helpful, although it is important to think about the process of achieving it.

Prime Minister Pearson, it is worth recalling, had very sound and far-sighted views with respect to Southeast Asia and our involvement in Vietnam. At the same time, I think it was a mistake to have expressed those views, as he did, in a speech in Pennsylvania while he was en route to Washington for a luncheon meeting with President Johnson. It was my misfortune to have been the third person present at that lunch, not the most agreeable experience of my time in Washington. The difficulty was not in what Pearson had said, but *where* he had said it.

Two alternatives were available then, and remain so today, for that kind of communication: private diplomacy or, with sufficient warning to the intended target of the criticism, the issuing of a statement in one's own country that clearly reflects the political necessity of such action by a democratic leader. In the end, that is simply a matter of tactics. The larger point to be made is that the requirement in the era of Pearson and Lyndon Johnson—that the protocols as well as the substance of Canadian–American unity be observed by the principals—is not the same now.

Even if we are entering a period of substantially increased tension between Moscow and Washington, it is unlikely that we will experience in the Western alliance the sort of esprit that may have affected the judgments and decisions of governments in earlier decades: that is, the sense that the allies must all rally round the United States because of the importance of being seen to support the Alliance leader. On the contrary, Canada will become a little less visibly the friend of the United States, a little more an independent voice. And that will be to the general good as well as to the advantage of the larger power. Not that the larger power will always perceive such independence in generous and enlightened terms; but that kind of irritation comes frequently, and it is seldom the test of international understanding. The fact is that, given the many currents of understanding, sympathy, and communication that flow across the 49th parallel, the risk of a breakdown in Canada–U.S. relations because of increasing Canadian self-determination is small.

The visitor from outer space would therefore judge correctly that the Canadian nation is exceptional and exceptionally favored, and that such a position is not by any stretch the least desirable from which to proclaim an independent voice in the world's affairs.

The scholar, the writer, and the artist in Canada, those who are in some ways most sensitive to the shape and direction of Canadian life, might be less optimistic about the future, as it often seems they are. I would not let that artistic or sociological judgment make me withdraw my optimistic assessment of Canada's promise on the world scene, any more than I would let the novels of Sinclair Lewis determine my view of America's behavior in world affairs as it might have been predicted at the time when Lewis's *Main Street* was first published in the 1930s.

But I would venture a concluding observation that the relation between the quality, spirit, and style of Canadian life today and the quite extraordinary, outsized role that Canada has played, and can continue to play, internationally in the years ahead, may pose an uncomfortable challenge for that society before the next century.

James H. Taylor

Bilateral Relations in the Global Context: A Canadian Perspective

National perspectives do not appear out of the blue; they are born of history. When the distinguished Canadian novelist, Robertson Davies, addressed an audience of Americans recently at the National Arts Club in New York, he said of Canada: "Our history is not like yours. You were born of revolution, our roots are deep in dogged loyalty." Confessing his United Empire Loyalist ancestry, Davies went on to say that "even now, when I visit New York, I have a haunting fear that I may be detected as an unrepentant Tory, and tarred and feathered." I trust, of course, that Americans stopped that unwholesome practice long ago.

Within this Western Hemisphere—a phrase which to this day does not come as easily to Canadians as to Americans—we Canadians have indeed clung to our roots. This is true of both my English- and French-speaking compatriots. British institutions, despite some adaptations to our national needs and character, have survived largely intact. Americans visiting Quebec will note the phrase "Je me souviens" ("I remember") imprinted on automobile licence plates. Those words encapsulate the feelings of French Canadians for the tumultuous history and change that have marked the evolution of modern Quebec. Nor is it only those of British and French stock who have sought this continuity. Canada's native peoples, many of whom never signed treaties with the British Crown, are negotiating to have what they see as their historical right to self-government entrenched in the Canadian Constitution.

The millions of immigrants who have journeyed to our shores in search of a better life and who are encouraged to retain their customs, though not their old feuds, round out what has been described as the "cultural mosaic" of contemporary Canada. Only through a process of give-and-take have Canadians been able to find strength in their diversity. Thus, we have become a nation of consensus-builders. Weaned on the often bruising realities of federal–provincial relations, we have been better trained than most for the hard bargaining of international diplomacy.

Canada's commitment to internationalism and the rule of law can be fully understood only through an appreciation of the history of our relations with the United States.

Canadians and Americans last crossed swords in the War of 1812. The only time since then that we have even come close to blows was in 1895, over a border dispute in South America. But those were aberrations in a relationship that has been remarkable for the peaceful resolution of disputes by negotiation and arbitration. Already, in the early years of this century, our border had become unique among nations, a dividing line so accepted that it has been described in recent years as the longest undefended cliché in the world. Canada and the United States were the archetypical "good neighbours."

Canada's experience with its more powerful but friendly neighbour gave rise to an almost unbridled optimism in the early 1900s. Canadians held fervently to the model of international relations that was then called the North American Idea. In 1914, William Lyon Mackenzie King, later to become, intermittently, Canada's longest-governing Prime Minister, declared at an international conference on arbitration that

> we have an opportunity to show the world by this unfortified line running between the two great countries, by this century of peace, [that] we on this continent have helped to work out the accomplishment of an epoch in the cause of Christianity itself.

Unmindful of King's words and his continental model, the European powers went to war a few months later.

In a sense, Canada came of age internationally when it signed in its own right the Treaty of Versailles ending the First World War. Hundreds of thousands of Canadians had fought in that bloody conflict. We were, however, bitterly disappointed when the United States failed to share our vision of the League of Nations and the balance of power. As Canadians saw it, this was a golden opportunity to remake the world on the basis of the North American Idea and to guarantee the peace by coupling the power of the United States with that of the British Empire. Then, as now, isolationism in America was anathema for Canadian foreign policy, a negation of our concept of a secure and just world order.

After the Second World War, Canadians were even more determined to contribute to the establishment of a stable world order. We had pulled our weight during six years of hostilities and emerged with some promising ideas and a useful degree of influence. All of our diplomatic resources and whatever ingenuity we possessed were committed to our universalist and Atlanticist visions, to the United Nations (UN) and to the North Atlantic Treaty Organization (NATO). We were driven all the more by the stark reality that, for Canada in the nuclear age, there could be no security without collective security. Renouncing nuclear weapons for ourselves, we exchanged them in effect for collective security. To protect North America from the growing Soviet missile threat, we joined with the United States in the creation of the North American Aerospace Defence (Command) (NORAD). Under the UN flag, we fought in Korea. Canada's commitment to collective peace-keeping has thus been deep and abiding: we are the only country to have taken part in every UN peacekeeping operation since that body first initiated them.

Canada was also present at the creation of the post-war economic order, which found expression in the General Agreement on Tariffs and Trade (GATT) and in the Bretton Woods agreements. Originally, the Canadian government had set its sights on an International Trade Organization with supranational powers, but in the end it settled happily for liberalized trade based on multilateral negotiation. The 1935

Canada–U.S. trade agreement, which helped lead the way out of Depression-era protectionism, became a building block for GATT.

Canada has always been a trading nation, exporting proportionally far more of its gross domestic product than the United States. Our economic security, like that of the United States, has depended on an open and stable international trade regime.

Although this is not widely known, Canada and the United States, immediately after the Second World War, were on the verge of concluding a bilateral free trade agreement, as they are now. Economic interdependence, however, had not reached the point that it has in today's world, and Canada withdrew, basically for political reasons. The idea of a special trading relationship with the United States had been a contentious issue in Canada since the nineteenth century, with Canadians averaging at least one major national debate on the subject every generation. In 1911, for example, the Liberal government of Sir Wilfrid Laurier fell as a result of advocating free trade between Canada and the United States. Therefore, the present (Progressive Conservative) government's initiative in proposing a major trade negotiation with the United States is in keeping with the long history of commercial relations between the two countries reaching back well over a century.

All this helps to explain our perspective on Canada–U.S. relations and the world. We remain deeply attached to our vision of a model bilateral relationship with the United States, within a broader context of multilateralism and collective security, the whole underpinned by the rule of law as well as by consultations and negotiated compromises in the conduct of international affairs.

Canadians, it is true, like to think of themselves as being positioned strategically in the middle of things: a middle power; a moderating influence; a peacekeeper; a helpful fixer; a bridge-builder. While sharing many of the same values and interests as the United States, we lay no claim to the reality of interdependence, and indeed our foreign policy is largely concerned with "managing interdependence." Call it altruism, self-interest or realism—that, in short, is the Canadian perspective on international relations. Above all, as a regional power without a region, we have had to learn to manage our North American interdependence with our sole neighbour, a country ten times as populous and rich as ours.

Canada's foreign policy under Prime Minister Brian Mulroney is firmly rooted in our internationalist traditions. Indeed, his policy is designed specifically as one of constructive internationalism, and a major parliamentary review, with public hearings held across the country, has confirmed that the great majority of Canadians subscribe to his policy's basic tenets.

In the UN, Canada has laboured hard to bring greater pragmatism and financial realism to that organization, for Canadians remain deeply committed to it and to working within it. For all its faults, the UN remains the authentic voice of the world community. Its specialized agencies perform invaluable work and, as a collective unit and the one forum that concerns all the world's countries, it is uniquely positioned to advance the international rule of law in such spheres as the Law of the Sea and the peaceful uses of outer space.

Canada also participates actively in an impressive array of multilateral institutions, including the Commonwealth and la Francophonie, an association of states that use French as their official language. In 1987, we serve as the host country for the summit meetings of both these groups, and in 1988 as host to the Economic Summit of the Group of Seven (G-7) nations (the United States, Japan, West Germany, Britain, France, Canada and Italy) for the second time since that institution was created.

Canada remains deeply committed to the concept of Atlanticism, to the coupling of North America and Western Europe, and to strategic deterrence. In NATO, we have increased our contribution of troops stationed in Europe and markedly improved their equipment. The number of Canadian servicemen there remains small but of high quality. As an effective military contribution to those forces at the disposal of the NATO commanders, they also demonstrate Canada's political commitment to the collective defence of the North Atlantic Treaty area. On this continent, we have renewed the NORAD agreement and embarked with the United States on constructing a state-of-the-art North Warning System in the Arctic to replace the Distant Early Warning (DEW) line. We are currently conducting a comprehensive review of our defence policy, which should lead in coming years to an enhanced contribution by Canada to the collective defence effort of the Western allies.

Our belief in collective defence leads us to insist that changes to Canadian strategic policies must be a matter for the most intensive intra-alliance consultations. The Reagan Administration's Strategic Defence Initiative (SDI) is one such issue. For its part, Canada has taken the position that SDI research is prudent in light of the Soviet Union's research in strategic defence. At the same time, we have urged the Soviet Union and the United States to continue to abide by the terms of their Anti-Ballistic Missile (ABM) Treaty, which in our view has been a stabilizing force for arms control, underpinning the prospects for arms reductions. We foresee the possibility of more important arms control and disarmament agreements that would ratify a new strategic balance, one that ideally would be more stable and fixed at a lower level of armaments. Meanwhile, Canada feels that the existing framework of agreements should remain in place until something offering greater security can be negotiated and installed.

East–West relations remain as primordial a concern for Canada as for the United States. The great strength of the West has been the active cooperation of the allies, which is based in turn, ultimately, on the support of public opinion in our countries. We are entering a period when unity of purpose within the Alliance could be more important than ever. Consultation will be critical. It will not be enough to support the presumption of an unchanging threat. We are witnessing a ferment of change in the Soviet Union today that may be without precedent since the 1917 revolution, or at the very least unprecedented since the early Khrushchev years. The Soviet leaders themselves appear uncertain as to what the change will ultimately produce. Who can say whether Gorbachev will be able to achieve the ambitious goals he has set for Soviet society?

We Canadians will remain cautious until we see concrete results—for example, in the international realm, Soviet disengagement from Afghanistan and Cambodia. We would then have more confidence in the possibility of a genuine détente, as opposed to the détente of the seventies that was founded on too many illusions about the speed with which East–West relations could be transformed.

The 1986 Reagan-Gorbachev summit meeting in Reykjavik was a seminal event. It indicated more clearly than before that, in arms control at least, parallel interests may be emerging in East–

West relations. For its own reasons, the Soviet Union appears now to be genuinely interested in reaching arms reduction agreements. President Reagan's "zero-zero option," which he proposed as long ago as 1981, and his proposals for radical reductions in strategic arms have become the focus of serious negotiations in Geneva. We remain hopeful that major breakthroughs will be achieved, especially in the area of strategic nuclear arms, which pose the major threat to Canada. We were heartened by the President's statement in his recent speech to the Canadian Parliament that, thanks to the firmness shown by the Alliance, the United States and the Soviet Union were now moving towards a breakthrough agreement that would dramatically reduce intermediate-range missiles in Europe and Asia.

Long active as well in North–South relations, Canada manages one of the world's larger aid development programs. This and our defence effort are the only two major programs that the government is allowing to expand; otherwise, its overriding priority is to reduce the nation's $30 billion deficit. We have recently put our aid program on an all-grant basis to improve the quality of our assistance. We have also authorized a moratorium on the repayment of aid loans by sub-Saharan countries that are willing to put their financial house in order. This last was an expression of our particular concern over the impact of huge debts on the development prospects of the world's poorest countries.

Over the years, Canada has forged an extraordinary network of links to the Third World, including those in regions where, historically, our nation has little trade or other direct stake. It began with India and Pakistan when those formerly British territories gained independence, and it continued with the progressive decolonization of the British and French empires. The ties remain strong, reflected in the Commonwealth and La Francophonie. Elsewhere, as in Latin America, Canada has similarly mounted growing aid and development programs.

With some frequency, too, we have been able to play a bridging role in North–South negotiations. Canada has always appreciated the sound relationship between development and security, but it has been less inclined than the United States to view regional problems through an East–West prism. In our view, many Third World conflicts, however they may become embroiled in East–West rivalry, owe their origins to local economic and social problems. The solutions to these problems, if they are to be durable, must also be local.

The Third World's experience, as colonies and dependencies of Western powers, has not always been an unremittingly happy one. Yet, it is to the West that most developing countries look first for support, even though they want to avoid getting caught up in East–West struggles. A superpower only in the military dimension, the Soviet Union has little to offer these countries except armaments. An economy that is under such strong attack from its own leadership hardly commends itself as a model for Third World development. It is incumbent on the West, then, to act responsibly and increase the effectiveness of its development assistance. We must continue to pursue coordinated, sensible and compassionate policies on Third World debt. At the same time, we must keep our markets open to Third World exports, for trade is more important to their development than aid. Our own economies also depend to some degree on the capacity of less developed nations to buy our products.

The recent nationwide hearings on our country's foreign policy revealed that Central America and South Africa were two of the areas of greatest public concern among Canadians.

In the Canadian perspective, economic and social conditions lie at the root of the conflict in Central America. The solution must come from the region itself. Canada has steadfastly opposed third-party intervention and the promotion of armed insurgency anywhere in Central America. At the same time, we have increased our development aid to the region and have strongly supported the regional peace initiative launched by the Contadora countries. We have also voiced our concerns about human rights abuses in certain Central American countries, and the spread of authoritarianism in Nicaragua.

In South Africa, the continuation of apartheid increases the prospect of the worst bloodbath since the Second World War. This was the unanimous conclusion of the Commonwealth Eminent Persons Group, which reported almost a year ago on the deteriorating situation. Canada, for its part, is trying to do its utmost to help convince the South African authorities to dismantle apartheid and enter into negotiations with authentic black leaders. The goal: formation of a non-racial and representative government. We have been active in developing measures by the Commonwealth governments to pressure Pretoria for change. The measures that have been adopted by the Commonwealth are similar to those subsequently enacted in the United States. Canada is prepared to go as far as breaking off all relations with the Pretoria government if fundamental change is not forthcoming in South Africa. Prime Minister Mulroney stated as much before the UN in 1985. So far, however, we have largely acted on a step-by-step basis in concert with others; that remains our preference.

We are substantially increasing our assistance to the victims of apartheid within South Africa, as well as to South Africa's neighbours. The repression in South Africa and the Pretoria government's destabilizing actions in the region have imposed heavy burdens on those within, as well as adjacent to, South Africa's borders. Over the next five years, Canada is committed to providing more than half a billion dollars in aid to Southern Africa to foster growth and reduce the economic dependence of the Front Line States on South Africa.

Prospects for progress remain dim, but we do not accept that descent into ever greater violence is inevitable. We are determined to keep communication channels open to all parties to the conflict, from the National Party to the African National Congress, with the goal of encouraging dialogue and peaceful change.

As for the international trading system, it is coming under some of the most severe strains it has experienced in the post-war period. The GATT contracting parties recently launched at Punta del Este what may be the most comprehensive round of multilateral trade negotiations ever. But burgeoning trade wars threaten to undo even what has been already achieved over decades. Protectionist pressures are growing, one reason for this being the failure among the major world economies to agree on policies.

In concrete terms, it is hard to envisage any lasting solution to trade imbalances that does not involve a massive reduction of the American budget deficit. Canada is deeply concerned by the draconian protectionist bills now before Congress because, in the long run, protectionism can only contract world trade and beggar everyone. We believe that we are getting it right in Canada by attacking our budget deficit, letting our dollar realign and keeping our market as open as possible. Meanwhile, we share the American view that Japan and Germany should consider stimulating more domestic demand and that Japan should open its market wider.

A bilateral free trade agreement, on which Canada and the United States have begun negotiations, would be to the great mutual benefit of both countries. For two nations sharing the largest trading relationship in the world—$130 billion (US) last year in goods alone— free trade would ultimately mean more investment and more employ- ment. An agreement between us would dismantle tariff and non-tariff barriers; our border would become duty-free as well as arms-free. The agreement would be compatible with our GATT negotiations, and could also spur trade liberalization through multinational companies by setting precedents for multilateral agreements in such areas as trade in services.

President Reagan has put the full weight of his Admin- istration behind a free trade agreement with Canada, describing it as a paradigm for all nations that now wrestle against the "siren tempta- tion of protectionism." The issues in the negotiations are many and diffi- cult, but we have reason to believe that, if Canada and the United States recognize what is in their own best interests, they will soon approve and enact an historic trade agreement.

We also have reasonable hope that the United States will join Canada in taking serious action against the scourge of acid rain. The issue is viewed in Canada as a litmus test of the government's approach to Canada–U.S. relations.

President Reagan has agreed to consider Prime Minister Mulroney's proposal for a bilateral accord that would provide a marked reduction in the transborder flows of air-borne pollution that cause acid rain. The proposed accord would extend a tradition reaching back to the Canada–U.S. Boundary Waters Treaty and the establishment in 1909 of our International Joint Commission (IJC). The IJC, long held up as a model for relations between states, was instrumental in the cleaning up of the Great Lakes, to cite but one example. Its signal advantage as a dispute-settling body lies in its ability to take politically contentious problems and deal with them dispassionately and effectively on the basis of expert advice. Acid rain, as a North American problem, demands another such North American solution.

The President and the Prime Minister have also expressed their determination to resolve the Arctic waters issue on the basis of mutual respect for sovereignty and our common security. The issue, a burning one in Canada, intensified after the voyage of the American Coast Guard vessel *Polar Sea* through the Northwest Passage in 1985. For Canada, sovereignty in our Arctic is indivisible, embracing land, sea and ice. But by asserting this we are, emphatically, not attempting to block all transit through the Northwest Passage. On the contrary, we feel confident that shared security and other interests provide ample grounds for an agreement that would reflect the tradition of Canada–U.S. relations while not jeopardizing American strategic concerns in other parts of the world.

Canada and the United States have developed a remarkable relationship—civilized in the best sense of the word. It is a relationship that, by tradition, has successfully accommodated the interests, and reconciled the differences, of two sovereign partners of totally unequal weight. It is a relationship from which force and the threat of force—too often still the law of the international jungle—have long been removed.

As the two nations extended their reach across the continent, they learned to settle their disputes by negotiation and arbitration. The last land frontier was fixed in 1904, and it has been nearly eighty years since we began sharing our boundary waters for purposes of irrigation and power development. The present generation of Americans and Canadians has had the good sense to adapt and apply this tradition of civility to new areas of concern: transboundary air and water pollution; delimitation of our sea frontiers and economic zones. Finally, through the shared experience of fighting as allies in two world wars, we have reached a profound understanding of what is required of both our nations to defend the peace and security of our North American inheritance, at the margins of the continent itself as well as overseas. Who among us, then, would forswear being a traditionalist when there is so worthy a tradition as this to defend?

Robin W. Winks

Canada and the Three Americas: Her Hemispheric Role

That Canadians are preoccupied with themselves should surprise no one: most peoples are self-preoccupied. That Canadian scholars engage in the same preoccupation is only slightly more surprising. Nor does it come as a shock that these same scholars, presumed to be worldly in outlook, spend so little time studying the nations south of the United States. What is revealing is the extent to which Canadians' obsessive focus on their nearest neighbor, the United States, or those nations across the Atlantic and Pacific oceans, to the neglect of the third America in this hemisphere, can be detailed.

Statistics can distort, and I am suggesting only a tendency, not a hard fact, by calling attention to them. There are many other ways to measure interest in foreign cultures than by simply asking how many professors may dance on the south end of a pin. Even so, in evaluating the number of scholars who devote a substantial portion of their efforts to Latin America, we must consider the question as a means of broaching the larger subject.

In 1980, within the forty-six universities of the United Kingdom, there were nearly 3 200 theses in progress on purely historical subjects. Of these only seventy-eight, some 2 per cent, were on Latin American issues. (To be sure, only sixteen, less than 1 per cent, were devoted to Canada.) By contrast, 150 scholars were burrowing away on African history. These figures no doubt reflect a continued awareness of Britain's recent imperial role in Africa, its lack of any such formal role in Latin America, and of course the widely held though mistaken notion that Canadian history is dull (a canard most extensively spread by Canadians themselves). No scholar, for example, was writing on Canadian relations with Latin America, although four were at work on the origins of Newfoundland. In keeping with a healthy xenophobia, nearly 1 700 scholars were writing on domestic British history. Or, put another way, more than 50 per cent of all fledgling historians in Britain were looking inward. One presumes they reflect the judgment of the market.

In the United States in 1981, some 2 000 doctoral dissertations in history were in progress, plus an estimated 10 000 Master's theses, and the Americans were just about as preoccupied with themselves as the British. One thousand, or 50 per cent, of the American doctoral aspirants were at work on purely American subjects. Perhaps reflecting its own imperial tendencies, the United States had 160 scholars at work on Latin America. There were six writing dissertations on Canadian subjects.

As for Canada in 1981, out of a total of 1 900 theses reported in progress, more than 1 300, or 70 per cent, were on Canada. One may conclude that this is simply another indication that Canadians continue to search for their identity, even when writing theses about the Anglican Church in Saskatchewan. British history attracted 167 Canadian scholars; American history, only fifty; and Latin America and the West Indies a paltry nineteen. Only two of those students were at work on Canadian relations with Latin America.

I draw several obvious conclusions from this exercise. Canadians prefer to study themselves. When they don't study themselves, they prefer to study their roots, British and French. Since at least some know a second language, usually French, they prefer to study French West Africa rather than learn Spanish. In the groves of academe, Latin America is simply not regarded as very significant. That is, from the Canadian perspective there are three Americas: themselves, the United

States, and all the rest. All the rest taken together comprise just 1 per cent of the total intellectual inquiry undertaken in Canada's universities. In short, the degree of Canadian ignorance about Latin America resembles the ignorance the United States is said to harbor about matters Canadian. Indeed, one cannot escape the conclusion that Canadian ignorance of Latin America is rather more profound than American ignorance of Canada.

The leading Canadian scholar in Canadian–Latin American relations, J.C.M. Ogelsby, concluded after extensive study that Canadians regard Latin America as a monolithic unit, a separate America unto itself. They perceive the Organization of American States (OAS) and Latin America as one and the same. And they become most aware of Latin America only in times of a crisis in American relations with one of that region's constituent parts, a crisis that permits Canadians to demonstrate their latent anti-Americanism and independence by virtue of their lack of involvement in Latin American affairs.

The best neutrality is based on ignorance. While one would scarcely regard Canada's Department of External Affairs as uninformed on Latin America, one may reasonably conclude that the frequency with which it issues statements, speeches, or informational materials on Canadian policy vis-à-vis Latin America reflects the Department's perception of Canadians' need to be informed about that part of the world. There have been ten such statements in five years, amidst a general flurry of some 250 public releases on foreign policy. Simply put, Latin America has warranted a comment from Ottawa on the order of twice a year.

It is trite but true to say that most American audiences who take an interest in Canadian matters are what Canadian historian John Holmes has called "internationalists of goodwill." That is, they are people who believe in international harmony and think it a bad thing for Canadians and Americans to be out of sorts with each other. Some think it particularly unfortunate if the source of disagreement is a lack of common attitude toward a third party, such as a specific nation that is the focus of what is fashionably referred to as the North–South debate. Most of these internationalists of goodwill are not, in fact, interested in Canada for itself. When one points out to them that Canada is a monarchy, or that its frontier movement differed utterly from that of the United States, so as to make the bases of American ideology quite irrelevant for Canada, they yawn. What they really wish to hear are the facts relating to acid rain, fisheries, natural gas, investment, oil, or whether Canada is about to deal with some regime that the United States seeks to quarantine.

Most internationalists of goodwill look for similarities between Canada and the United States, believing that those of us who find the differences more fascinating and profound are somehow subversive of their intent. The result is tokenism: the journals *Foreign Policy* or *Foreign Affairs* give their readers an article on Canada every two or three years; the article, read closely, is almost always about the American relationship to a Canada that is misunderstood. In short, it is not clear to me that there is a true *American* perspective on Canada except one shaped by the desires of American foreign policy or the American business community. While such perspectives have their own legitimacy, they are at best partial in both senses of that word. Why, then, should we expect Americans to think of Canada's relationship with Latin America other than in terms of the autonomous ethic that arises from the specific concerns of finance, resource allocation, or foreign policy goals?

What must be reiterated is that Canada *is* different from the United States. It has long marched to different drummers. The forces at work in American society, which historians of the United States regard as most fundamental, are not at work and have never been at work in Canadian society. If we accept even rudimentary assumptions about the nature of cause and effect, we must see that Canada is one of the three Americas, not an upward extension of the dominant America.

Most historians would agree that the United States was fundamentally shaped by a trinity of causations. First was the existence of the belief in a vast western frontier by which a separate American identity was molded and through which a unique American security was originally assured, since every move westward carried the American identity one further evolutionary stage away from its European legacy. Second was the presence of a remarkable natural cornucopia that brought onto world markets precisely the right products at the right times, ensuring both an economy of abundance and the right to assume a prosperous future for each and every citizen. Thirdly, there flourished a security that was free of charge, since distance, mobility, and abundant resources meant that Americans did not have to temper their independence. They did not have to enter into entangling alliances with other powers. They were under little pressure to slow their movement toward isolation or to expend any appreciable portion of their national income on the apparatus of security, whether in the form of a standing army, a Maginot line, or a formal overseas empire.

None of these three influences is at work in the United States any longer. Yet, they remain deeply buried in the psyche of American expectation. Such influences, however, were never lodged in the Canadian psyche. There was no westward movement of significance, and such movement as there was tended to weaken rather than strengthen the Canadian identity. There was no economy of abundance: the Canadian economy developed on the basis of a succession of staples. Therefore, at least the central core of argument by the *dependencia* school of Latin American scholars is quite relevant to the Canadian story. And Canada has never experienced a security free of either compromise or expense. In short, Canada is markedly distinct.

As a nation, Canada not only lacked the three most important influences that helped mold America's character; it experienced three historically different influences which proved to be countervailing forces in their own right. These were the monarchical tradition, the bicultural commitment, and the fact that national independence and identity were achieved through evolution, not revolution. These factors, clichés of Canadian historiography, require no analysis here.

Thus, Canadians have tended to see themselves as rather unlike the United States and distinctively unlike Latin America. They have seen little reason to do better by Latin American cultures than the United States has done by Canadian cultures: that is, Canadians are aware of Latin America only in the context of Canada's relationship with the United States, or in terms of Canadian foreign relations or investment opportunities, rather than in terms of the history of Latin America itself. At this superficial level of observation, most Canadians have therefore concluded that they have little in common with Latin America.

That region's traditions are revolutionary rather than evolutionary; its social structures and political systems have often been non-democratic and hierarchical; and, for English-speaking Canada, any implication of cultural proximity might be exploited by those Québécois who tend to insist they are generically Latins, to possibly divisive ends.

Viewed from a perspective that is neither Canadian nor Latin American, however, the fabric of Canadian history seems more *like* than unlike that of Latin America. Canada is, as they say, a vertical mosaic of cultures; so are many Latin American societies. Canada's economic history has, until recently, been shaped by dependence on staples; so has the history of most Latin American nations—dependence on beef, leather, and wheat in Argentina; on sugar in Cuba; on copper in Bolivia. Within these two Americas there is also a shared sense of cultural superiority to, and varying degrees of dislike for, the United States. Indeed, were I to engage in a genuine comparative study of cultures, it would not be the United States and Canada, or Canada and Australia, or Quebec and the Transvaal that I would examine most closely: it would be Canada and Argentina.

Given the similarities and affinities, Canadians could play in this hemisphere the same role they have always assigned themselves more broadly in the world. Canadians were, they felt, the golden hinge between the New World and the Old, the linchpin between fading empire and newborn sovereignty. They acted as the interpreter of India to the United States, because they shared an imperial past and Commonwealth present with the former, a North American environment and standard of living with the latter. These are cherished notions in Canadian diplomatic history and political rhetoric, although examination of the record does not suggest that Canada has been all that successful in interpreting two such diverse nations as India and the United States to each other. Nonetheless, having chosen the role of interpreter, go-between, international coordinator, or facilitator, Canadians might well decide to apply this role to their relations with Latin American nations, with which Canada has more in common historically than it has noticed, and to apply the role specifically vis-à-vis the United States.

Of course, this will not happen. Canadians do not want to be seen as interfering in American foreign policy. They do not wish to enter into areas ripe with the potential for conflict when Canada has sufficient ethnic and linguistic conflict within its own borders. Nor will they commit any substantial resources to developing expertise on Latin American problems. Canadians lack code words or even a vocabulary for dealing with Latin America. In John Robert Colombo's massive compilation of Canadian quotations on almost every conceivable subject, he offers deathless epigrammatical statements by Canadians on South Africa, South Bay, even on the South Porcupine, but none on South America, Latin America, or the Spanish language. In happy proof of my argument that Canadians view all lands south of the United States in the context of their own relationship with the fabled elephant, even Colombo's three quotations on the West Indies focus those islands through a perceptibly American lens.

Nor, in this argument, can one ignore the issue of race relations. Canada has not been free of the taint of racism that exists, if in larger measure, in the United States. During the short period in the 1880s when there was ostensibly serious discussion of whether the larger West Indian colonies might join the Canadian Confederation, the issue of race continually intruded. By 1919, the Jamaican *Gleaner* had concluded that Canada was hostile "towards people of African descent."

It is not an historical red herring to suggest that, even though Canada's record on matters of race is a relatively good one, the resistance by its Western provinces (and, for other reasons, by Quebec) to including truly entrenched protections for minority groups in the newly patriated Constitution, reflected an attitude which detoured the development of closer Canadian contact with the West Indies and South America in the nineteenth century and, refracted through the language issue, still does so today.

There are, then, three Americas, and Canada sees itself as comprising one. In its international relations, this third America has traditionally lagged in the development of ties with the Commonwealth, Western Europe, and the Pacific Rim nations and, where Latin America has drawn serious attention, economic issues largely have been at stake. For a time, Canadians paid close attention to Mexico and Venezuela, as the politics of oil and the OPEC (Organization of Petroleum Exporting Countries) nations assumed ever greater importance for a northern nation and especially for the oil-importing provinces of Eastern Canada. Oil aside, the politics of economics are not of key significance to Canadians when they look to Latin America: since 1946, there has been no year in which annual Canadian exports to Latin America have been more than 5 per cent of the Canadian total; if one omits Venezuelan oil, Canadian imports from Latin America have been even smaller. Although Prime Minister Trudeau sent a mission to Latin America in 1968, it was historically viewed as no more meaningful than missions sent as early as 1866 or the five missions sent between 1930 and 1953.

Certain changes that coincided with the mission of 1968 and those of subsequent years, however, have given the Latin American relationship the appearance of greater importance. The most obvious, though least remarked upon, is the exponential rate of increase in news stories about Latin America's crises and problems; other people's troubles make for comforting reading or television viewing at home. As Ogelsby and others have observed, the amount, if not the quality, of Canadian coverage of Latin American events has increased substantially. What Ogelsby did not add is that the sheer amount of public expectation for news everywhere has increased at least as rapidly, and it is unclear whether or not the Latin American portion of this total coverage has really increased or improved. More aggressive development of Canadian business interests worldwide has been reflected in Latin America as well, though not to any exceptional degree.

Most of the steps taken toward closer relations with Latin America have been in the context of the Third World and the North–South dialogue. When Trudeau sought to strengthen Canada's position in Latin America, he referred to the move as a step toward a stronger position in hemispheric affairs generally—a dispassionate way of suggesting that Canada might offer technologically less developed Latin American nations a high-technology option to the United States. Canada sought Permanent Observer Status in the OAS and, from January 1972 onward, attended meetings of the Inter-American Economic and Social Council. The primary reason given for not seeking full membership in the OAS was Canada's frankly stated concern that it should not further complicate its most important bilateral relationship with the United States.

Thus, another theme basic to Canadian history has dominated Canada's approach to the nations south of the Rio Grande: namely, Canada's preoccupation with her immediate southern neighbor.

The history of Canada can be written only in the context of the Canadian–American relationship. While it is true that most of the precedents by which Britain developed the steps for decolonizing her overseas possessions were first worked out in response to Canadian issues, those issues in turn generally arose over problems inherent in the relationship with the United States. Canada was the Mother Dominion, the first former colony to pass through all the stages of preparation by which the historian demarks the rites of passage to independence. In due course, almost all these precedents were consciously borrowed from the British–Canadian experience and applied by the British to the Gold Coast or Nigeria. Thus, one cannot fully comprehend Nigerian history without a knowledge of Canadian history—one way in which Canada serves as a true linchpin—but it is also true that one cannot understand these Canadian precedents outside the context of the Canadian–American relationship.

In fine, there is no Canadian relationship with Latin America except as determined by the overriding Canadian concern for the United States. Fear that the OAS might radicalize its position on the question of "collective economic security"—a code phrase meaning a concentrated effort by all members to raise the living standards of Latin American nations by redistributing other people's property—had caused concern in the board rooms of Massey-Ferguson, Alcan, and other Canadian multinationals which, in Latin American eyes, were indistinguishable from their American counterparts. The prudent path was taken and Canada applied for membership in the Inter-American Bank.

The period of most rapid Canadian growth in Latin America was in the mid-1970s, when numerous missions ventured south of the Equator. In 1976, Prime Minister Trudeau visited three nations, key to Canadian interests. One of these was Cuba, through which Canada managed to establish a firm symbolic distance from the United States in its approach to Central and Latin American issues. Another was Mexico, with which Canada had always felt an affinity based on the old "three Americas" argument of Herbert Eugene Bolton and others. The third was Venezuela, where the politics of oil merited a dominant consideration. Two other South American powers, Argentina and Brazil, were also of growing importance to Canada because of their automobiles and their resource-based commodities: wheat, aluminum, asbestos, and newsprint. Nevertheless, Canada's exports to Latin America over the decade increased less than 1 per cent of the total, for the gross gain had to be read in the context of general Canadian expansion and increased Latin American consumption. In the same period, setting aside oil, there was no growth whatsoever in Latin American exports to Canada. (In the last few years, Canadian banks have given greater attention to Latin America, and the Canadian government has mounted a developmental assistance program as part of its general concern for *le tiers monde*.)

Latin Americans seem to display an enthusiasm for hemispheric matters but, reciprocally, show a lack of interest in what lies north of the 49th parallel. During the American bicentennial, when I was charged by the State Department and the United States Information Agency with organizing an inter-American conference on American Studies, the Latin American nations sent far more delegates than Canada. Nearly two-thirds of the Latin American scholars who professed some form of study of the United States routinely included Canada in the scope of their interests. Yet, although the conference was scheduled to be held in South America, not one of the Canadian scholars professed any interest in Spanish-speaking America. At the same time, during a visit to a CIDA (Canadian International Development Agency) project in Mexico City, I found a group of *dependencia* theorists working on a study of high technology in North America and making little theoretical distinction between Canada and the United States. They envisioned but two Americas and happily accepted Ogelsby's appellation of Canadians as "Gringos from the Far North."

In sum, much that is known in Latin America about either Canada or the United States is badly known, although the ignorance, to one's surprise, seems equally distributed despite so small a Canadian economic presence in Latin America.

This is not the place to argue that it is in Canada's self-interest to help with Third World development, and to help disproportionately, as I would urge. Nor is this the place to assert that Canadians ought to learn Spanish when the majority of them are still trying to decide whether they wish to learn French. Nor is this the forum to engage in a rehearsal of Canada's trade relationship with Cuba or its interaction with the OAS. One may express delight, however, that the Americas Society has added a Canadian program to its structure. One may be grateful that Canada's Prime Minister and Secretary of State for External Affairs have spoken out on Latin American and West Indian matters. One may hope that, in the future, more Canadian universities will establish programs in Latin American studies.

Yet, these steps remain hesitant, small, and circumscribed by the dominant Canadian preoccupation with itself and with the United States. In the fast-paced world of international relations, it seems not far wrong to suggest that Canada is about where it was in 1967 when those early students of Canada's relationship with Latin America, Irving and Richard Brecher, remarked that Canada was more or less stuck at dead center. We know what the issues are: energy, finance, trade, food, aid—constructive revolution. But the infrastructure of knowledge, by which international goodwill is translated into action, still remains to be built. Canada has the same stake in promoting peaceful revolution in Latin America as have other highly developed nations. For, if peaceful revolution is not possible, violent revolution will be inevitable.

Perrin Beatty

The New Look in Canadian Defence: Outward and Upward

The roads that nations follow through history are scattered with milestones marking various critical stages in their development.

The second half of the last century in the United States, for example, was marked by a transfer of attention to the world beyond America's borders. Near the end of the 1800s, that world-renowned American theoretician of naval power, Admiral Alfred Mahan, wrote of his emerging nation: "Whether they will or no, Americans must begin to look outward." So, too, must Canadians as the decade of the 1980s completes its course.

A new tide of confidence is running in Canadian affairs. The economic indicators show that capital investment in manufacturing rose 21 per cent in 1986 and will probably rise 15 per cent more this year. Among the G-7 (Group of Seven) nations, Canada showed the strongest growth in 1987. The new spirit manifests itself in our determination to secure a historic free trade agreement with our largest trading partner, the United States. And it is manifested particularly in our current approach to national security and defence matters.

Our thinking on defence issues has crystallized within the harsh context of international tensions. The world should rejoice

at the progress made by the United States and the Soviet Union in achieving, for the first time, the elimination of a whole class of nuclear weapons.
Canadians strongly welcome the agreement on intermediate-range
nuclear forces. We hope it turns out to be the first in a series of agreements that will enable both sides to attain security at much lower levels
of armament.

As we strive for further progress towards stable peace,
however, we recognize that the journey is far from over. We have
entered the fifth decade of an armed and uneasy peace between the
superpowers. Across the gulf of conflicting values and ideology, the
nations of the West confront the Soviet Union and its Warsaw Pact
allies—nuclear-armed, equipped with huge conventional forces and,
despite domestic reform and tactical variations, still committed to
Communist hegemony.

In this situation, Canada's policy rests on two basic principles. First, we are not neutral. We reject the concept of moral equiv-
alence between pluralistic democracies and one-party states. The political
values at stake are our values. We are of the West; we are with the
West. Second, we believe peace is synonymous with survival and that
the way to preserve it is to place no temptations for quick gain in the
path of the adventurous.

We believe that the peace has held for more than forty
years because of the strength, realism and resolve of the West. Canada's
policy is consistent with this assessment. We have no nuclear arms and
we seek none. We are, however, members of the North Atlantic Treaty
Organization (NATO), as well as partners with the United States in the
defence of North America. Because we, too, are sheltered from war
by the Western deterrent, we deem it strategically unsound and morally
indefensible not to accept a share of responsibility for its effectiveness.

For this reason, our ports are open to nuclear-equipped
ships of the Western alliance, while we cooperate with American armed
forces in the testing over Canadian territory of the Cruise Missile, a
weapon designed to offset the Soviet Cruise Missile which has been
not only tested, but deployed. We believe, in short, in the pooling of
effort and the sharing of strength among the Western democracies, both
in NATO and in other alliances and conventions.

Beyond fulfilling our international treaty obligations, we

face the requirements of directly defending our own national land mass and, in Canada's case, these are immense. Physically, our country is larger than the United States, outstripping in size every other country but the Soviet Union. Our coastline is the world's longest. At the same time, we are situated geographically between the two superpowers.

Thus, Canada's new defence policy must, in effect, meet this dual set of needs: obligations to collective security and responsibility as a sovereign nation to contribute to the defence of our territory.

The policy recognizes a dilemma common to all the Western democracies: the need to carry a shield strong enough to deter, but not so heavy that it stunts economic development. To accomplish this, we must make the best possible use of every resource. Within NATO, for instance, we are re-deploying Canadian land and air units assigned to Europe in order to give us a better concentration of forces. We are taking new approaches in the use of personnel, tripling the size of our reserve forces and equipping them on the same basis as the regulars. We have also completed a detailed stocktaking of the nation's industrial base, working with industry to develop a plan under which this powerful resource could be swiftly utilized for defence production in a wartime emergency.

For the Western nations, conventional or non-nuclear deterrence must begin in the research and development laboratories. The Warsaw Pact outnumbers NATO by two to one in manpower, tanks and armed helicopters, and by more than that in artillery. NATO's conventional forces have compensated for this quantitative imbalance by maintaining a technological advantage. Through a combination of complacency and illegal transfers of technology, however, we have seen that advantage slip. Canada and the other NATO nations are committed to reversing the trend. We are working with our NATO partners on several advanced projects, including a NATO frigate, specialized aerial communications systems and air-to-air missiles. A good example of military–industrial cooperation within the Alliance is the case of Oerlikon Aerospace of St-Jean, Quebec. The Canadian company was selected by the United States Army to fulfill part of its low-level air defence program because of Oerlikon's technical expertise in this field.

Indeed, we are determined to ensure that Canada's armed forces will be as advanced as any in the world. We are increasing our inventory of CF-18 fighter aircraft so that squadrons can stay up to strength in the face of peacetime losses. We are increasing the size of our aerial patrol forces. We are expanding our capabilities in underwater surveillance.

The greatest changes, however, will come in our naval forces. Canada, as a three-ocean nation, needs a three-ocean navy. Its backbone will be a fleet of ten to twelve nuclear-powered submarines. Soviet naval power is a factor in all three oceans, and the detection of Soviet submarines in waters off Canada is by no means an uncommon occurrence. From the Arctic, deep submarine channels lead to the Pacific and east to the Atlantic Ocean where one of Canada's assigned wartime missions under NATO is to keep the sea lanes to Europe open. Nuclear-powered submarines are uniquely effective in these circumstances. They can operate under the Arctic ice pack. Unlike the diesel-powered submarines we have now, they can travel at high speeds for long periods; we will thus be able to deploy from area to area more easily when we need to. The two existing nuclear-powered types under consideration are the British *Trafalgar* and the French *Rubis*, either of which could be modified for Canadian use. Most of these vessels will be built in Canada, the first to be launched in 1996, with additional ships coming into service every eighteen months.*

Canada's goal is essentially to maintain the same mission it has today, patrolling the waters adjacent to its shores and protecting its convoys to Europe. But we will accomplish this mission more effectively than we are able to do now with a navy that is on the verge of rusting out. We will be markedly improving our ability to defend our own waters.

All these improvements will strengthen our sovereignty, making us less dependent on others for our own defence. They will also make us a more reliable contributor to the common defence of

---

*As this book went to press, the nuclear submarines took a fatal dive as a result of the government's 1989 federal budget, which recognized a new era of severe budget restraints and shifts in spending priorities.

the West, because Canada intends to be a strong and resolute partner of the other democracies and not a protectorate. The price of contracting out the defence of Canada is simply too high: for our allies, who have long felt we should shoulder our fair share of the burden, and for Canadians themselves, who increasingly recognize that a nation cannot be unwilling or unable to defend itself and still be considered truly independent.

I welcome the support the United States government has given Canada as we begin to implement our new defence policy. In peace and war, in many great and common undertakings, our two countries have walked the same road for generations. With mutual respect for one another, we will continue to do so.

Nicholas Stethem
Alliance, Independence and Power: Defending Canada

       In Canadian political terms, defence has become a subject that matters.

       In the government of Prime Minister Mulroney between 1984 and 1988, the Defence Minister and his department gained a level of power and importance not seen since the 1960s. The opposition Liberal Party's inability to generate a coherent defence policy argument in the same period proved a political liability, perhaps a consequence of the period of Liberal government in the 1970s and early 1980s when interest in defence was not the route to success. The lack of a logical policy mattered little when defence was a non-issue, when the department was weak and when a succession of Defence Ministers, following the 1971 White Paper, were only minor players in government.

       The 1980s marked Canada's return to a national logic of "defence in alliance," that which had heralded the birth of the North Atlantic Treaty Organization (NATO). The concept, developed in the late 1940s, had grown uncertain during the defence debates at the end of the 1950s and become utterly scrambled during the apparent enlightenment of the late 1960s. Though piously proclaimed, defence in alliance had become in Canada a hollow public posture cloaking a profound indifference to the problems of defence and to strategic logic.

Only after the Canadian armed forces had grown visibly incapable of meeting commitments—and the Canadian public had witnessed the collapse of détente, the invasion of Afghanistan and the increasing prominence of a score of smaller wars worldwide—was the government forced to re-examine its policies.

Oddly enough, in the early 1980s, it was the peace movement's questioning of Western defence policy that turned out to be a determining factor. Their criticism forced a return to the logical roots of Canadian defence policy in justifying government action or inaction. Thus, it is one of history's small ironies that major credit for the restoration of a consistent and strong defence policy may have to go to those who at one time attacked the defence establishment most strongly.

By the time the Progressive Conservative government was elected in 1984, entering office with a promise to rebuild the armed forces and meet Canada's alliance commitments, much of the homework required to implement a more muscular policy had already been done. The two-year delay in publishing a new White Paper on Defence resulted less from Ottawa's need to determine what had to be done than from political problems and a rearguard action fought by advocates of a "Canadacentric" policy that included withdrawal from central Europe. What they were opposing, in the name of a "made-in-Canada" policy, was in fact an historically consistent development of a very Canadian defence policy. That this policy's modern incarnation involved the stationing of forces in Europe, rather than in defensive positions in Northern Canada, was the deliberate result of an approach to defence, independence and power that is as certifiably Canadian as the land which both sides of the argument wished to defend.

Since roughly 1776, Canada has continuously belonged to a larger defensive structure. Beginning as a prominent part of the most powerful empire of its day, then evolving into the first independent dominion within an imperial defence structure, and finally emerging as a fully independent member of the Western alliance during and after the Second World War, Canada has never been in a position where it alone had to defend itself. On the other hand, it has frequently had to contribute to the distant defence of a larger structure—starting with the individual English and French Canadians who fought for, and helped to build the furthest parts of, the British Empire, and ending with a nation that was counted as the third-largest Western military power after 1945 and one of the developers, with the United States and Britain, of the atomic bomb.

In the late 1940s, Canada began a deliberate diplomatic campaign in cooperation with the British and a few sympathetic American officials. The aim was to produce an alliance that would tie North America and Western Europe into an almost organic defensive relationship. At the time, the United States was considering the extension of less entangling security guarantees, while a number of influential Europeans, seeking to achieve the goal of a united and powerful Europe, were determined to avoid American dominance. The diplomatic campaign, reinforced by the events of the late 1940s, resulted in the birth of NATO.

In addition to securing the defence of Canada and that of the nations to which we were tied through bonds of history, kinship, culture and interests, our national aim was to ensure the future independence of Canadian foreign and defence policy. Alliance may seem an odd key to independence but, in the late 1940s, a close Western alliance was a means of ensuring that Canada would not be left alone in North America with the United States. Geography, history and the strategic imperatives of the nuclear age meant that Canada and the United States would remain close allies after the war. Canada's traditional alliance relationship was fading rapidly: the concept of imperial defence was over, Britain's power having been vitiated by the war. Within a few years, thanks to the Suez crisis, whatever last thoughts were entertained about a British–Canadian connection possibly again counterbalancing the American colossus would disappear.

The prospect of a purely bilateral alliance with Canada's much larger neighbour, now brimming with self-confidence as the dominant world power, was claustrophobic. The struggle—first military, then economic and political—to remain separate from the United States was one of the historic themes in Canada's national development. Another theme was the evolution of independent, national control of our foreign and defence policies, the final elements of which had been achieved in the world war just ended. These could fade within the consumingly protective shadow of American power. Fortress North America presented a forbidding prospect.

Within a larger Western alliance framework, however, Canada would not be, or be seen to be, tied to the United States in a lopsided bilateral alliance. The inevitable question of American domination would have to be asked in terms of the West as a whole, not in terms of North America alone.

Canadian policy would have room to manoeuvre in the larger forum. In the post-war world, we would institutionalize the transatlantic perspective, the reach outwards from North America that had helped shape the world view of Canadians in a manner significantly different from that of the more continentalist, inward-looking Americans. Within NATO, the independence of Canadian foreign and defence policy could be as authentic, and be seen as such, as that of Britain or France. That determination to preserve national independence, real and perceived, remains a powerful force in the politics and management of Canadian national security policy.

NATO solved the problem of national defence so effectively that it grew difficult to imagine any conventional military threat to Canadian territory, or any nuclear threat short of all-out nuclear war. In effect, the strategic deterrent possessed by the United States became Canada's nuclear deterrent, and our key defensive positions moved roughly a dozen degrees east of Greenwich.

When the 1987 government White Paper ("Challenge and Commitment: A Defence Policy for Canada") stated that defence policy would " . . . continue to be based on a strategy of collective security within the framework of the North Atlantic Alliance, including the continental defence partnership with the United States," it defined Canada's contribution to that overall framework in functional rather than geographic terms. The problem was not defined in terms of the defence of Canada, the defence of North America and the defence of NATO, concentric circles forming a classic defensive structure that the Caesars would readily have understood. Instead, defence was described in terms of strategic levels. Four global levels, and one specifically national level, were defined through contributions to:

—maintenance of strategic deterrence
—credible conventional defence
—protection of Canadian sovereignty
—peaceful settlement of international disputes
—effective arms control.

Canada's contributions to strategic deterrence, provided in common with the other members of the alliance, comprise political support along with a sharing of the moral burden inherent in reliance upon nuclear weapons. Unlike the other non-nuclear members of NATO, however, Canada has a direct national involvement in the structure of the United States' strategic weapons.

There are no large-scale conventional military threats to North America. We sit firmly beneath the umbrella of nuclear deterrence: a major conventional attack upon Canada or the United States would invite strategic nuclear retaliation.

Distance, geography and climate give Canada an unmatched set of natural defences. Small attacks upon North America are logistically and operationally possible. Compact, self-contained attacking forces could be used to draw larger forces into costly defensive campaigns or to attack vital installations such as the radar stations of the North Warning System. In a short, conventional conflict, however, there would be little time for diversionary attacks to affect the outcome as effectively as the same resources used closer to the front lines of the conflict. Raids on vital facilities such as air defence or communications systems would also risk immediate escalation to the strategic nuclear level, destroying any limited conventional war strategy. In an extended conventional war, a conflict measured in months or years, disrupting and diverting the industrial and mobilization base of North America's defence might be a reasonable strategic objective. But this type of conflict is only a remote possibility, demanding as it does the removal of the nuclear deterrent from the strategic equation.

Basically, North America is where the conventional defence problem *is not*. The key is to deal with the remote possibilities that do exist without being diverted from the central aim.

The aim of any contribution to conventional defence must be to prevent a potential enemy from believing that conventional force can be used successfully against the Western alliance. The value of conventional forces must be measured in terms of their ability to support this aim, and thus in terms of their ability to get to where the war might be at the right time and with the right support behind them. The only area where NATO itself faces a credible threat of conventional force is Europe. Having no conventional defence responsibilities outside the alliance area, Canada's effective contribution to conventional defence must therefore be weighed in terms of the conventional balance in Europe.

By late 1988, the bulk of Canada's regular armed forces had been committed to that balance. True, the commitment of an army brigade and two fighter squadrons to reinforce Norway—originally made to reduce the impact of withdrawing half the Canadian brigade from West Germany in the early 1970s—was dropped. But the Canadian brigade already stationed on the central front was strengthened, while the brigade formerly committed to Norway was switched to the central front on a flyover basis, and the two fighter squadrons were assigned to reinforce the three squadrons of CF-18s already based in West Germany. It was a logical consolidation of combat forces committed to the alliance in Europe.

The rebuilding of Canada's navy was also oriented towards alliance commitments. The White Paper deliberately placed the rebuilt navy in the context of, first, the North Atlantic, "...the ocean of primary strategic importance to Canada and its NATO allies"; second, the Northeast Pacific; and, third, the Arctic Ocean, offering as it does the possibility of concealment and strategic transit of nuclear submarines. The fleet, beyond the year 2000, would number sixteen frigates, ten to twelve nuclear submarines, plus numerous ships and minehunters.

The addition of nuclear-powered submarines would solve a multitude of problems. The submarines possess the range and speed to permit a small fleet to cover a large area. Because of their relative ease of concealment, the number of areas that a potential enemy must assume to be covered by them is multiplied. Their speed makes possible a rapid concentration of naval force in any single area, a further force multiplier. Given the navy's dual requirement in the Atlantic and the Northeast Pacific, the nuclear submarines' ability to range effectively throughout the Arctic offers an alternative to the strategic bottleneck of the Panama Canal or the southern tip of South America. This flexibility avoids the re-allocation of a greater proportion of surface ships from their primary role in the North Atlantic to the Pacific, where there is a growing strategic requirement. It also avoids the commitment of naval resources to a specialized Arctic capability that would be of limited use elsewhere.

It was predictable that the submarine program would become the focus of sharp public debate. The word "nuclear"—even though it refers exclusively to the submarines' form of locomotion, not armament (Canada has eschewed a nuclear arms capability from the beginning)—propelled peace activists into the public forum, dispensing once alien arguments on the relative merits of diesel-electric submarines and frigates. Antinuclear nationalists called for the mining of the Northwest Passage in preference to a less belligerent proposal that might somehow be seen to subvert Canada's stand on nuclear non-proliferation. The submarines were also a natural focus of attack as the single most expensive program mentioned in the government's White Paper, although the planned spending was spread over two decades. The submarines became a symbol for the new policy. When that policy collided with the demands for spending cuts in 1989, their symbolic importance far outweighed their cost, which would not have become significant for several years. Lost in the uproar was the fact that the cumulative cost of an equivalent number of surface vessels required in the Atlantic, as well as the cost of increased fleet air-defence capabilities, a larger surface fleet in the Pacific, plus the commitment of a specialized Arctic capability, probably made nuclear submarines the cheapest naval alternative available.

The dominance in public debate of a tertiary defence consideration, the protection of Canadian *sovereignty* (as well as a tertiary

naval priority, the Arctic Ocean) was equally predictable. Deployment
of a nuclear submarine force, as political symbol and strategic imperative,
could be both ridiculed *and* supported because the issues of sovereignty
and defence pose two such different challenges. Neither defence policy
nor the submarine program is driven primarily by concerns over sovereignty, but Canadian sensibilities are such that the concept of sovereignty
can form a volatile part of any debate on national security.

In 1987, the sovereignty issue quickly pre-empted in the
public's imagination the larger strategic logic proposed in the White
Paper. Canadian sovereignty, a problem of national civil authority and
international legal recognition, was conceptually fudged into the defence
of Canada proper, the securing of the nation and its vital interests against
the threat of armed attack. The concept of defence suddenly narrowed
to the guarding of Canadian turf; the broader, more complex view of
defence in alliance lost ground to something far simpler and more
emotive in the public debate.

To the degree that "Canadian sovereignty" is concerned
with the established control of national territory, the extension of the
apparatus of government and the fabric of national society counts far
more than submarines or patrolling aircraft. The presence of a Royal
Canadian Mounted Police constable, a public health nurse or a Customs
officer is worth more than a company of infantry in establishing the
fact of sovereignty. Each represents the responsibility assumed and authority routinely exercised by the state within its own borders. The infantry
company, the long-range patrol aircraft and the submarine represent
a different type of power.

At the same time, the intrusion of a foreign military
aircraft or submarine does not necessarily disestablish sovereignty. Soviet
submarines off the coast of Sweden may constitute a military threat
and a trespass in Swedish territorial waters, but they do not perforce
throw into question Swedish sovereignty. Sweden's vulnerability in the
event of war, the effectiveness of its naval defences, the security of
its facilities and the degree of force Sweden is willing to use in peacetime may all be open to question, but nowhere in the international
community is there a suggestion that the waters around the Karlskrona
naval base are rendered any less sovereign by the clandestine entry of

Soviet submarines. Nor is it suggested that these waters might have been rendered more sovereign had the Swedish navy blown the submarines out of the water. More effectively controlled or defended, perhaps, but not more sovereign.

By the same token, Soviet or American or British or Patagonian submarines passing undetected through the Canadian Arctic should not throw into doubt the ownership of those territorial waters. Such passage establishes vulnerability, a weak point in terms of surveillance and control; but the extension of Canadian civil authority is by no means as challenged by such clandestine military activity as by, for example, the open transit of foreign ships which refuse to acknowledge any Canadian civil jurisdiction in the Northwest Passage.

In the Canadian context, however, sovereignty is not simply a question of civil power and international legal recognition. It is also a question of nationalism and self-confidence, elements deeply embedded in the amorphous popular concept of sovereignty which can baffle the best of Canada's friends. Preserving Canadian sovereignty thus becomes, in the eyes of many Canadians, the ultimate defence of Canada as a driving cause and measure of their self-esteem. It is this element of sovereignty that is most threatened by Canada's inability to control the Arctic waters, by the passage of foreign submarines, and by a military imminence which in fact is really marginal to the overall defence of the nation.

The arguments it generates may seem bizarre, but this aspect of sovereignty is as much a part of Canada's political reality as the "Stars and Stripes" is of America's. And, just as contradictory and illogical arguments can be wrapped in the flag south of the border, so can they be enfolded in sovereignty to the north. That the submarine program, draped in the mantle of sovereignty, could be cancelled in 1989 demonstrates that current defence policy is not primarily driven by this lesser priority. Still, in any discussion of national policy, the issue of sovereignty sits waiting in the middle distance, ready to loom large. Just try suggesting, for example, that any allied submarine requirement in the Arctic Ocean can be filled by the United States fleet.

When it is not confused with conventional defence, however, the contribution to the protection of Canadian sovereignty is straightforward. The Canadian armed forces possess equipment and capabilities that can support the exercise of civil power in the surveillance, control and policing of a vast expanse of land, sea and air. Since the armed forces are required to support our contribution to the conventional defence of Canada, their involvement in support of the civil power is a logical use of national resources, providing that primary defence commitments are not imperilled. Change the phrase "contribution to the protection of Canadian sovereignty" to something like "aid to the civil power," and this third priority becomes a national role common to most armed forces, whether they are patrolling remote border areas, fighting fire and flood or rattling sabres over the rights to cod fisheries.

Contributions to the peaceful settlement of international disputes and effective arms control, the fourth and fifth roles cited in the White Paper, are logical complements to the first and second, Canada's contributions to strategic deterrence and conventional defence. Arms control maps and manages the structures of nuclear deterrence and the conventional force balance; the peaceful settlement of international disputes stabilizes the global framework within which these structures exist. In both areas, defence provides knowledge and experience in support of diplomacy. In the special cases of peacekeeping, truce supervision and emergency relief operations, defence provides the resources and skills which make Canadian participation especially sought after.

While the determination to preserve national independence is an obvious force in Canadian defence policy, our equal desire to contribute to the settlement of international disputes and arms control, as well as our implicit desire to influence the evolution of the international framework, may seem at cross-purposes to some Canadians.

Canadians see themselves as working for the common good multilaterally, bilaterally and occasionally on their own, helping to solve problems from Third World debt to the security of international air traffic. We enjoy participatory roles in European security and arms control negotiations, in multilateral and United Nations (UN) peacekeeping operations. We take for granted consultations involving us within the Western alliance and the Group of Seven (G-7) major industrialized nations. Our diplomats, most Canadians believe, bring to bear policies and skills which enhance international deliberations and ensure that Canada's positions are clear and present within the most powerful councils of the West. It seemed perfectly logical that Canada should lobby for a seat on the UN Security Council in 1988: Canadians believe this is where Canada belongs and where it can function more effectively than most other nations. Since Canada historically has gained and exercised its power through multilateral structures, acquiring institutional experience along the way, all this is not entirely a national conceit.

It is, of course, the exercise of a different kind of power from that of the nuclear giants—the power to influence, sometimes the power to shape, and always the power to ensure that the national view or interest is recognized, if not protected. Whether it is exercised for the noblest of reasons or for the most selfish of national motives, whether it is exercised directly or indirectly, at the centre of the international stage or in the back corridors, it remains a force to be regarded with respect. Canada's quest for power may be less visible than that of its more formidable allies, but it is no less real.

In the 1990s, the possibility of enhancing Canada's position through increases in its commitments to strategic deterrence, conventional defence, protection of sovereignty, arms control or the peaceful settlement of international disputes will be limited economically and strategically. Unfortunately, opportunities to reduce Canada's effective power and real independence arise all too frequently.

Alliance defence budgets everywhere will be under economic pressure. National debts, social programs, industrial restructuring, international competition, changing demographics, competitive tax structures—all suggest the reason why the upper economic limits of Western defence efforts are increasingly defined by a general constraint on government spending.

Canada's lower limit is specific to a nation which spent 2.2 per cent of its gross national product on defence in 1986 and has occupied a position near the bottom of the NATO spending list for more than a decade. Although Canada is now ahead of Denmark and tied with Spain and Italy on that list, it is unlikely that it will move above the lower third of NATO members in the 1990s. Given the probability of continued American demands for greater sharing of the alliance burden, which the European allies will likely respond to, and Canada's particularly abysmal defence record in the last two decades, any cuts in our own spending plans will be perceived within the alliance as more drastic than they may appear to Canadian planners. The vision of Canada ducking defence burdens is too easily revived among its allies.

The impact of that vision is easily underestimated. Late in the 1988 election campaign, both the Liberal and New Democratic parties argued for the diversion of money from defence to rationalize proposed budgets for social programs. Yet, at precisely the wrong moment in our history, such positions could hobble Canada's effective power within NATO and other Western multilateral structures. In economic terms, during a period of critical restructuring in Europe and North America and within the global trading system, the lower limit of Canada's contribution to conventional defence may be defined by its need for all the power and influence it can muster on the global economic front in the 1990s. That we may have crashed through this lower limit, critically damaging our national position with the budget cuts of 1989, is a risk that appears to have been recognized only after the budget implications had had time to sink in both inside and outside the government.

The strategic boundaries are obvious in the case of Canada's direct contribution to the nuclear deterrent. The systems and programs required to ensure that the bomber threat remains a marginal factor in the context of general strategic attack are being put into place. An increased commitment of resources to NORAD (the North American Aerospace Defence [Command]) would produce only slight improvement in a marginal factor, with no net gain in terms of strategic deterrence. A *decrease* in commitment, however, risks opening holes in the system that could erode the theoretical integrity of the deterrent, seriously undermining the entire structure. There is little manoeuvring room.

Based upon the plans in effect prior to the 1989 budget, Canada's contribution to conventional defence would have improved throughout the next decade. Its armed forces in the 1970s shrank to roughly 78 000 servicemen, backed by a reserve of about 20 000 of which 20 per cent or less were actually deployable in the event of war. By 1990, regular strength would have increased by 15 per cent to 90 000 personnel; by 1992, 25 000 former regular force personnel, immediately available as reinforcements for the regular force, would have been organized into a new Supplementary Ready Reserve. By the year 2003, the overall strength of Canada's primary reserves, which constitute the basis of immediate wartime expansion, would have increased more than 300 per cent to 65 000 service men and women.

By the summer of 1989, somewhere between half and three-quarters of Canada's regular combat forces would have been committed to the European theatre. Two of its three regular army brigade groups were committed to the central front with the First Canadian Division. The airborne/airportable Special Service Force was to provide a flyover battalion with prepositioned equipment to a composite NATO force in northern Norway, leaving the remaining airborne formation to act as a quick-reaction force defending from conventional attack, in cooperation with the United States, NATO's North American flank. Added to these commitments was one regular brigade group in Western Canada, along with the revitalized formations of the primary reserve forces. Five of the air force's eight operational CF-18 fighter squadrons were committed to the European central front, two to NORAD. The primary commitment of Canada's navy—with six new frigates by 1992, plus another six along with its first nuclear submarine by 1996—was to remain the protection of the sea lanes in the North Atlantic, with forces in the Arctic and Pacific covering more remote threats to NATO's flanks.

In effect, Canada had thrown everything in its arsenal directly into the conventional balance. We may contribute less before the end of the next decade—the 1989 budget makes this a virtual certainty—but it is difficult to see how we could have planned to do more.

Perhaps the 1990s will still see the development of northern airfields in Canada for NORAD fighters; the opening of an Arctic warfare training base at the eastern end of the Northwest Passage; and the revitalization of the Canadian Rangers. This special militia operates small patrols out of settlements across the far North, acting as the eyes and ears of defence and as guides for larger forces like the Canadian Airborne Regiment parachuted in from the south.

All this activity is designed not only to ensure that the strategic bomber and conventional threats to the North remain marginal factors, but to develop Canada's national capability to move, fight and survive in the North, decisively turning the vast distances and climatic extremes to its defensive advantage. It represents as well the extension of the state's internal business, enhancing the national presence and the armed forces' mission to aid the civil authority in the remoter regions of Canada's North.

Defence, in short, contributes to that aspect of sovereignty that is a function of nationalism and self-confidence. The belief that Canada is doing a reasonable job of defending itself and playing its part within the alliance should generate positive feelings among most Canadians. The question of control of Arctic waters may not be legally resolved in the next decade, and pride will no longer be satisfied by the thought that commanders of allied submarines heading north request liaison or joint exercises with patrolling Canadian submarines, in order to avoid diplomatic misunderstandings. Neither the desire for sovereignty nor defence will be satisfied when commanders of potentially hostile submarines operate on the comfortable assumption that, where they intrude, no Canadian submarines prowl.

For those nationalists who view alliance membership as hobbling Canadian independence, or as subordination to the United States, the very basis of our defence policy will, of course, seem a violation of sovereignty. The immediate nationalist reaction to the budget cuts of 1989 illustrated nationalists' inability to understand or debate problems of defence and foreign policy beyond narrow ideological confines. For the majority, though, defence will probably seem less a factor in the sovereignty debates of the 1990s than, for example, our economic strength or the integrity of our cultural and social policies. The contribution of defence to sovereignty will be increasingly taken for granted, provided that the overall policy is credible. It is the failure of the national defence policy's credibility, rather than any specific program such as that of the nuclear submarines, which may provoke the next wave of concern over sovereignty.

For Canada to assist in the peaceful settlement of international disputes in the next decade is an aim reasonable in principle but unpredictable in practice. Where, when and how defence may be able to support such actions are functions of chance, diplomacy and circumstance. Defence policy can only ensure that the way is there when the will and opportunity exist. As battlefield observers, or as peacekeepers patrolling between warring communities, the stronger, better-equipped Canadian armed forces of the 1990s, if they emerge from the budgetary confusion of 1989, should constitute a more flexible and useful instrument of diplomacy. If weaker forces emerge, then the real capability to support such operations will be problematic.

As for arms control, Canada's involvement has been intimately linked with its contributions to strategic deterrence and conventional defence: our role in nuclear force planning in Europe coincides with our participation in limiting European-based nuclear forces; we offer a credible voice on conventional arms control because we are part of the balance of conventional forces between the Atlantic and the Urals. Our voice in the world's multilateral fora assumes greater weight in discussions of security and arms control because of our position in the councils of the Western alliance. To put it crudely, from an arms control point of view, Canada remains part of the solution because it is an integral part of the problem.

If the policy of 1987 survives the budget of 1989, Canada will be doing more for defence in the next decade than it has done in twenty years, yet our armed forces will still be operating at something close to a minimum national level. Any proposal, therefore, that Canada withdraw its ground forces stationed in Europe early in the process of balanced-force reductions would be tantamount to proposing that Canada withdraw from a major role in subsequent talks on conventional stability in Europe; the effect would also be to cut the physical link which has guaranteed Canada's independent North American commitment to conventional defence. To suggest symbolic reductions for whatever motive—cost-cutting or advancing arms control—is to suggest substantial cuts: Canada's forces are too small to permit cuts without a critical loss of capability. For the Soviet Union or the United States, to cut a division or two may reasonably encourage the arms control process; for Canada, to cut a division is to scrap the regular army.

Reducing defence expenditures to less than 3 per cent

of the gross national product on both sides of the East–West balance by the year 2000 would be a truly ambitious goal for the arms control process. As it happens, Canada is already there. Such a triumph of nuclear and conventional arms control would simply bring the vast majority of Canada's allies and potential rivals down to its relative level or, at least, to less than 1 per cent above it. Canadian defence cuts over the next decade would in truth contribute as little to the process of arms control as the rebuilding of the armed forces will to the global military balance. The plain fact is that the earth does not move when Canada makes a serious defence decision.

We are in a position, however, to help those whose decisions will shape the future of the military balance and, at the same time, help ourselves. By bolstering the political strength of the Western alliance during a period of transition, we can serve the interests of our allies, of old enemies and of ourselves. If the alliance is united in terms of fundamental principles and policy, that will reduce any perceived risk or danger during the transition to lower force levels. Steadiness in NATO policy will decrease the temptation of those in the Soviet Union and Warsaw Pact who would use Western divisiveness as an excuse to alter the commitment to stability and arms reductions. For Canada, the alliance will continue to be a useful means of influencing the formulation of conventional defence, strategic deterrence and our own international role.

By shouldering as much of the changing defence burden as our rebuilt forces are able, Canada can help bolster the alliance's political strength and further the process of arms reduction. Our forces on Europe's central front are both a symbol of commitment and hostage to our rhetoric. Their strengthening may not tip the military balance, but it evidences our determination to sustain the alliance. Our willingness to undertake a relatively greater share of the overall burden, as the larger allies cut back their forces, will help smooth the process of force reductions, particularly if other NATO members with small military establishments can be persuaded to hold steady while the big battalions shift.

Canada's firm commitment on the ground throughout

the force reduction process could help in small ways to stem the lingering fear that North America may be severed from the security of Europe as American forces shrink under the political pressure back home to discontinue so huge and costly a deployment in so prosperous a Europe. Finally, should the future turn bleaker than we had envisioned, Canada will still be a part of the central problem with the potential to assist in its solution.

None of this necessitates a major change in policy, but it will demand a steadiness of purpose that has not been a characteristic of defence policy and that is not evident in the defence budget of 1989. It will mean a turning away from the academic temptation to seek "new directions in national defence" before we have finally sorted out the old ones. An Australian strategist has remarked that the best thing Canada can do for the security of the Pacific is to make sure that NATO does not fall apart. That may well demand the level of multilateral skill and strategic insight displayed by those Canadians who helped build the Western alliance in the late 1940s. It will be a tall order.

In short, the strategic task for Canada in the 1990s is to ensure that the alliance which has served our national purposes for forty years continues to do so. If it changes in the wrong way, relations with our European allies will come into question. What is less obvious with such change is that our fundamental relationship with the United States may also become a problem.

Imagine, at some point in the next decade when television shows the President welcoming the first American soldiers who have flown home from Europe, a Canadian government having to forgo a similar political triumph, resisting the temptation to bring its own troops home from Europe. How much less politically satisfying and more difficult it will be for the Prime Minister to have to sell the virtues of steadiness, to have to explain why Canadian soldiers are still abroad. As commentators enthuse over the dawning of a hopeful new age in East–West relations, how less comforting it will seem to have to revive in words the meaning of steadfastness and the value of that enduring relationship between alliance, independence and power.

Part VI

Canada and the United States: The Next Decade

Divining the future of Canadian–American relations begins with an appreciation of how the partnership has progressed over this past decade.

A refreshing degree of maturity has characterized the management of the relationship in the 1980s. So, too, has a willingness to take risks in large causes, as the consummation of the free trade agreement has demonstrated. Much of the pettiness that soured relations at the beginning of the eighties has dissipated. A greater awareness of and sensitivity to the problems and fears within each society have marked the conduct of diplomacy on both sides. This is not to suggest that all major sources of disagreement have been resolved, or that many of the old psychological attitudes overshadowing the relationship will not endure like weeds.

Americans better understand than they did a decade ago the profound differences between themselves and the system, the philosophy and governing priorities of their neighbors across the 49th parallel. In their relations with Canadians, Americans have grown up and away from the "just one big family" ideal that technicolored their vision of Canada and Canadians for much of the post-war era. The pervasive Hollywood caricature, the old-boy-network ethos that tended to narcotize Washington–Ottawa diplomacy, the easy sense in American business circles that Canada was ripe for picking—all this has changed, along with Canada's own sense of esteem.

Canadians have not only grown confident as their earlier internal crises have abated and their economy has soared. The wiser among them have also observed and sought to take advantage of the new forces changing the face of governance in Washington. In quiet ways, watching America's slips and slides in its relations with Central and South American states, Ottawa has sought to exert a more definitive role for Canada in the region. That is why, in 1988, Brian Mulroney became the first Canadian Prime Minister to receive the Pan American Society's Gold Insigne medal at an Americas Society dinner in New York. The award, as he saw it, was "a recognition of Canada's growing role in this hemisphere, a symbol of Canada's partnership in the Americas."

Prime Minister Mulroney is one of a trio of distinguished Canadians who bring this book to a close with assessments of the past decade in Canada–U.S. relations and of what the developments bode for the decade ahead. Allan Gotlieb summons the ghost of de Tocqueville to survey the current state of democracy in America. And John Holmes, in one of the last articles he wrote before his death in August 1988, takes note of how the veils have dropped, the old illusions and simplicities dissolved, among Canadian and American diplomats over the years.

Allan E. Gotlieb

Democracy in America: A Sequel

In his *Democracy in America*, Alexis de Tocqueville wrote what remains the seminal work on America by a foreigner. Despite the fact that his visit to the United States came in the exuberant, even riotous Jackson era, or perhaps *because* it came then, much of what de Tocqueville wrote is as sound today as the day he recorded it—Americans' belief in equality, their devotion to individual liberty, their enthusiasm for commerce, their suspicion of government and wariness of the outside world.

De Tocqueville had much less to say about Canada and it was largely negative. Happily, however, what he did say has mostly proven wrong.

While many of the core elements of de Tocqueville's observations about the United States remain reassuringly valid, this nineteenth-century genius would doubtless be the first to agree that there is an enormous amount of material left for a sequel to *Democracy in America*.

It would be presumptuous to attempt, in the manner of de Tocqueville, to chronicle our times. But, as Canadian Ambassador in Washington, I do work in that expanding space where American and Canadian interests meet or clash. So, as one appointed nearly seven years ago to occupy this privileged post, I offer some observations on the changes I have observed taking place in our two societies, and on the nature and management of our bilateral relationship. That relationship is, and in some respects must be, the prototype of the future. Indeed, I see the Canada–U.S. free trade agreement as an integral part of the future architecture of our relationship.

On balance, de Tocqueville would be pleased by what he would see in America were he to return today to write the sequel to his classic.

Militarily, in the course of two world wars, America became the superpower de Tocqueville believed it would. His prediction that the United States and Russia, backwater nations at the time, "would sway the destinies of half the globe" indicates astonishing prescience. Economically, thanks to the industrial and information revolutions, and through the sheer energy and genius of its people, the United States grew into the world's foremost economic, cultural and military power, far outdistancing the European states of de Tocqueville's frame of reference. Politically, with its core beliefs in equality and justice for all, along with its instinct for forming effective associations to solve world problems, the United States led the way in the creation of many of the great institutions of the twentieth century—the League of Nations, the General Agreement on Tariffs and Trade (GATT), the International Monetary Fund (IMF), the United Nations (UN), the North Atlantic Treaty Organization (NATO) and the Organization for Economic Cooperation and Development (OECD).

While impressed by the energy, enterprise and ambition of the new nation, de Tocqueville was no mere cheerleader. He confessed to irritation with America's unabashed patriotism. He accepted the concept of the sovereignty of the people, while warning of its potential excesses. He marked the clamour of "a thousand simultaneous voices demanding the satisfaction of their social wants." He voiced doubts about the adequacy of America's system of checks and balances to cope with the challenges of the emerging world.

Were de Tocqueville, with his dispassionate eye, to

retrace his steps today, he would be immensely impressed by the power and accomplishment of America. He would also detect trends that would trouble him.

De Tocqueville would probably record a certain tentative, even defensive, state of mind among Americans. He would note, as evidence, levels of defence expenditure and armaments approaching those of wartime; attempts to restrict immigration; anxiety about huge public deficits and debts to foreigners; persistent protectionist tendencies in international trade; and mounting dissatisfaction with the nation's education system. He would no doubt observe that American economic and technological leadership has been seriously challenged as much of the nation's long-held comparative advantage and its dynamic efficiencies have shifted to other areas of the world.

The importance of these trends must not be underestimated. America's unity was forged as millions of immigrants took their place in the greatest production line of consumer goods the world had ever seen. This immense industrial superiority became the hallmark of American genius and the flag of American national identity.

Today, de Tocqueville would be surprised to see that the American self-confidence he thought so remarkable has been shaken. He might wonder whether a certain crisis of identity was being caused by the very preference Americans are now showing for the consumer products of other nations' industrial genius. At the same time, he would see signs that America is beginning to face the challenge of declining and uncompetitive industries, that there is a growing recognition of and a readiness to address the problems of education and training, of work attitude and management.

The cure, however, lies ahead in the long term. Meanwhile, alas, de Tocqueville would discern a pronounced tendency among American politicians and much of the public to view the main problem at hand as one of unfairness on the part of America's trading partners.

Perhaps most importantly, de Tocqueville would be struck by how America governs itself today. While Americans' cultural mores, social habits and lifestyles have never been more unified—drawn together, as they are, by the electronic impulses that reach out to every home in the land—the national system of governance has become more fractured and entangled than at any time in history. The changes in the system have come about in response to the myriad public policy preferences voiced by an ever-growing universe of societal groups that have been established along local, regional or other lines, each pressing for satisfaction. Congress has consequently become a vast and expanding arena for the advancement of special interests—de Tocqueville's "thousand simultaneous voices."

The significance for Canada in all this is nothing less than immense, for if the United States has grown beyond even de Tocqueville's imagination to its present vast and problem-creating size, Canada has developed in many ways even more dramatically. In fact, de Tocqueville did not expect much of Canada, viewing it as a country with a small population "divided into two inimical nations," locked up for all intents and purposes during the six months of winter. Possibly he was too influenced by Voltaire's dismissal of the place as a "few acres of snow." And we did develop slowly: it was only about sixty years ago that Canada sent its first Ambassador abroad, to Washington.

And today in 1988? There has been a diplomatic and political transformation of impressive magnitude. Canada has just hosted the Commonwealth Conference of Heads of Government (CCHG), as well as a similar conference of Francophone Heads of Government, a relatively new institution for which, as for the CCHG, Canadian diplomacy can claim sizable credit. Canada will shortly host the annual summit meeting of the seven leading industrialized powers, the so-called G-7 nations, in Toronto.

Quietly, Canada has become a major power in its own right, one of a small core of countries with serious world interests and the means, unilaterally or multilaterally, to advance them. Most countries have to satisfy themselves merely by expressing positions on the cardinal issues of our time, knowing that they are largely powerless to effect their resolution. Canada, like the United States and a handful of other nations, must concern itself with outcomes and consequences.

In international affairs, however, perceptions are slow to catch up with reality. Most Canadians are still content to view their country as a middle power, a position that implies material comfort and imposes only modest responsibilities. It is a view that defies reality, for most other nations no longer see us in those terms.

They see, instead, a country with the eighth-largest economy in the world. They see one of the world's most effective and least costly social systems. According to *Fortune* magazine, three of the ten richest people in the world are Canadian.

Since the beginning of 1983, Canada's overall growth rate has been the highest of the seven economic summit countries. In 1986, it was about 3.5 per cent, the highest in the West; in 1987, it was nearly 5 per cent, again the highest. Our rate of job creation has been unequalled among the Western nations and all this has been happening despite a prolonged decline in natural resource prices.

Although Canada lays strong claim to its role as a resource superpower, it would be a mistake to assume that resources will always be in oversupply. In a world shaken by the stock market crash of October 1987, and wary of government paper, natural resources represent solid value over the longer term. Canada's strength here lies in its possession of the world's largest reserves of zinc, potash, sulphur and asbestos, and the world's second-largest reserves of silver, tungsten and nickel. We are also the largest exporter of energy to the United States, as well as the world's largest exporter of minerals. No one else exports as much lumber and newsprint as Canada, and it is also the second-largest exporter of wheat on the globe.

Nor should anyone doubt that our firms can successfully compete abroad. Seventy-five per cent of Northern Telecom's sales, for example, go to foreign markets, as do 75 per cent of MacMillan-Bloedel's, 85 per cent of Alcan Aluminum's, 85 per cent of the International Nickel Company's and 92 per cent of Seagram's. By 1985, manufactured products amounted to about 70 per cent of Canadian exports. Canada exports 30 per cent of its gross national product, more than any other major industrial state. In *Fortune* magazine's ranking of the 500 largest non-American industrial companies, Canada has nearly as many entries as France and three times as many as Italy.

Canada also imports—and in a big way. We now consume almost 25 per cent of *all* American exports. In 1986, Canadian purchases, per capita, of American goods amounted to $2 173, compared to the $166 spent, per capita, on European purchases. Thus, imperceptibly, the United States has come to place a lot of its own eggs in our basket, according us a considerable degree of influence.

As to foreign investment, the scope of change is so phenomenal that most people have barely begun to recognize it. The flow of Canadian direct investment to the United States now exceeds the flow of American direct investment to Canada. By 1985, the total amount of Canadian-controlled direct investment in America equalled about three-fifths of the total of American direct investment in Canada. That kind of penetration has increased Canada's presence abroad while extending the nation's influence.

Canadians at last are beginning to catch up with the reality of their prominence. We have always been conscious of our role and influence in the context of the UN. Yet, former American Secretary of State Dean Acheson once dismissed Canada as a regional power without a region. In fact, we are determinedly emerging from our shell, becoming more conscious of our interests and potential role, not only on the North American continent, but in Central America, the Caribbean and elsewhere in the hemisphere.

Conceptually, we are coming to grips with our North American character as we enter into the largest bilateral trading agreement ever, one covering even more trade than the European Community did when the Common Market was created.

Whatever these stirrings and debates among Canadians portend, they are not the hallmarks of a mere middle power. Were he to retrace his steps today, de Tocqueville would marvel at the vast relationship that has mushroomed between Canada and the United States, much of it having developed in the last twenty years.

Arnold Heeney, that distinguished public servant, served two terms as Canada's Ambassador to the United States—from 1953 to 1957 and from 1959 to 1962. During his years in Washington, he was occupied primarily with the ending of the Korean War, the Suez crisis, the issue of recognition of China, and the Cuban Missile Crisis of October 1962. Economic issues were close to non-existent. In his memoirs, Heeney says he reported to the Prime Minister of the day that there were no important economic problems between the two North American neighbours.

When I glance at *my* bilateral agenda for the past six years, it reads like a description of the Canadian economy: uranium,

copper, asbestos, oil, gas, steel, lumber, fish, pork, beef and cattle, pota-
toes, pharmaceuticals, films, wheat, potash, corn, textiles, wine and
beer—not to mention the extensive environmental, boundary and coastal
issues between the United States and Canada, or the regulatory, defence
and foreign policy issues. Heeney, let alone de Tocqueville, simply would
not recognize the state of relations between the two countries.

During his stay in Washington, Ambassador Heeney journeyed to Capitol Hill only once, and then only as a last resort to try
and head off a piece of Congressional legislation particularly troubling
to Canada. On that visit, he called on a single Congressman, Senate
Majority leader Lyndon Johnson, at the suggestion of the State Department. Senator Johnson gave his word to Heeney that the bill in question,
concerning the diversion of water from the Great Lakes, would not pass.
And it didn't. The anecdote only illustrates how profoundly things have
changed in the two decades since Ambassador Heeney left Washington.
We have witnessed the diplomatic equivalent of a neutron bomb attack:
the buildings remain standing, but everything else has changed.

Arnold Heeney called on one Congressional leader on
one occasion only. In ten days alone, I have paid eight calls on Congressmen. In my more than six years in Washington, I have made hundreds
and hundreds of personal calls on Capitol Hill; my colleagues at the
embassy have probably made a thousand or more. Heeney solved his
problem by talking to one person, the Senate Majority leader. Today,
on such an issue, I would not even seek a meeting with the Senate
or House Majority leader, competent and honourable men though I
know them to be, so decentralized and dispersed has decision-making
power become on Capitol Hill.

The American political system, having undergone rapid
change in recent decades, finds itself under increasing strain. In Congress,
the seniority system has ended. Party discipline has eroded as television
advertising campaigns and political action committees (PACs) have
strengthened the independence of individual members. Only one party
commands widespread allegiance: the re-election party. Political bosses
are no more; the legislative agenda is largely run now by greatly increased
numbers of committee and subcommittee chairmen who are perhaps
the most powerful players in the system. As one astute former Congress-

man told me, a chairman of a Congressional subcommittee who knows what he is doing can write the laws of the land. The end result may be "gridlock" or, alternatively, open season for special interests. The legislation that Congress approves is often part and parcel of huge spending packages that lend themselves to deal-making among the law-makers, often in the dead of night.

In America's executive and judicial branches too, the dispersal of power provides other convenient avenues for special inter-ests to seek narrow fixes. Declining American industries, for example, are able to harass foreign competition via litigation before autonomous agencies and, increasingly, before the courts. These entities, in turn, have little institutional competence in the field of trade and less experience in foreign affairs.

De Tocqueville recognized that the policy process in democratic societies must mediate among competing interests. Indeed, any representative government must be responsive to domestic interests. From my experience, however, I am convinced that it has become increasingly difficult for the interests of outside countries to be fairly recognized and effectively brought into play at critical times. Foreign governments deal with these problems as best they can. For Canada, the problem is more acute because of the unparalleled level of interlock-ing interests between it and the United States.

When we examine the regulation of the environment, regarding air quality and acid rain, when we study the trend towards deregulation of communications, trucking, air and other transportation services, when we analyze changes in banking, investment and financial services, we see that many of our conflicts arise on the American side of the border, because of *domestic* as opposed to foreign policy interests. That is why I conclude that, in Canada's case, the term "American foreign policy" is largely a misnomer. In reality, American foreign policy vis-à-vis Canada is more an aggregation of American domestic policies.

No more vexing problem divides us than acid rain pollu-tion. At least half of the noxious sulphuric emissions that fall in Canada emanate from smoke-stacks in the United States. When Congress regu-lates air quality in America, it accordingly regulates it for Canada as well. Yet regulation (i.e., the Clean Air Act) is viewed in America as largely a domestic policy matter. If Canadian diplomats seek to influence the scope or nature of such regulation, they are thought by some to be interfering in American domestic affairs.

But "interfere" we must, whether by calling on Congress, the Administration or government regulatory bodies, or by presenting our case to the media, making speeches, writing op-ed pieces or whatever. This is the diplomatic equivalent of the full-court press—or more accurately, in this era of protectionism, of a blitzing defence.

Arnold Heeney's more restrained brand of diplomacy would have struck a familiar chord with de Tocqueville. For that matter, it would have been familiar to the Pharaohs, to the Inner Kingdom, to the Sun King and even to the Court of St. James. In this historical context, what we and more and more embassies are now doing in Washington *is* revolutionary. Some Americans may be shocked at the extent to which we appear to be involved in American domestic affairs. In Canada, some are shocked about this, too, although others are shocked that we are not more involved.

The reasons for this new state of affairs are worth noting. First is the development and expansion of the international economy into one vast world market. Second is the explosive post-war growth in the Canada–U.S. relationship. Third is the impact of domestic laws and regulation on Canada's interests. Fourth is the shift in the balance of power from the Administration to Congress over the disposition of most issues, but especially trade. One may add to this last: the collapse of the post-war consensus in the American government on foreign policy issues; the breakdown of trust between the executive and legislative branches; the creation of a whole new public service, numbering some 40 000 people, on Capitol Hill; the ascendance of a dramatically expanded "persuasion" industry in Washington, led by a cohort of 46 000 lawyers in addition to the 20 000 or more professionals already engaged in lobbying and the 2 500 associations located in the capital, which promote special interests.

Because Canadians are the most affected by American policies and regulation, we are in the vanguard in establishing ways to deal with them.

The Canada–U.S. predicament is simply described: on

either side of the border, members of two intensely democratic societies frequently express opposing policy preferences; politicians on either side, representing these policy interests, pursue them vigorously. Given the two nations' independent ways and the fact that their central authorities, even when they have the power to act, are reluctant to override domestic interests, especially to satisfy foreigners, our disputes fester. In an era of virulent protectionism, they also tend to expand into new fields. On top of this, the global market has spawned intense competition leading to economic disputes that institutions, national as well as international, cannot resolve. The cliché of interdependence is as true as it is troublesome.

Traditional diplomacy and even the more recent efforts at diplomatic lobbying have, in my opinion, reached the outer limits of their effectiveness in dealing with these conditions. Innovation is necessary; new methods need to be broached.

Whether or not de Tocqueville contemplated the kind of world I have described, he would have appreciated the response by Canada and the United States—a free trade agreement (FTA) creating new institutional methods for settling disputes between them. The FTA is not just an accord about tariffs, though their elimination will bring substantial benefits. It is an agreement about how two nations will conduct economic relations with each other. It is intended to address deeply entrenched forces in two modern democracies that are ever more reliant on each other—forces that make it increasingly difficult to accommodate diverging political pressures and to reconcile conflicting policy goals.

The Canada–U.S. FTA is much more than a defensive system: it offers a framework for the management of the most complex trading relationship in the world. At the same time, it sets out principles for ushering the North American economy into the twenty-first century. In opting for an institutional approach to the settlement of trade disputes, the FTA marks an historic transformation of methodology in the Canada–U.S. relationship. In the past, our two countries have rarely used formal mechanisms for consultation and for resolution of disputes. Exceptions like the International Joint Commission (IJC) are few and far between.

The world has changed profoundly, the United States and Canada with it. Our relationship has come a long way, and I have, too. I have moved from being one of the most persistent doubters of the value of formal dispute-settlement institutions to being one of the most persuaded advocates of this agreement as an idea whose time has arrived. If reason prevails, it will be approved and implemented in the two countries—a "win-win" proposition that stands to benefit both signatories. It will benefit the world as well, because the FTA is not merely supplemental to GATT. It is integral to it, if that institution is to become fully relevant once again. Indeed, this bilateral pact could constitute the underpinning of a renewed world trading system.

Let Canada and the United States choose cooperation over confrontation, facilitation over interference, progress over protectionism. Let both sides make it possible for de Tocqueville's sequel to chronicle the confidence and genius of North America, allowing it to record for posterity our wisdom and leadership in the world.

Brian Mulroney

Cooperation and Leadership in the Americas

It is a great honour to receive the Gold Insigne. I accept it with special pride because it is the first time it has been given to a Canadian Prime Minister.

I also accept it on behalf of Canada. I see it as a recognition of Canada's growing role in this hemisphere, as a symbol of Canada's partnership in the Americas.

Canada is a dynamic country, a proud and active member of the international community, in which our perspective is as diverse as our geography. It is also a nation that is building better and closer relations with its hemispheric neighbours.

Better relations with Latin America and the Caribbean are an important facet of our foreign policy. Canadian missionaries forged links with Latin America that flourish to this day. Canada established embassies in Brazil, Argentina, Chile, Cuba, Peru and Mexico not long after sending its first Ambassador to Washington. Two-way trade with Latin America today has yielded Canadian exports of more than $3 billion and imports exceeding $4 billion. Direct Canadian investment is more than $4 billion. Our assistance program to the developing countries of the region is large and growing.

Canada also plays an important and constructive role in the Caribbean through the United Nations (UN) and its agencies, as well as through the Commonwealth and La Francophonie. We actively support the Commonwealth countries of the Caribbean (CARICOM) through increased development assistance, along with special arrangements for tariff reduction and trade facilitation under the 1986 CARIBCAN Agreement between Canada and the CARICOM countries. On a per capita basis, the Caribbean countries receive the highest level of Canadian aid in the world. We are impressed by the determination of the people in the region to build their own democracies. Nowhere has the yearning for democracy been greater than in Haiti; nowhere has it been more cynically thwarted. We have pressed, and will continue to firmly press, the Haitian authorities to develop genuine democratic institutions. We profoundly regret that the aspirations of the Haitian people have been frustrated for so long. Nor will they be satisfied with the illusion of democracy, because the Haitians, who have sacrificed so much, are resolved to possess the genuine article.

We are sensitive as well to the aspirations of the Central American peoples for economic progress and peace. We believe that the fundamental cause of the problems in Central America lies in social and economic conditions. That is why we have responded with development assistance programs to all countries in that region: some $200 million over the past five years. We recognize that solutions depend on political will and political consensus. As the Nobel Laureate Oscar Arias recently told an Americas Society audience:

> Domestic tranquility and external security may be attained in our hemisphere only if freedom and democracy prevail in all of the countries.

That is why Canada supports the Central America Peace Plan, as we supported the Contadora process before it. That is why I am pleased to report that, consistent with its tradition, Canada stands ready to undertake a peace-supervisory role anywhere in the region, provided that the Central American governments desire our involvement and create a framework for effective action. Our policy is clear: we shall support any initiative which contributes to the stability of the region, to self-determination for its nations, to peace for its peoples.

I have no doubt that the Central American countries can find, out of their long experience as sovereign nations, exemplary models of freedom and social progress to emulate, as well as examples of oppression and stagnation to avoid. Only in a stable, free, productive environment can the regional economy develop and new trade links be fostered. Trade results *from* peace, just as it results *in* prosperity.

Canada and the United States have lived in peace for over 175 years. How many neighbouring nations can make that claim, in this hemisphere or any other? We have our differences of policy, of view and approach. We have disagreements that are deeply felt and prerogatives that are vigorously defended. We are sovereign nations with interests that sometimes diverge or collide. But given these realities, consider our evolution together.

A 5 000-mile border between our nations is unguarded. Not a single soldier, not an expression of might, are to be found any-where. Our two nations are founded on the principles of freedom and democracy. In somewhat different but genuinely remarkable ways, Canada and the United States have stayed true to those values and, in the process, contributed significantly to the improvement of mankind. Fifty years ago, Winston Churchill said it best when he described our relationship thus:

> That long frontier from the Atlantic to the Pacific Ocean, guarded only by neighbourly respect and honourable obligations, is an example to every country and a pattern for the future of the world.

When my government was elected in 1984, one of our most urgent priorities was the refurbishment of relations with the United States. Barriers to expanded trade had been established, particularly in the field of investment. Canadian foreign policy had drifted from funda-mentals that had long anchored our international activity. None of these things, in my view, respected Canadian traditions or served Canadian interests.

We promised Canadians that we would restore our country to its former role of full participation in our historic alliances and the international community. We have carried out that promise. The driving force behind growth and job creation is a dynamic private sector. We restored fiscal responsibility, reducing the federal deficit every year since 1984, largely by controlling expenditures. We deregulated the transportation and energy sectors. We dismantled the National Energy Policy (NEP), with its abusive intervention in the marketplace. We opened financial markets and stimulated greater competition in financial services. We sold a number of Crown or public corporations to the private sector. We created Investment Canada to encourage and welcome capital from abroad. We introduced major reforms to the tax system that will lower personal and corporate tax rates.

Canadians have responded to these policies. Since 1984, our growth rate has led those of all other major OECD (Organization for Economic Cooperation and Development) countries. Our job creation rate leads that of the industrialized world. We can therefore look back on the last three and a half years with some satisfaction. The Canada–U.S. relationship is where it ought to be, conducted in an atmosphere of mutual respect and understanding. These results have entailed hard work on both sides. President Reagan and I agreed to devote special attention and priority to the task through annual meetings at the highest level. But if this relationship is to remain sound, it will require further effort.

The obligations of neighbourliness include the steward-ship of our natural environment. The boundary between us may be political, but the environment pays it no notice. Nowhere is this clearer than on the issue of acid rain, which is devastating North American forests and lakes, ours as well as yours. Our environmental heritage and our economic development are both threatened by this blight, which demands urgent action.

Some 14 000 Canadian lakes are already dead; 150 000 others are being acidified, while 150 000 more are vulnerable. Acid rain has killed nineteen salmon-bearing rivers in one province alone—Nova Scotia. Almost 85 per cent of the best agricultural land in Eastern Canada receives unacceptably high levels of acid. More than 50 per cent of the forests in this region grow in areas where rainfall is acidic. Even our maple sugar industry is in jeopardy.

This is a vast, accelerating tragedy. It is also entirely pre-ventable. We cannot solve this problem by ourselves, however, because

50 per cent of all the acid rain falling on Canada today comes directly from the United States. You are a major part of our problem and a vital part of the solution. My government has enacted tough legislation and concluded agreements with our provinces that ensure we have cleaned up our own act. Now, nothing less than targeted, mandated reductions in acid rain emissions in the United States will suffice.

Yet, we are told, in the face of overwhelming scientific evidence to the contrary, that the issue needs more study—all to avoid action. America must do its part. Friendship has inescapable costs. One of them is bearing whatever burdens are required to avoid polluting your neighbour's property with destructive wastes. I have raised the acid rain issue at every meeting with President Reagan. I will raise it with him again. I will raise it with his successor, if need be. I will raise it until we get it resolved, until the damage is curtailed.

Canada and the United States have built the largest trading relationship in history and two of the most prosperous economies in the world. Nearly 80 per cent of our exports go to the United States; fully 25 per cent of America's exports go to Canada. Some two million American jobs depend directly on exports to Canada. Between our countries, we conduct annually some $160 billion worth of trade and commerce in goods and services. After dividends, interest payments and retained earnings are factored in, the commercial account between us results in a rough balance. So, our two-way trade is fair and mutually beneficial, the only kind that Canada wants for its partners and itself.

In January, President Reagan and I signed the Canada–U.S. Free Trade Agreement, a dream as old as the century and one which has eluded successive generations of leaders in both countries. The American trade representative, Ambassador Clayton Yeutter, has called the agreement

> a truly historic document . . . as significant in the economic sphere as the arms control agreement [signed between the Soviet Union and America in December 1987] is in the national security area.

Until recently, it was widely assumed in the United States that Japan was America's largest trading partner. In fact, Canada, not Japan, is America's largest trading partner, by a country mile. And one of our provinces, Ontario, is America's *second*-largest export market. The commercial dialogue between us is hugely varied, and Canada, as a superpower in terms of its natural resources, contributes impressively to that dialogue.

> —Supplier of fully one-third of the world's newsprint, Canada is the source of 90 per cent of the *New York Times* newspaper, while most of the *New York Daily News* derives from my home town of Baie-Comeau, Quebec.
> —Canada and the United States conduct the world's largest energy trade—in oil, gas and, increasingly, in electricity.
> —In New York, the Canadian firm of Olympia and York has become the city's largest landlord, leading one prominent local to observe:
>> There have been two great real estate deals in the history of New York. The first was when the Dutch bought the Island of Manhattan. The second was when the Canadians bought [it] again.
> —Canada remains by far America's best customer, with the value of American exports to Canada nearly equalling its sales to the other five G-7 (Group of Seven) partners combined. Canada buys more than twice as much from the United States as Japan does, and nearly twice as much as West Germany, Britain and France combined.

Now, under the Free Trade Agreement, our trade will increase even more. All tariffs, without exception, will be abolished or phased out over a ten-year period beginning January 1, 1989. Among the other precedents established by this agreement are: rules for two-way trade in services; a bilateral agreement in the financial services sector; rules on bilateral investment activities; and a unique binational mechanism for settling trade disputes.

Some in Canada feel we have gained too little and given away too much. Some in the United States feel we have gained too much and conceded too little. The voices of special interests, sectional interests and vested interests are raised, seeking favours and protection. But there are other, stronger voices, those of your national interest and ours, calling on their governments for the vision and courage to make history, not to shrink from it. If this agreement is not completed now, when it is within our grasp, such an opportunity will not soon arise again. If the Free Trade Agreement becomes a reality, on the other hand, North America will assume new strength.

Our two countries must never turn away from an historic opportunity to improve the world's prosperity by enhancing our relationship with one another. I believe that the Free Trade Agreement will be strongly endorsed on both sides. I believe that the vision of a bigger and bolder future will prevail. I believe that leadership and confidence shall triumph over protectionism and fear.

An agreement between the world's two largest trading partners is exceptionally important in multilateral terms. Indeed, our agreement is crucial to the outcome of the multilateral trade negotiations in the General Agreement on Tariffs and Trade (GATT).

Serious strains persist in the international economic system that can only be addressed collectively. Progress must be made on economic policy coordination and on trade liberalization. At the forthcoming Economic Summit of the leaders of the G-7 nations in Toronto, my colleagues and I will have to try to provide momentum for the Uruguay Round of multilateral trade negotiations. We can do that by committing ourselves to, and making progress on, agricultural reforms. I attach particular importance to the problems plaguing agricultural producers and the need to reform the subsidy practices, which are escalating out of control and run counter to the most elementary principles of efficiency and comparative advantage.

Finally, we must deal with the issue of Third World debt. We must build on the progress that was achieved at the Venice Summit on the problems of the poorest countries. Canada has recently written off $600 million of African debt; if the other G-7 countries took similar steps, the Official Development Assistance debt of these countries would be reduced by 15 per cent. Canada has also channelled its assistance to the poorest countries entirely on the basis of grants, not loans.

The situation of middle-income debtor countries should also preoccupy us, and not only out of concern for the impact of defaults on our own financial institutions and of shrinking markets for our exports. It should concern us because of the debilitating impact on democratic institutions and on the hopes of young leaders in the Third World nations when interest and debt payments consume most, if not all, of their foreign exchange.

The G-7, of which Canada and the United States are members, is a community of industrialized democracies accounting for more than 50 per cent of the world's economic output. We *must* find the capacity to act in concert on those tough issues where individual action is either impossible or ineffective. It is in all our interests to ensure that the democratic values we cherish continue to flourish; that the obligation to preserve our natural environment is met; that the trade channels, so vital to growth, remain open and vigorous; and that the institutions which enrich our societies do not collapse under the weight of financial burden.

The challenges call for cooperation and leadership. Canada, in confidence and pride, will do its part.

John W. Holmes

The Disillusioning of the Relationship: Epitaph to a Decade

The 1980s have been a great learning experience in international relations: East–West, North–South, Canadian–American.

One might say, optimistically, that we have been getting down to brass tacks: the actual reduction of nuclear weapons; concrete schemes for debt reduction; the nitty-gritty of trade barriers. There are more signs of maturity at the leadership summit. It just might be that Canadians and Americans are moving towards the more mature relationship that President Nixon called for when he visited Ottawa in the early seventies.

There was not much maturity in the confrontational attitudes of the early eighties, as reflected in my somewhat acerbic lecture to the Americas Society in 1981. I made a plea then for "pragmatism and tolerance, qualities that have led Canadians and Americans to set an example to the world." Without much confidence, I added: "If we can avoid the abstractions and sit down at the table, if we can subdue the rhetoric and look at the facts, we will better serve the interests of both peoples." Well, we have spent a good deal of time in the mid-eighties at the drawing boards, working our way from those abstractions to the case studies. This has been most notable, of course, on trade and investment. Whether or not the free trade agreement turns out to have been a good thing, a lesson in pragmatism may have been learned in spite of all the tumult and the shouting over the issue.

We have worked our way through illusions and simplicities that frustrated progress in our relations. We should have learned, in particular, that mood and personalities are less important factors than we had been led to believe. The changes of government in both countries have been illustrative of this: much has altered, but not necessarily because new governments took over. Conflicts persisted because they were real. Circumstances changed because of shifts in the world economy, world strategy, and alterations of the domestic political balances in both countries, especially Canada.

In the early eighties, the confrontation was being blamed on Prime Minister Trudeau by Americans and by a good many Canadians. If those pinko Liberals in Ottawa could only be replaced by Conservatives to match the Reagan blue in Washington, all would be well. It was forgotten that, in the early sixties, the solution for confrontation had been to turn out the anti-American Tories of the Diefenbaker regime and replace them with friendly Liberals. The changes that Americans and many Canadians wanted in Ottawa's policy, particularly in the case of the National Energy Policy (NEP) and the Foreign Investment Review Agency (FIRA), were already underway before Trudeau left office. (It is worth noting that, while the Tories changed the name of the odious FIRA, they retained the agency, which still places restrictions on foreign investors.) The "nationalist" trends in Canadian economic policies in the seventies were less the consequence of partisan conviction than a widely felt response by Canadians to what had seemed to be a swing in Washington towards economic nationalism, as dramatically revealed in the protectionist measures of the Nixon–Connally regime.

When the change came in Ottawa in 1984, there were great expectations on both sides of the border. Many Canadians were convinced that a more friendly disposition towards the United States would dissolve outstanding bilateral problems. In the United States, there was a widespread assumption that, with the anti-Americans out and the pro-Americans installed in Ottawa, Canadians would be causing less trouble. So, we had a smiling summit meeting between Reagan and Mulroney in Quebec City, but not much progress on the issues. Acid rain still blew north, the Maritime Boundary Treaty remained stalled. A more amiable attitude, however, undoubtedly smoothed some operations. Goodwill is an essential element in this kind of relationship, particularly when it involves unequal countries, one of which, Canada, is obsessively preoccupied with the other and one, the United States, for which domestic and other foreign relations always command a higher priority. Goodwill does not just remove conflict on its own, for conflict is more than an emotional issue. In this case, there was danger that the collapse of fond expectations would provoke bitterness. It did, but less seriously than one had feared. The backlash may have been directed into healthy disillusionment, a more sophisticated grasp of the paradoxes of the "unfortified frontier."

It should be noted that changes in Canadian foreign policy overall were considerably less under the new Mulroney regime than might have been expected. Whether they liked it or not, Canadians had tended to assume that Canada's foreign policy would draw closer to that of the United States. The expectation was probably shared by those few officials and others in the United States who are aware that Canada *has* a foreign policy. At the time the new government decided to go for a free trade agreement, it was widely accepted that policies or attitudes offending the Americans would be in poor taste. Yet, there are greater differences between the *weltanschauung* of Canadian and American conservatives, in their perceptions of their respective national interests, than readily meet the eye.

The Prime Minister and his Secretary of State for External Affairs promptly reaffirmed Canada's traditionally internationalist approach to world order, in particular its dedication to the United Nations (UN) and other multilateral institutions, at a time when Washington looked very critically on multilateralism. Mulroney appointed as Ambassador to the UN a man whose views on that institution as well as on other major issues differed notably from Washington's. Canada's concern over American policy in Central America was expressed on various occasions. It was voiced politely and non-confrontationally, but the message was clear to those who understand the language of diplomacy. Intergovernmental collaboration on America's Strategic Defence Initiative (SDI) was tactfully rejected on the ground that it did not fit Canada's line of research.

In the UN Assembly, Canadian delegations played a leading role in seeking to avert the financial crisis precipitated by the American default, while expressing some sympathy for the causes of Washington's discontent. Canada's voting record in the UN during the Mulroney years differed from that of the United States more markedly than in some other periods. In contrast to the American approach, Canada did not withdraw from the United Nations Educational, Scientific, and Cultural Organization (UNESCO) during the controversy over that body, but chose to work for reform from the inside. And, at a time when the Reagan Administration was notably souring on North–South issues, Canada not only increased its aid, but took a lead in focusing special attention on African concerns. In particular, the Mulroney government has actively pressed for sanctions against South Africa, contrary to the views of President Reagan.

This stubborn persistence in divergent foreign policy approaches is significant, given Canadians' paranoid fear that their need to preserve good economic relations with the United States would compromise their ability to conduct an independent foreign policy. The evidence of the past few years, despite a strong compulsion to keep Congress happy, ought to modify that illusion.

Regrettably, the differentiation in Canadian and American policies is too little acknowledged by those Canadians who insist that differences between the two countries—if they are to carry any political weight—must be total and noisy. There has been little evidence, of course, that Canadian policies on Nicaragua or South Africa have attracted attention beyond the Canadian desk in the American State Department, and there has been no indication that they had the slightest impact on the negotiations for a free trade agreement. Congress might have eschewed a trade agreement had Ottawa begun sending tanks to the Sandinistas or joined the Soviet Union in a bilateral agreement for Arctic disarmament. But these are not policies a Canadian government would be disposed to pursue in any case.

There have been fewer and fewer reasons for differing

on North Atlantic Treaty Organization (NATO) matters. Canada's increased defence appropriations were a response to criticism from all the allies, not just the United States. Primarily, however, they are the expression of a growing belief that Canada, to maintain its sovereignty, must play a larger role in collective defence. Despite dire predictions of conflict between Europeans and Americans over missiles and conventional weapons, the alliance itself has been working quite smoothly. Its role, after all, is not to exorcise disputes but to cope with them. In spite of the unilateralist gestures of some outspoken American military men and politicians, and the contempt they frequently show for their entangling alliances, those Americans actually responsible for negotiation and policy have been fairly sensitive and have brought their allies along remarkably well on arms control.

When there is movement in East–West negotiation, as there has been in the late eighties, we get down at last to specifics and face the contradictions that cannot be denounced away. The actual prospect of prudently dismantling a military confrontation, constructed over four decades, concentrates the mind remarkably.

In highly important areas, Canadians have become less critical of American policies because those policies have changed. Two issues, for example, on which Canadians and Americans once had opposing views—China and Vietnam—have ceased to divide us because the United States retreated from an aggressive policy in East Asia that had consistently worried Ottawa. At the same time, Canada has always evinced a strong interest in arms control and persistently pressed the superpowers to get on with it. Without being neutral, Canadians have tended to see the danger not simply in terms of a Soviet attack but rather in terms of the circumstances that would trigger a nuclear exchange. Early on in the Reagan regime, we were alarmed by the effect on the paranoiac Russians of the "evil empire" rhetoric. That was the prime reason for Trudeau's peace crusade which, in the waning months of his government, got wider public support than he did.

Not surprisingly, then, Canadians have been almost universally enthusiastic about the President's activist policies on arms control and East–West dialogue during his second term. Congressional opposition to military assistance for the Contra rebels also diminished Canadian criticism over Nicaragua. None of this is to suggest even faintly that American policy buckled under Canadian pressure, although our voice was part of the collective advice of many concerned friends and allies. Nevertheless, because the stronger rather than the weaker power altered course, Canadian and American policies at the end of the decade have become closer on important issues—a development that must be disconcerting to those Canadians for whom independence is the highest priority.

On the North American defence front, there has been a deliberate effort by Ottawa and Washington to rationalize provisions for surveillance and achieve some workable understandings. Symbolic of a new, more pragmatic approach was the agreement reached about the disposition of surface ships and submarines in Arctic waters. On the vexing issue of sovereignty in the Arctic, the two sides resorted to one of the most sensible formulae for diplomacy, an agreement to disagree. It was an absurd situation that the natural collaboration of allies in the northern seas had been inhibited by a disagreement over the sovereignty and the rights of passage which had more to do with the precedent supposedly set for the Indonesian archipelago than with the realities of Arctic ice. So, we set aside ideology and passions to find something with which we could live and work.

In the course of negotiations over the trade agreement, a number of illusions have been discarded. We had been dogged by the North American reliance on the quick fix, the ready assumption that there is a simple formula or device to make trade uninhibited, unfettered, and self-regulating. That alluring vision of a border removed, of free trade, free enterprise, and free love faded as a lengthy and complex text full of qualifying provisos was hammered out. At the same time, the fears of those who saw Canada losing the essentials for protecting its soul were assuaged or at least directed to the fine print. It became clear that any agreement within reach would be laced with checks and balances, possibly to the extent that it would not in the end seem worthwhile. What has been sought, after all, is not a formula for eliminating conflict but a more satisfactory process for resolving it, bearing in mind that the new agreement would multiply rather than diminish the number of conflicts.

It is clear that the ultimate sovereignty of Canada and the United States has to be accepted even if their freedom of action is bound by new obligations. The hope of some Canadians for an international commission that would bind the two governments to decisions reached on trade disputes evaporated quickly when put to the test. Obviously, new rules would have to be accepted by Congress and by federal and provincial governments, but they would have to be freely accepted. It was an aberration, in any case, for Canadians to argue that an international commission should make binding decisions instead of recommendations; traditionally, as with the International Joint Commission (IJC), Canada had always insisted on the right in principle of each government to decide whether to take action in accordance with IJC recommendations. Canada had always recognized that it should never be entrapped in a supra-sovereign continental institution in which the will of the stronger power was bound to predominate.

We should talk less about "closer relations" between the two countries and more about "better relations," which are not necessarily the same thing. Nature has made us about as close as we could possibly be and this has made it all the more necessary that relations should be carefully structured. One could only wish that the debate on trade had begun not with utopian visions but with a simple recognition that there were bound to be ways of improving the trading relationship if we just sat down and examined the list of problems. Had we started from this perspective, the draft agreements could have been assessed on their merits rather than in the high-flown context of a giant step for the liberation of North America or the demise of Canada.

The utopian illusions were closely associated with the zealous free-enterprise ideology of early Reaganites and in the rhetoric, if not the practice, of some Canadian Conservatives. Heavy emphasis was placed on abolishing government intervention. However, while governments that talk that way may privatize large sections of the economy, they do not forgo, with subsidies and quotas, tariff and non-tariff barriers, support for banks and currency management—often on the demand of those very industrialists who want government off their backs. Though it deplores international interference, the United States government, when in need, frequently turns to such UN bodies as the International Monetary Fund (IMF), the International Bank for Reconstruction and Development (IBRD), and the General Agreement on Tariffs and Trade (GATT).

Canadians have found it easier to accept limited governmental management in principle, while keeping it to a minimum in practice, because they have always recognized a role for government to do those things an underpopulated country needs, while they have consistently regarded international institutions as necessary guardians of the interests of lesser powers. As America's hegemony has dwindled, its people, too, have demanded that their government do something. This has, however, hardly entailed a conversion to socialism which, in any case, has proved a universal failure, existing only as a bogey word for hard-pressed ideologues.

The sweet illusion of a self-regulating world may have died of shame, a victim of the crass hypocrisy of every Western government that charged another government with the kind of regulation and restriction it practised itself. An honest recognition that Canada, the United States, and other nations are bound to try and manage their interests in an interdependent world might help us make that management as intelligent and limited as possible.

Another illusion being shattered is that we on this continent can operate on our own. Americans have always seen "free trade" with Canada in the context of a new GATT round, leaving Canadians to temper their dream of a bilateral solution. The relative global decline of the two North American economies has dissipated the latent assumption that we could, if necessary, build a satisfactory continental economy on our own. Canadians have perhaps been more addicted than Americans to this fancy; they have not hankered after a continental economy in which they recognize they would be subordinate, but the notion has always clung there as a last resort. Still, both countries have now become massively indebted and they cannot just declare bankruptcy. The internationalization of business and finance proceeds at a dizzying pace. The prospects are of a terrifying complexity, but at least we may both have shed the image of isolation.

There may still linger in Canadian minds the possibility of one last solution: application for membership in the American federation. The intense debate over the trade issue has revealed, however, that "manifest destiny" is not exactly a live issue in the United States. Americans seem to have as many vested interests in protecting themselves against the Canadian economy as Canadians have traditionally had in the other direction. Just as Canadians want to resist the extension northwards of certain American laws and customs, not to mention a homicide rate five times their own, so many Americans may fear the socialist contamination of medicare or marketing boards. National differences are cherished on both sides. Bilingualism is right for Canada, but would be contrary to the deeply rooted convictions of Americans about their nation. Moreover, the United States, already weighed down with enormous national and international responsibilities, would just as soon not take on more ice and barren lands, along with such problems as native land claims, the maintenance of communications over even vaster areas, and the thorny and still unresolved matter of language rights in Quebec and certain other provinces. None of these profoundly Canadian issues would just fade away with annexation. Canada would be a large and difficult lump to swallow. One can envision, following union, a Canadian Liberation Front with terrorist links to Belfast and Tripoli. Therefore, a realization that Americans do not actually want Canada may indeed encourage Canadians to adopt more rational approaches in the ordering of a continent irrevocably divided by four centuries of history and accumulated cultural and regional interests.

It is not hard, of course, to take a pessimistic view of relations between Canada and the United States in the late 1980s. There is much to be said, though, for regarding with some approval the considerable progress through our actions, if not necessarily through our rhetoric, in recognizing the profits of disillusionment.

In the world at large, we have approached a degree of rationality that could never have been foreseen as the decade began. The fact that we have a long way to go, with many uncertainties, ought not to obscure the transformation in East–West relations. Leaders in all countries have had no alternative but to face up to the stark facts of life: nuclear escalation veering out of control; Third World debt collapsing the international financial system; environmental abuses threatening the earth's ozone layer and climatic stability. Soviet leaders say openly that they had no alternative to change, that they have had to abandon their notion of a capitalist versus a socialist world and seek their place in a global economy.

The mounting debt burden has affected the calculations of military powers, left and right. Scientists, regardless of iron curtains, are collaborating intensely on the threats to our environment. The People's Republic of China and the World Bank are working jointly on plans to improve the Chinese economy, an endeavour in which ideology appears irrelevant. Gorbachev's proposals bewilder us with their apparent good sense. The five great powers in the UN's Security Council agree on at least a basic approach to ending the Iran–Iraq war. An agreement is worked out over Afghanistan. In Washington, the pragmatists, led by Secretary of State Shultz and Treasury Secretary Baker, gain the upper hand over the simplicists.

Pragmatism can, of course, become an ideology too. We are noting only a change in direction. Negotiation is better than angry confrontation, but it is also a lot more exhausting. Facing the issues at the conference table is certainly better than facing them from the rostrum, but the formulae are not easy to assemble and there is no guarantee of success. Patience is required; lack of trust can trigger panic all too easily. In North America, failure to approve a trade agreement could sour attitudes in both countries and inspire domestic divisions. Canada and the United States are not necessarily entering an era of good feeling. Still, failure on trade would force us to return, somewhat the wiser perhaps, to the search for ways of conflict resolution, because conflicts between us are not going to go away.

With our eyes fixed on ways and means rather than visions, we might make better progress than we did in the cacophonous early years of this decade. The more one looks back to the early eighties, the more one is aware of how greatly the situation has changed and how great are the opportunities ahead of us.

Have we advanced in mutual understanding? That is always the stated priority of good bilateral resolutions, the *sine qua non*. The controversies over trade have no doubt familiarized more people in both countries with the hard realities of the relationship; progress has been on a very narrow front. Of course, we go on working for better understanding, but we must limit our expectations that enlightenment will become the great resolver of conflict. Fair-minded Canadians admit that they do not understand the United States as well as they claim. Yet, they understand that country a great deal better than Americans understand Canada, or ever will. That inequality is in the nature of things and we must accept it with a minimum of exasperation. Good working relations cannot wait until every American schoolchild identifies the capital of Canada.

All the same, the extension of Canadian studies in American universities during this decade has been encouraging. To have a larger number of America's foreign policy élite better aware of and informed about Canada's economy, its political system, and its psychoses, helps a great deal. Among other things, it helps spur the kind of give-and-take dialogue that eases the paranoia of the more intense Canadian nationalists. It is for such important reasons that the good work of the Americas Society has been a far from negligible factor in the progress we have made in the eighties.

Postscript

On November 8, 1988, Americans elected a new President, Republican George Bush, to carry on the Reagan legacy of economic and social conservatism, assertive foreign policy, and freer trade. It was the Reagan Administration, supported by a Democratic Congress, that had negotiated and approved the Free Trade Agreement with Canada.

Two weeks later, on November 21, 1988, after one of the most bitter election campaigns in modern Canadian history, Prime Minister Brian Mulroney and his Progressive Conservatives won a second mandate from the voters. In winning re-election with another sizable majority in Canada's House of Commons, Mulroney accomplished a feat that no Conservative Prime Minister had managed in Canada for nearly a century. The Canadian election was fought on the transforming issue of free trade—whether or not Canadians would choose to take a leap of faith by approving the Free Trade Agreement that Mulroney and his government had negotiated with the Americans. His victory ensured parliamentary passage of the Agreement and the dawn of a new era in Canada–U.S. relations.

About the Editors

LANSING LAMONT is an author, journalist and public affairs executive. He was for many years a Washington and foreign correspondent for *Time* magazine, serving as *Time*'s chief correspondent in Canada and head of its Ottawa bureau in the early 1970s. He is the author of two books, has co-edited a third, and has written numerous magazine and newspaper articles. He is a trustee of several educational and cultural institutions and a member of the Council on Foreign Relations. He is currently a vice-president of the Americas Society and managing director of its Canadian Affairs program.

J. DUNCAN EDMONDS, Professor, Faculty of Administration, University of Ottawa, has served as a senior policy adviser in several Canadian governments, has written extensively on Canadian and North American issues, and has lectured at a number of American and Canadian universities. He is a director of several companies and president of his own international public affairs consulting firm in Ottawa. He was Visiting Associate of the Americas Society in 1985 and from 1986 to 1988 was Adjunct Associate Professor of Political Science and Chairman of the Committee on Canadian Studies at Yale University.